WOMEN IN SCIENCE

WOMEN IN SCIENCE

Meeting
Career
Challenges

Edited by
Ángela M. Pattatucci

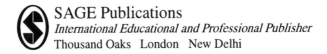
SAGE Publications
International Educational and Professional Publisher
Thousand Oaks   London   New Delhi

For information:

 SAGE Publications, Inc.
2455 Teller Road
Thousand Oaks, California 91320
E-mail: order@sagepub.com

SAGE Publications Ltd.
6 Bonhill Street
London EC2A 4PU
United Kingdom

SAGE Publications India Pvt. Ltd.
M-32 Market
Greater Kailash I
New Delhi 110 048 India

Printed in the United States of America

Library of Congress Cataloging-in-Publication Data

Main entry under title:

Women in science: Meeting career challenges /
edited by Ángela M. Pattatucci.
   p. cm.
Includes bibliographical references and index.
ISBN 0-7619-0048-9 (cloth: alk. paper)
ISBN 0-7619-0049-7 (pbk.: alk. paper)
1. Women in science. I. Pattatucci, Ángela M., 1951-
Q130.W655 1998
508.2—ddc21   98-9052

This book is printed on acid-free paper.

98 99 00 01 02 03 10 9 8 7 6 5 4 3 2 1

Acquiring Editor:	Margaret Seawell
Editorial Assistant:	Renée Piernot
Production Editor:	Sanford Robinson
Editorial Assistant:	Nevair Kabakian
Designer/Typesetter:	Janelle LeMaster
Cover Designer:	Candice Harman

To Teresa, Robert, and Sasha

Contents

Preface

This volume is a book within a book. Like most edited volumes, it contains contributions by a diverse group of authors able to provide unique insights on a particular issue. Unlike most edited volumes, this work contains a substantial contribution by the editor. The reason for this is twofold. The first reason is because I have a lot I want to say about the subject of women in science—and more broadly, women in professional careers. The second reason is structural. I departed from the traditional practice of outlining the chapter topics in advance and then inviting contributors to compose an essay within that framework. I felt that this approach was too confining for authors. My concern was that by constraining their contribution to fit within a specific, predetermined area of focus, I might inhibit the authors from sharing their most valuable insights. I therefore opted for a more open-ended approach, asking contributors to simply write an essay about their experiences as women in science. The focus of these essays could be anything. I then looked for commonalities among the essays, grouped them into chapters, and weaved my own contribution around them to ensure continuity. (Juncture points are clearly demarcated in the text, indicating where a contributor's essay ends and my contribution continues.) I am satisfied that as a result of this approach the volume presents a more complete picture than otherwise would have been possible.

I designed this volume to be read by anyone; no special knowledge of science is required. Jargon, when used, is explained with common language.

Despite its focus on challenges and boundaries to success encountered by women in science, this volume has broad applications to all professional fields. In this respect, science and engineering can be thought of as providing the best vehicle for exposing common factors contributing to the global derailment of women from professional career tracks. Thus, this volume has several levels of utility that may not be readily apparent from its title.

College and university faculty in several subject areas will find this volume a beneficial addition to course work and theoretical discussions. Managers concerned about the productivity of those under their supervision, whether it be in a scientific laboratory or automobile assembly plant, will gain valuable insight from this volume. Those occupying senior-level policy positions in government and industry concerned about creating a nonthreatening, respectful work environment for all employees will find the grassroots information contained in these pages useful. Parents reading this book will gain valuable insight and strategies for supporting and nurturing the development of their daughters in a social setting in which they regularly receive messages of devaluation, as well as raising their sons in such a way as to teach them to respect and value women as individuals. Parents can create a sanctuary within the home, a place where girls, embattled by outside prejudicial assumptions, could check reality. Along these lines, fathers could particularly benefit from reading this volume, as they will learn about the tremendous impact they have on the development of their daughters. Successful professional women, including many of the contributors to this volume, report an unconventional rearing by their fathers ("My father raised me like a son"). By *unconventional,* the contributors usually mean that the father did not "lower" his expectations of them. Parents concerned about the positive development of their daughters will take an important cue from this trend. Interested men, in general, will find value in these pages, because they will learn how the destructive behavior of males, which is often characterized as "innocent" and "light-hearted," can have an extremely negative impact on the lives of women. Finally, the obvious groups will profit. Faculty and others guiding students along career tracks will benefit by using the accounts and recommendations of the contributors to create a learning environment in which all students can excel and strive to reach their full potential. Women reading this volume will enter scientific (and other professional) career tracks better prepared to recognize gender-based challenges and boundaries to success, and they will carry a set of strategies for transcending them.

Although the volume is easy to read, it is definitely not light reading. Rather than speculating about the problem, this volume takes a grassroots approach to examining reasons for the general underrepresentation of women in science-related careers and the disproportionate number of women exiting the scientific career track. Challenges and boundaries to success are exposed that must be addressed if women's participation in scientific disciplines is to increase and stabilize. There is hope on the horizon. A small number of women have reached policy-making levels in government, academia, and industry. These women are in a position to be heard and effect change. It is our responsibility to support them and provide others with relevant information about the challenges and boundaries to success that professional women encounter. In addition, new and innovative programs designed to support and nurture women along the science career path are springing up in various localities. Whereas policy can legislate how things are supposed to be, the programs can create an environment in which women's success is supported even if policy expectations are not entirely met. This volume provides a glimpse of two such programs that can be used as a valuable reference for those wishing to establish similar programs designed to support the success of women in their locale.

It is every author's wish that her work be read and taken seriously. I am no exception. It is my hope that this volume will serve as a springboard for further research and discussion. I believe that if we are ever to improve the system for women, we must listen to the voices of women presently in it.

Acknowledgments

I would like to acknowledge the three mentors who guided and had a profound impact on my career: Dr. Jules Lerner at Northeastern Illinois University in Chicago, Dr. Thomas Kaufman at Indiana University in Bloomington, and Dr. Dean Hamer at the National Institutes of Health in Bethesda, Maryland. In addition, I would like to acknowledge the contributions of three women to my career: Ellen Dempsey, a corn geneticist at Indiana University, who had a rich research career spanning more than 40 years, though she never directed a laboratory of her own; Dr. Kathy Matthews, director of the Drosophila International Stock Center at Indiana University, whose support has been an integral part in the success of hundreds of researchers; and Stella Hu, a laboratory technician at the National Institutes of Health, who has unselfishly supported the career development of countless graduate students and postdoctoral research associates while simultaneously having a highly productive research career of her own. The three of you exemplify what this volume is about: Women negotiating through challenges and boundaries to forge successful, productive, and fulfilling scientific careers. Though I never studied formally with any of you, you have influenced me more than you will ever know.

I am grateful to Alex Schwartz, formerly at Sage Publications, who enthusiastically supported this project at its inception, and to Margaret Seawell at Sage Publications, who patiently supported its completion. Many thanks to Dr. Daphne Patai at the Univeristy of Massachusetts, Amherst, for her encouragement and for helping me tie up some loose ends with this project. I would also like to sincerely thank the faculty and administration at Trinity College in Hartford, Connecticut, who provided me with a forum to express the thoughts and ideas that evolved into this volume. Finally, I would like to express my sincere appreciation to each of the contributors to this volume. Your efforts and dedication to this book have made composing and compiling this volume a magnificent journey.

—ÁNGELA PATTATUCCI

1

Trespassers on Private Property

How about a school for Token Women? Why not teach these otherwise well prepared women how to deal with the powers-that-be who make important decisions in the men's room or who vote at a cocktail party to replace "that uppity Ph.D. in the nursing office" with "one of our own diploma graduates who knows her place"? Why not teach our competent women that tears of frustration and anger need about the same measure of apology as a man's cursing, swearing, and throwing of instruments? Should women not learn that when they "change their minds" the process is exactly the same as the more noble sounding male operation called "adjusting to the situation"? Competent, well educated women do not need lessons in logical, clear thinking. What they do need is a method of dealing with men who insist on confusing female logic with charm—or the lack thereof. What these women especially need to learn is to stop blaming themselves for the barriers erected against them. (quoted in Kelly, 1976, p. 7)

—Dorothy N. Kelly, editor, *Supervisor Nurse*

Science captures the imagination. Who can forget the heated debates surrounding the DNA evidence presented at the controversial double-murder trail of O. J. Simpson, or the spectacular photographs of Saturn and Jupiter transmitted by the *Voyager* space craft? Who has not at some time in her life contemplated the existence of extraterrestrial life, the theory of evolution, the effects of the desecration of the world's rain forests, or the outcome of global warming and the depletion of the ozone layer? In the process of growing up we imagine ourselves as medical doctors healing the

1

sick, astronauts walking on the moon, and inventors on the cutting edge of technology. We are captivated by movies and television shows with scientific themes. Whereas the realities of everyday life constrain our thinking, science offers us endless possibilities. Science invites us to dream. For girls, this is at the level of a true fantasy because there are few visible examples of successful women scientists. Boys, however, grow up surrounded by men in positions of authority and leadership, which instills within them a sense of entitlement that is largely absent for girls. Thus, for boys the dream is not a fantasy; it is solidly within their grasp.

- Of course I could be an astronaut. Neil Armstrong walked on the Moon.
- Of course I could be a physicist. Sir Isaac Newton discovered the principles of gravity.
- Of course I could be a biologist. Gregor Mendel founded genetics.
- Of course I could be an engineer. Benjamin Franklin discovered electricity.
- Of course I could be an inventor. Thomas Edison invented the lightbulb.
- Of course I could be a medical doctor. Jonas Salk developed the polio vaccine.
- Of course I could be a mathematician. Euclid founded geometry.

Of course. Of Course. OF COURSE!

Science is male territory. A built-in system of support exists at both the institutional and social levels that nurtures the interest, motivation, and success of males in science. This support system permeates virtually every aspect of our culture—from the presentation of gender-stereotyped toys by parents during infancy to the selection of astronauts for space shuttle missions. As the excerpt that follows indicates, when we think of scientists, we think of men.

One weekend afternoon I asked my daughter to draw a picture of a scientist. She sat down, pencil in hand, and sketched me a scientist. A while later, my son emerged from his room and I asked him to draw a scientist. . . . The two drew precisely the same figure. The styles were different, of course, but the scientist was essentially the same: a white male, alone in a lab, with a stethoscope and a slightly mad look in his eyes. (Mann, 1994, p. 106–107).

Countless numbers of parents have dreamed of their sons becoming medical doctors or scientists, unlocking the mysteries of life and the universe. But this dream is rarely envisioned on the birth of a daughter. Instead the hope is often that she will grow up and marry a man who is a medical doctor or a scientist.

In her book, *The Difference: Growing Up Female in America,* Judy Mann (1994), a columnist for the *Washington Post,* reports that from kindergarten to college, boys and girls in industrialized nations consistently portray scientists as white men in lab coats wearing glasses. This image is reinforced in school textbooks, where the contributions of women scientists are often overlooked or presented as tangential to the big picture—which is invariably the brainchild of male scientists. Science textbooks consistently portray girls and women as onlookers, while the boys and men do the "real" experimental work. Media representations reinforce the concept that science is conducted by men. For example, scientists are characteristically portrayed by men in movies and on television programs. Even on those occasions when medical doctors and scientists are played by women, they are typically attached to a male authority figure and when a crucial opinion is needed, they defer to him.

Parents also contribute to the image that science is a masculine endeavor. For example, the results of a British study focusing on achievement in mathematics found that parents have lower expectations for their daughters than for their sons and that this difference is noticeable as early as the first grade (Entwisle & Baker, 1983). Parents often subtly, or perhaps not so subtly, channel their sons toward, and their daughters away from, academic study and activities that would encourage interest and potential success in scientific-oriented endeavors.

These factors, along with many others, work together to produce the strong message that scientists are men and science is masculine—a concept that both boys and girls grasp at an early age and tend to hold throughout their lives. However, the message carries a different meaning depending on the gender of the recipient. For boys, it is encouraging and inspiring. Science is something that they can and should do. Science is their private property. For girls, the same message is discouraging and obstructive. Science is not only something that they supposedly *cannot* do, it is an endeavor that they *should not* even attempt. Women aspiring for scientific careers can therefore be characterized as trespassers on the private property of males.

Given these circumstances, it should come as no surprise that most women choose not to embark on a scientific career, and that this is reflected in a severe underrepresentation of women in scientific disciplines. Explanations traditionally have focused on two areas: (a) females have been alleged to be less adept at abstract reasoning, a requisite skill for success in scientific endeavors; and (b) women exit the scientific career track in disproportionate numbers to heed nature's call to the maternal instinct. The letter below, appearing in the interdisciplinary journal *Science*, exemplifies this bias.

> Suppose we took a random sample of 1000 women starting careers in science, quantified their "mortality" (numbers leaving the field) over time, and compared this mortality with that of a control group of men assumed to have equal intellectual capacity? What do you think the result would be? I'd be willing to bet plenty that the mortality among the ladies (resulting from marriage, babies, and so forth) would be much higher than that of the controls. I can't prove it. But if I were hiring people of equal capacity, I'd want to select those whom I felt would "stay with it" longest. In this situation the *long-term* value of the commodity determines its price, not the immediate value. Lab directors just don't want and won't pay the same prices for people whom they suspect have a high chance of leaving. (Davenport, 1971, pp. 521-522)

The following letter to *Science* further reveals that an absence of data to support such contentions does not stop men from harboring, and voicing, stereotypical assumptions about women in science.

> When hiring a scientist, male or female, the employer must look to the future. What is the productive life expectancy of the individual? What is the probable productivity of that person in terms of what the employer wants? How much will the individual cost per unit of output? And, could some other procurable person give comparable or more satisfactory service at the same or a cheaper per-unit cost? In view of the apprenticeship required for maximum productivity on most [scientific] jobs, probable absenteeism, retirement and disability benefit costs, and so forth, these are valid considerations. . . . *I have seen no data* comparing the relative per-life-unit-output cost of men and women in science, nor in any other occupation. *I have heard* that (i) most young women work only until they can find husbands; (ii) most mothers are engrossed with their families and not with their jobs; (iii) women are of uncertain tenure because their husbands move; (iv) pregnancy and parturition decrease the working woman's usefulness on the job; (v) women are not as dedicated to getting ahead as men are and, consequently, are not worth as much; and (vi) women cause more friction and conflict than men. (Jensen, 1971, p. 522; emphasis added)

There is little doubt that some women having an interest in science choose not to pursue it as a career as a result of dislike or difficulties with abstract reasoning applications such as mathematics. Moreover, some women in scientific careers actually do choose to refocus their priorities toward family responsibilities. An exhaustive search would unquestionably turn up examples of women affirming each of the six points listed previously. What is in dispute is that these are the sole, or even the major, factors contributing to the underrepresentation of women in scientific careers.

Those in the field of epidemiological science are familiar with the paradox of the "Texas Sharpshooter." An individual predesigns the dimensions of a target (e.g., radius of the bull's-eye and each surrounding concentric circle), then fires 100 rounds of ammunition into the side of a barn. Using the target dimensions, the individual scans the field of bullet holes in the barn to determine the area of greatest density. The target is subsequently drawn around this area and then calculations are made to determine the person's shooting accuracy. It requires no scientific training to realize that the sharpshooter has "fixed" the experiment and that his or her shooting precision estimates will be worthless. Likewise, in attempting to account both for the general underrepresentation of women in scientific disciplines, as well as the disproportionate exodus of women from these fields, the scientific establishment has committed a similar error. The bull's-eye has been drawn after the fact around the easy explanations, those based on stereotype or coincidence, in preference to examining all possible factors. After all, who can judge a woman for ending her scientific career to focus on tending to the needs of her family? Nature is the perfect scapegoat. It allows all parties to evade accountability, and the status quo is maintained. However, just as with the fallacious reasoning of the Texas sharpshooter, it does not necessarily follow that a woman choosing to exit a scientific career, who happens to have a family, is doing so because she is heeding a call to the maternal instinct. This may be the explanation that the academy *wants to hear,* because this explanation abdicates them from any responsibility for her career derailment, but it may not be the major contributing factor at all.

The scientific establishment has addressed the issue of women in science in a very *un*scientific manner, choosing to rely on speculation rather than on a systematic gathering of data. Extrapolating isolated incidences and elevating them to a level of commonality for the subsequent justification of a conclusion represents a fundamental error in logic that would render the reporting scientist a laughingstock in most circles—that is, except when the topic of discussion is women's underrepresentation in science. I find it astounding that the "problem" is supposedly being addressed by the academy, but no one has really bothered to ask *women* why they believe that their early interest in science as children did not blossom into careers; no one has bothered to ask *women* why they are abandoning science careers in disproportionate numbers.

This volume represents a first attempt to fill this void. It was spawned out of a growing sense of uneasiness as my own scientific career has progressed, coupled with feelings of despair as I have watched numerous women colleagues exit their scientific careers. Through it all, a glaring inconsistency has emerged. The traditional explanations forwarded for the disproportionately low numbers of women in science have not been confirmed by my experience. Women I have known have not ended their scientific careers because the subject matter was beyond their ability. These were highly talented and capable women. They also have not left for family-related reasons (although this has sometimes been expressed as an afterthought). Instead, these colleagues abandoned science careers because they had finally reached their threshold of tolerance for what I will call the *extra stuff*—a blanket term encompassing all gender-related challenges and boundaries faced by women in science *over and above* those inherent to the field and experienced by all persons aspiring for a career. On my speaking with these colleagues, a picture of frustration and disillusionment with science emerged. Although each story was individual, they all had the common theme of burnout, not with science itself, but with the extra stuff. The boundaries to success for women in science were determined to be too great.

Whether the point of saturation comes early in high school, after completing a long arduous journey through graduate school and postdoctoral research, or when battling for tenure at an academic institution, the result is typically the same. Women who have reached their threshold of tolerance for the extra stuff leave without a word—often blaming themselves for their apparent "failure." Disillusionment is expressed even by those women who have managed to be successful in the system. It seems that women in science face an even greater challenge than mastering the rigors of a given discipline. For most women, this represents a minor ordeal compared to overcoming the boundary of their gender. It is the consuming effects of simultaneously fighting battles on two fronts—the relentless, indiscriminate application of gender-related social stereotypes about women coupled with the strain associated with mastering a body of technical material inherent to a field—that often results in a woman deciding to end a scientific career.

Bernadine Healy, former director of the National Institutes of Health, commented on the situation faced by women in science:

> When I was in medical school in the 1960s, it was a widely held view that women should have children before age thirty. Illnesses like endometriosis were seen as punishment for delaying. Today, few in the biomedical professions would admit

to holding such unscientific views. In fact, now the punishments come to women who do have their children while in their 20s, at least among women in the sciences.

One study of 460 former National Science Foundation postdoctoral fellows showed that women who had children during their postdoctoral years did not attain as high academic and leadership positions as other women and men. But let's not blame the babies. Both married and single women scientists and engineers also have higher rates of un- and underemployment than do their male counterparts. As in so many other fields, women in science eventually hit either the "mommy track" or a "glass ceiling." (Healy, 1992)

The extra stuff confronted by women in science has been conspicuously ignored by the academy because to give it recognition would be tantamount to accepting responsibility for the underrepresentation of women in scientific fields—something that the scientific establishment apparently wants to avoid at all costs. They prefer to portray the problem as a mystery yet to be solved. However, this stance is absurd. It raises imagery of a mischievous child hitting his teacher squarely in the back of the head with a giant spitball, and then staring innocently upward toward her glaring eyes, gurgling, "Who, me?" through a mouth full of slobbering wet paper. Although the teacher will undoubtedly hold the child culpable, the scientific community is accountable only to itself. Rather than accept responsibility for creating and perpetuating the harsh environment that women in science encounter, the academy has instead traditionally blamed the victim. Returning to the spitball illustration, it would be preposterous to suggest that the teacher was responsible for the projectile striking her in the back of her head. No adult would be willing to accept the excuse that the spitball was intended to assist the teacher in her lesson on the principles of gravity or that she spoiled everything by having a head so enormous that it was impossible to avoid hitting it. However, analogous statements are made and accepted about women's derailment from science-oriented endeavors, be it women in professional careers or girls in a third-grade classroom, on a regular basis (e.g., girls are not good at math; women are too emotional to think logically; she is too feminine to be a good scientist; she was not serious, she was only here for an "MRS" degree). By blaming the victim, the scientific establishment feeds into the same stereotypes that form the boundaries that women in science face in the first place. Thus, a vicious cycle ensues in which stereotype fuels stereotype, fuels stereotype. I propose that the academy stop asking what is wrong with women in science—that large numbers leave the field—and start asking the question what is wrong with the scientific environment—that large numbers of talented women choose to leave rather than participate in it?

This volume is about the extra stuff confronted by women in science. It makes no pretense to be comprehensive, but instead is a sampling of authors representing a cross section of scientific disciplines and come from varied class, ethnic, and racial backgrounds. In addition, the authors are a cross section of points along the scientific professional continuum, ranging from the undergraduate level to associate dean. A few have chosen to exit the scientific career path. Most have altered their original plans. It is interesting to note that not one woman in this group cites mastering the large body of technical material inherent to succeeding in science as an overwhelming task. However, a majority indicate that the lack of institutional support and the relentless application of social stereotypes about women are at the least distracting, and at the most suffocating, to their success in the field. Whereas men can be characterized as in pursuit of a scientific career, women are best represented as *embarking on a crusade.* It is my contention that it is the exhausting effects of the crusade—the constant campaigns to fight off overt and covert applications of gender-related stereotypes, harassment, discrimination, sexism, assaults on self-esteem and threats to personal well-being, and overall lack of support—rather than the alleged "acts of nature" that cause the interest and motivation for science by girls and women to derail at various points along the continuum.

Dr. Healy has offered some suggestions.

In view of some negative treatment in the classroom and discouraging employment and funding prospects, the astonishing thing is that young women pursue careers in science and medicine at all! But it is fortunate—and important—that they do. By the year 2000, women and minorities will account for 68% of new workers. And, if current trends continue, the United States will face a shortage of scientists and physicians by the end of the century. It is safe to say that sustaining America's scientific preeminence will depend on attracting—and retaining—talented women and minorities.

When British women were trying to win the right to vote 80 years ago they played by men's rules: They broke windows in Parliament Square. Their leader, Emmeline Pankhurst, defended the women's action, saying, "Why should women go to Parliament Square and be battered about and insulted, and . . . produce less effect than when they throw stones? . . . After all, is not a woman's life, is not her health, are not her limbs more valuable than panes of glass? There is no doubt of that, but most important of all, does not the breaking of glass produce more effect upon the Government?" (quoted in Pankhurst, 1914, pp. 212–213)

Although I am not advocating that American women resort to such behaviors—or even to the breaking of test tubes—it is clear that all of us in the scientific community have a lot of breaking to do—especially old rules, self-defeating habits, and glass ceilings. (Healy, 1992)

The extra stuff faced by women is pervasive and exists in the system at all levels. Highlighting one aspect of the problem, several studies have pointed out how girls are short-changed in early education and that they are selected out of the sciences early through multiple avenues of discouragement. Thus, the last decade has seen the inception of several programs aimed at capturing and holding the interest of young girls and women in science. One such program was started out of necessity by Maureen Castellana. She was concerned that her daughter, then in the fourth grade, would become yet another casualty of the educational–social system that selects against girls developing and maintaining an interest in science. She therefore organized the Auburndale Girls' Science Club out of the pool of girls in her daughter's fourth-grade class at school. The single-gender environment allowed the girls to explore and make mistakes without worrying about what their male contemporaries thought. When the girls reached the sixth grade, they gained national prominence by competing with some of the nation's best engineering minds at the Massachusetts Institute of Technology's seventh annual battle of LEGO robots. The object of the contest was to design an autonomous LEGO robot, guided solely by sensors and internal programming, that would move as many foam-rubber blocks as possible into specified areas. Several competitors designed aggressive robots aimed at preventing their adversary from securing blocks. However, the sixth-grade girls designed a simple machine programmed to detect a light above the goal and move any blocks that it encountered toward that direction. This modest yet elegant approach was sufficient to defeat more than half of the MIT robots (Travis, 1993)!

The previous example illustrates a point supported by a lot of contemporary research: Girls learn best in a cooperative, nonjudgmental atmosphere. This usually translates to an environment in which there are no boys. Castellana has been criticized for excluding boys from the science club she founded. However, a father of one of the members says that he believes that including boys in the design of the LEGO robot would have altered the group dynamics significantly:

The girls would be less willing to take risks and make mistakes. Many of the girls surprised themselves at how well they did . . . if there were boys there, it wouldn't have worked as well. The girls would have been inhibited. (Travis, 1993)

As an aside, I find it curious that separatist accusations tend to be expressed only when all-girl efforts are successful and receive media attention. Prior to this point, all-girl environments are typically ridiculed and discounted as frivolous.

Castellana's example also demonstrates that efforts aimed at capturing and nurturing an interest in science by girls need not be elaborate, formal, and well-funded programs, weighted down by bureaucracy. It is possible to get a lot from very little. Conventional wisdom holds that science programs for girls such as The Auburndale Girls' Science Club will increase the pool of women with aspirations for scientific careers, which in turn should eventually result in a greater overall representation for women at the professional level. I commend and support these long-term efforts, but seriously question if they will be sufficient to increase the overall percentage of women in science.

Often overlooked in the focus on early education is that the elite complement of women, who survive the multiple avenues of discouragement present in the primary and secondary education systems and embark on a science career, still leave these fields in disproportionate numbers compared with men. As Joe Alper aptly put it in a recent article appearing in *Science*, "The pipeline is leaking women all the way along" (Alper, 1993, p. 409). Thus, the critical challenge as I see it may not be capturing girls' interest but convincing women that they *can succeed* in the sciences—that there is a place for us and that our contributions are valued. In fact, the brute-force approach of the early education programs may be somewhat naive in that the focus is on increasing numbers—the logic being that by fueling early interest in science, more women will want to enter the science career track, resulting in an eventual increase in the number of women scientists, and finally culminating in the attainment a *critical mass* of women in science. An inherent assumption of this approach is that the impediments to success are greatest at the bottom and taper off as one moves up the science career track. However, the essays contained in this volume, along with data from several recent studies, suggest that this is not the case. Women face unique challenges and boundaries to success in the sciences at every stage of the process. Although a good starting point, the focus on early education may be a gross oversimplification of the problem.

Given its reputation as a discipline advanced by logic, reason, and objectivity, one might predict that science would be a haven for women, that their status would be significantly better in science than in other career tracks.

However, nothing could be further from the truth. Although the data indicate that percentages of baccalaureate, master's, and doctorate degrees awarded to women have shown an overall steady increase, closer scrutiny reveals that women are disproportionately selected out at each level. Furthermore, among doctoral students requiring 6 to 8 years to complete their dissertation research, the percentage of men steadily went down from 1972 to 1991, whereas the percentage of women has risen steadily (Vetter, 1994).

It seems clear that the road to a graduate degree contains more impediments and detours for women compared with men. As mentioned previously, the "easy explanation" embraced by the scientific establishment accounts for this disparity by ascribing it to the forces of nature: Women make an exit out of the science pipeline to have families, or minimally family responsibilities account for the longer period to earn graduate degrees. Thus, the integrity of science as an institution is sound and should not be questioned. However, most women in science choose to postpone childbearing until their careers are established and a substantial minority choose not to bear children at all. Furthermore, the focus on family responsibilities conveniently detours around the major issue. Regardless of marital and family status, women in the pipeline typically occupy lower-level positions relative to their male counterparts despite having comparable levels of expertise. For example, women on average spend significantly more time in postdoctoral positions than men. The most severe aspect of this process is demonstrated in employment data, where women have their strongest representation in non–tenure-track academic positions, but higher up the career ladder, women's representation steadily declines. Equally discouraging is the fact that women on average earn substantially less than their male counterparts at every period of their scientific careers, and the gap widens at the highest levels of experience and responsibility (*Science, 255,* 1376).

Laws and policies may make it seem on the surface that things are better for women, but in reality they tend to drive deeply ingrained social attitudes and stereotypes underground rather than foster genuine change. Despite current trends making it "politically incorrect" to engage in discriminatory practices or publicly express stereotypical views, overall attitudes about women's inferiority to men and their "proper place" in society are solidly in place. For example, a report by the Feminist Majority Foundation (1991) has projected that at the current rate of advancement, it will require another 475 years for women to reach parity with men in the executive suite!

Attainment of a critical mass of women scientists has been advocated by many as the primary solution to the problem of increasing women's overall representation in scientific disciplines (Mason, 1991; Osborn, 1992). A *criti-*

cal mass has been defined as the precise point at which the presence of an adequate number of individuals effects qualitative improvement in workplace conditions and expedites reorganization in a positive direction. This threshold has been specified as a strong minority constituting a minimal level of 15% (Osborn, 1994). On the surface this seems reasonable. In theory, as the critical mass level is approached and finally achieved, women's ability to organize and safeguard their livelihood from within should increase substantially, resulting in a progression to an accepted presence without a need for outside influence, in a self-perpetuating process (Gutek, 1985; Kanter, 1977). The quote that follows, from a female graduate student, certainly supports this utopian view:

> I wish we had a woman [on the faculty] because the men don't understand the issues that the women [graduate students] are concerned about. I thought about going to the chair and telling him to put all the new graduate students in the same area of the building because it's really helped us get through the first year. But he may say, "why?" Maybe that's not important to the men. But if there was a woman who was higher up then I could say this is really cool to have some companions, some support system here, and she might say, "Yeah, that's a really nice thought" (Etzkowitz, Kemelgor, Neuschatz, Uzzi, & Alonzo, 1994).

Critical mass is one of those buzz words that people parrot to impress others without adequately thinking through its implications. Embedded within the critical mass theory is the fallacious assumption that women are a unified group with a common set of goals, rather than a diverse collection of individuals. Henry Etzkowitz and his colleagues (1994) compared departments in which the criterion for a critical mass of women was satisfied to ones in which it had not yet been achieved and found that as the number of women faculty members in a department increased, they separated into subgroups that could be in philosophical disagreement with each other. Thus, despite attainment of a critical mass, departmental organizational structures and the separatist mentality they generate continue to isolate women. The researchers also found that the narrow focus of senior female scientists mirrored the general philosophy and work ethic of established male faculty and failed to fulfill the needs of most younger women. Furthermore, despite the presence of several women faculty in a department, the priorities of male students and faculty may still prevail and impede change. Women entering departments, either as students or faculty, where women's representation approaches or has achieved critical mass levels, are thus often dismayed at the unexpected realization that the critical mass is *not* a cohesive group.

> The scientific role thus bifurcates along generational and gender fault lines. These developments have significant unintended consequences for the socialization of female scientists, for example, the availability of relevant role models. As long as the relatively few women in academic science were willing to accept the strictures of a workplace organized on the assumption of a social and emotional support structure provided to the male scientist by an unpaid full-time housewife or done without, issues of women in science were not attended to. A modest increase in the numbers of women in science, without a change in the structure of the scientific workplace, creates a paradox of critical mass. (Etzkowitz et al., 1994).

Until the extra stuff women in science confront is acknowledged and addressed by the scientific community, accompanied by the establishment (or revamping) of institutional policies concerning recruitment and retention, slowing the tenure clock, crediting mentoring functions in tenure reviews, child care, and parental leave, women will continue to be underrepresented in scientific disciplines. Furthermore, tokenism must be abolished. Etzkowitz and his colleagues (1994) found that many institutions showcase a few female superstars while the remaining women waned in continued discrimination.

I want to emphasize that this volume does not concentrate on personal horror stories involving overt and intended acts of discrimination against women in science. These are certainly sad and unfortunate occurrences. However, most institutions presently have established procedures for addressing such predicaments. Instead, this volume focuses on the more diffuse aspects of the problem, things that a majority of women face to some degree, tending to eat slowly away at one's self-confidence. They are hidden, and by the time of their discovery the situation is often without recourse. Thus, the main work of the contributors of this volume is to explore what these boundaries to success are and how they might be transcended to eventually create a scientific environment in which women can thrive. More than anything, they state that it is the cumulative effect of the application of social stereotypes that serve to isolate women and undermine their ability to successfully negotiate through science career tracks.

This volume is more than a mere statement of the problem. Women need long-term strategies—ones that will lay the groundwork for future generations of women to be empowered on their journey along the science career track. However, I caution that we must not become so intoxicated by a vision for the future that women currently in the scientific pipeline are neglected. These women need practical, realistic strategies for transcending boundaries to success *now*. Furthermore, we must acknowledge that the current pool of women scientists will form the infrastructure and provide advocacy for the development and implementation of long-range projects designed to increase women's representation in science. Therefore, both short-term and long-term strategies for meeting challenges and transcending boundaries to success are crucial and are a focus of this volume.

Within the structure of science programs are support networks for men. They are so commonplace, and male participation in science is so abundant, that they are largely taken for granted. Therefore, men can often have their needs for support met within the context of being a scientist, whereas women typically must seek support from the outside, creating an illusion of weakness and the false notion that we require extra help. This affords men a privileged status and renders women underprivileged. We are largely left to fend for ourselves in a system that selects against us every step of the way. Although there are some within the scientific establishment sympathetic to the barriers women in science confront, most have historically subscribed to the "let them eat cake" philosophy forwarded by Marie Antoinette. Programs for women in science are therefore often cast as superfluous, pandering to special interests, and giving women an unfair advantage in an already highly competitive environment. However, in reality they simply seek to create a level playing field, to develop networks of support and opportunities for women in science similar to those that men already enjoy.

Science in its myriad of disciplines is both exciting and rewarding. The challenges and boundaries encountered by women in science outlined in this volume have no quick solutions. Making science hospitable for women will require a clear commitment on the part of those in the academy to critically examine the field and honestly accept responsibility for creating an environment in which women face numerous barriers to success over and above those genuinely inherent to a field of inquiry. I look forward to the day when these barriers will no longer exist and women are full contributors and valued participants in the scientific process. Until then, those of us in the scientific community must work to assist women in meeting challenges and transcending boundaries along their journey to a scientific career.

2

As a Woman Thinketh

Society has very different expectations of how women should use their intellectual capabilities . . . many parents do not have the same goals in mind for their daughters, for their life-long careers, as they do for their sons. (quoted in Cutler & Canellakis, 1989, p. 1784)

—Dr. Mary Ellen Jones, University of North Carolina, whose research focuses on the biosynthesis of pyrimidines

I f the development of girls and women within the current social structure is evaluated, the following scenario emerges. Most begin school eager and ready to achieve. Girls, in fact, begin with decidedly more zeal and aptitude compared to age-matched boys. Girls are generally more mature and prepared to learn. As a group, girls score higher on standardized tests at the beginning of their education compared to boys. However, something happens to a majority of girls during their primary and secondary education. By the time they graduate high school, their scores on standardized tests are generally lower compared to boys. Their eagerness to learn and motivation to achieve is replaced by a profound loss of self-esteem. Young women graduating high school are convinced that they have limited options regarding what they can do in life, whereas boys envision a world of possibilities. Somewhere along their journey to adulthood, girls' wings are clipped and they stop trying to soar (Mann, 1994). This represents the first great wave of casualties.

A minority of women emerge out of high school full of optimism and a passion for learning. They enthusiastically enroll in undergraduate science and mathematics courses with aspirations for careers in engineering, science, and medicine. However, a majority of these women get their fingers stepped on along the way, and they quit climbing toward their goals. Most are detoured into other "more feminine" majors, leaving few women graduating college with science- and engineering-related degrees. This represents the second great wave of casualties.

By this time, a scant number of women are left in the system. Those that remain must survive a third wave of casualties in graduate school, a fourth wave during the ever-expanding postdoctoral stage, a fifth wave during the tenure–probationary period of their first professional position, and a sixth wave marked by the period in which one's contributions to the field are recognized and rewarded with a senior-level position. It is not surprising that very few women survive all six waves, and among those that do, most carry scars. One might argue that men are selected out of the system at each of these points as well. This is, in fact, true, but there are proportionally far fewer male casualties at each step than there are female (Alper, 1993), resulting in a gap that exceeds a male to female ratio of 30 to 1 at the senior level in some subdisciplines (Vetter, 1994).

I use the term *casualties* because the environment women in science face is often characterized as like being in a war zone or on a crusade. Moreover, *casualties* invokes an image of fighters rather than quitters. A casualty is someone actively striving for a goal, but who is eliminated by outside opposing forces. This accurately depicts many women's experience in science and engineering fields.

In fact, many women struggle so hard to make it in the current system that they subscribe to the belief that they must be spectacular just to be considered average. My own experience provides an apt illustration. I was so grateful for the opportunity to earn a university education that I never questioned how women were viewed or treated at the various schools that I attended. I realized that sexism existed, but like many women did not have a personal horror story to share and therefore erroneously concluded that sexism had not touched my life. At the same time, I was acutely aware that opportunities were not equally afforded to women and men in our society and that this disparity was particularly evident in the so-called hard science fields. However, my early years taught me to expect that life would neither be fair nor egalitarian. Thus, my strategy to combat sexism and prejudice was to be outstanding. Simply stated, I strove *to be so good that I could not be denied.*

I naively subscribed to this philosophy throughout most of my educational career, living somewhat in denial, because I regularly observed occurrences, and had a mounting catalog of personal experiences, suggesting that my logic was flawed and not based on reality. There was one occasion, during my third year in graduate school at Indiana University, that nearly ended my career. I attended a seminar given by an eminent woman scientist and came to the painful realization that the members of the audience surrounding me had listened more intently to the man introducing her than they had to the seminar speaker herself. In a fleeting instant, my carefully constructed reality was shattered. I had to face the fact that despite my professed acceptance of the notion that life is not always fair, deep down I had expected life to be fair *to me*. I was forced to come to terms with my idealistic view that those at the top, those who worked hard and excelled, would not face discrimination.

Up to that point, I had taken sexism and discrimination as a given and was convinced that the only way to combat them was to be so good that I could not be denied. This is common among women, particularly those in the sciences. By applying this notion, we rationalize whatever discrimination we face as being our own fault: We simply are not working hard enough.

By itself, this experience may seem trivial, but it was not an isolated incident. Instead it represented one among many experiences in my life—all of which I had denied in lieu of the hope that I would one day be established and no longer face such incidents. However, this particular experience represented a watershed specifically because it left me with no hope. Witnessing an eminent scientist not being afforded the respect that she had earned did not make me feel good about my future prospects. For the first time in my career, I realized that my PhD was going to carry a different meaning and be viewed differently from the same degree earned by my male counterparts. I was filled with anger and despair. The experience left me so upset that for several days after the seminar I contemplated ending my graduate career. It was a silent struggle—my colleagues were unaware of my pain and rage. Nevertheless, as time distanced me from this experience, I was able to gain greater perspective. I had faced many obstacles in procuring an education, and I was not about to let this barrier stop me. I decided that I could both nurture my passion for science and also be an instrument for change.

This kind of positive outcome from such an experience, unfortunately, is rare. The casualties far outnumber the successes. Girls and women are silenced at each point along the science career track. They are vanquished and inundated. Those that remain learn to be acquiescent and submissive. They learn to wait, to take the last place in line, to be as unobtrusive as possible.

In her book *The Difference*, Judy Mann (1994) accurately depicts the challenges faced by girls within the current social framework.

> Our daughters have more options than we had, and they are coming of age with better and more varied role models than we had. But these are footnotes in the travel guide they need. They are still coming of age in a foreign country, where the customs and currency are male. Males still map the terrain, and young women have to figure it out. The signals mothers try to send their daughters about the options they must demand are undermined by the subtle and not so subtle signals they get from school, from rock music, from traditional religions, from the books they read, the movies they see, the television programming they watch, and the political dialogue they hear. (Mann, 1994, p. 12)

There is much that remains to be done to create an environment in which girls and women can excel, in which their accomplishments are acknowledged and they are viewed equally valuable to society as are their male counterparts. Psychiatrist Jean Hamilton provided the following insight.

> As a ubiquitous consequence of sexism, women's sense of identity is developed within a framework that defines woman as a devalued group. One of the most damaging effects of subordinate status is an impairment in self-esteem. That is, women—as members of a subgroup that is devalued and disadvantaged in comparison to men—have greater difficulty in maintaining a separate, valid, or reliable sense of their own worth. (Hamilton, 1989, p. 39)

The false elevation of boys' self-esteem at the expense of girls' starts at an early age and continues to adulthood. To be successful, women must unlearn the messages of devaluation and inferiority. It is a recovery process, one characterized by self-discovery and learning to become a whole person. Mann (1994) asked what would happen to girls if their development was not undermined and they were valued. What would happen if girls were raised to be self-reliant, independent, critical thinking women? What would happen if boys were reared to respect girls as equals, to listen when they speak, and to value them as friends?

Jennifer Cramer provided a glimpse of what such a woman might look like in the essay that follows.

I Dared to Be Different

_____ *Jennifer M. Cramer* _____

The purpose of this paper is to address some common concerns that arise when considering a school with small engineering or computer science departments and few or no female professors. I hope to show that such concerns are unwarranted and convince readers that they should dare to be different: a female in a male-dominated profession.

I dared to be different four years ago. I am now a fifth-year electrical engineering and computer science dual major at Ohio Northern University. Ohio Northern is a private university located in Ada, Ohio—which is halfway between Dayton and Toledo—and is primarily an undergraduate institution. The total enrollment is fewer than 3000 students. When I complete my baccalaureate, I hope to pursue my dream of becoming a college professor.

Women are not very heavily represented at ONU in either the College of Engineering or the Computer Science Department. The College of Engineering as a whole has only one female faculty member, and she is considered a lecturer. The Mathematics and Computer Science Department has two female professors, neither of whom teach computer science courses. When I entered the Computer Science Department as a major just a few years ago, I was the sole woman majoring in computer science. There are now two other female computer science majors, one of whom transferred in as a junior last year.

It would be easy to assume that because women are not heavily represented in either the faculty or the student population of these two departments that women would be treated poorly or at least very differently. That has not been my experience at ONU. Professors, in general, are very helpful and as a whole the students are close. However, there is one instance in which I have regularly seen male students treat female students differently. It occurs on the eve of the due date for computer programming assignments. Despite seeing a female classmate working confidently, without difficulty, males seem to have a very hard time asking a woman for help with a computer program, even when they recognize that they need help! This may be because they think that all women naturally know less about computers or it may just stem more from the fact that they do not want to lose the computer "guru" image. I am not sure. Nevertheless, I have noticed that men seem to be more at ease asking a woman for help after she first has sought help from them on several previous occasions. For example, two male classmates, who started with me as a first-year student in computer science, never requested help from me until last year, even though I had sought needed assistance from them numerous times throughout our tenure at ONU. Now that I am a senior, their hesitation seems to be gone, but the first- and second-year males are as stubborn as always.

Open-door policies and men who treat women as equals. Is it real? Yes, in my experience it is. I also believe that much of this is not unique to Ohio Northern. I propose that one can find these characteristics in many schools with small departments. At the time of writing, I am working at the University of New Hampshire, and the environment seems to be much the same here. Some people believe that the number of women on the faculty of a particular school will determine how hospitable the environment will be for female students. I disagree. An environment in which professors view students by their academic ability rather than their gender, previous knowledge, or family background makes it hospitable for both women and men.

A small department helps women because of its friendly, cooperative environment. One thing the professors at ONU emphasize is teamwork and cooperation. In today's industry, teams are frequently used. Members of a class do not always get along with each other. Nevertheless, the philosophy at ONU is that we should learn to work together regardless of the existence of differences. For example, each student is required to complete a major senior project, with most of the work being done in teams. In addition, one professor includes a group-learning section in his class, including a group test as a part of an exam. Another professor chooses laboratory partners out of a hat and rotates them every couple of weeks so that students will have an opportunity to work with someone with whom they are compatible, as well as someone they absolutely cannot stand. Because women are outnumbered, we are not typically working with other women. This prepares us to go out and work in a predominantly male workforce without being intimidated. It teaches us how to work with men as colleagues. As we enter the working world, we will be prepared to work cooperatively with others in a variety of situations.

If you are good at mathematics and science and are interested in engineering, then the most important thing to remember is that women are equally capable and intelligent as men. My class at ONU, consisting of three women, is a perfect example. When it came time, as juniors, for Tau Beta Pi (the engineering honorary society) inductions, all three of us were inaugurated.

Furthermore, when the class graduated at the end of last year, two of those women were among the top five members of the class. (I did not graduate with this group because of my dual major.) Of course, this does not mean that one has to be a "super brain" to be in engineering! In my graduating class, there is a mix of women. There are four of us and we span the range from the top of the class to struggling at the bottom.

A small school with all-male faculty does not seem like it would be the most hospitable place for a woman. Do not be deceived. Every school is characterized by a unique blend of attending students, faculty, administration, other employees, and community members. Do not rule out a school by size, or engineering as a profession, because of your gender. Women can and should pursue computer science and engineering as careers. Do not be discouraged by the male dominance in these fields. Women are just as capable as men and should pursue careers in these fields. Engineering is fun. Computer science is fun. Try them!

Over the years I have participated in several events, during which at some point the following chant spontaneously arose: "Say it loud! I'm a woman and proud."[1] It is difficult to be present at one of these gatherings and not be caught up in the electrifying emotion of thousands of women shouting together in unison. However, I have always found it curious that the effect is short-lived. I would encounter participants at a later date and notice that they did not appear to be nearly as proud to be women as they were during the chanting session on the day of the event. On contemplating the matter, it occurred to me that despite generating excitement, the chant provided those in attendance with no substance. Although they sound good, without substance the words have no power, and consequently no lasting effect. The lesson is clear. Merely tell me to be proud, and it might last for an afternoon. However, provide me with information and allow me to arrive at the conclusion myself, and my pride will last a lifetime.

I raise this point because I have recognized a disturbing trend among girls at the primary school age level. They readily parrot the phrase, "I can be anything I want to be," often adding that they could even be president of the United States of America. However, when other occupations traditionally held by men are suggested as potential careers, such as scientist, professional baseball player, engineer, carpenter, or mathematician, a typical response is, "Oh, I can't do that! It's too hard!"

Why would a young girl proclaim that she could be president of the United States of America, but in the same breath state that engineering is too hard? A logical explanation is that, similar to the chant, the girls have learned the words, but they have no substance. The well-intentioned campaign designed to raise the self-esteem of girls by providing them with catchy phrases to chant is in my opinion extremely irresponsible. It fails to recognize that girls exist in an environment in which they constantly receive the message, both explicitly and implicitly, that their gender represents the greatest impediment to their achievement. This cultural message *is* one of substance, whereas the chants and catchy phrases are not. Despite the obvious success of campaigns to teach catchy phrases such as, "I can be anything I want to be," girls still measure self-esteem by popularity and their ability to charm boys, not by scholastic achievement and their potential for self-sufficient living (Mann, 1994).

Exposing girls to women scientists, engineers, and mathematicians can provide possible role models and reinforce the concept that it is conceivable for women to succeed in these fields. However, a single exposure may not be sufficient to sustain motivation, and girls often find it difficult to project themselves into the roles—a crucial step if they are to genuinely believe that they can follow in the footsteps of the role model. Thus, the notion of becoming an engineer, a carpenter, or a scientist may remain an abstraction even in the presence of suitable role models. The message to girls must be personal and one of substance if it is to last and blossom. As a starting point, networks of support must be established at the family, school, and community levels that will help girls (and women) to make realistic assessments of their abilities by dismantling the link between gender and performance. It is my belief that girls need to receive this support on a daily basis. Simply telling girls that they can be anything they want to be is not enough. We need to specifically relate the message that girls possess the *ability* to master the basic skills needed to be a mathematician, an engineer, a biologist, and so forth, and then support them through a series of positive experiences to personally arrive at the conclusion that they *are* capable of excelling in these career areas. This means that networks not only need to be available to celebrate successes but also to support women in a realistic evaluation of their failures. If we can help women to transcend the boundary characterized by acquired feelings that we must be spectacular in order to be acceptable, and that anything short of spectacular is equivalent to failure, we will go a long way to increasing the participation of women in science.

The importance of helping girls and women to make realistic assessments of their failures as well as successes cannot be overemphasized. An often neglected consequence of an unbalanced cultural emphasis on male achievement is that females are for the most part deprived of the many benefits arising out of meaningful sports competition. One of these is learning to fail, and more important, learning that failure is not necessarily final. A boy striking out his first time up to bat at the beginning of the Little League baseball season may be disappointed, but he knows that his failure to successfully hit the ball on this particular occasion will not mark the end of his baseball career.[2] He will be afforded many more opportunities to succeed throughout the season. Moreover, his performance will be averaged, an outstanding record judged as failing in more than two thirds of his attempts![3] Valuable experiences such as this carry over into other areas of life. As a result, men tend to view challenges in perspective, whereas women see each attempt as a watershed event. Carol Hollenshead, director of the Michigan Center for the Education of Women and a strong advocate for well-coached team sports for girls, reported that she was shocked to learn that her husband's experience in taking the Scholastic Aptitude Test (SAT) was radically different from her own. She was panicked, feeling that her entire future was on the line. In contrast, her husband viewed the experience as a game (Mann, 1994).

Women tend to internalize an event to a far greater degree than men. I believe that this can be directly connected to the fact that girls are not provided with life experiences in which they fail and can still walk away feeling good about themselves and motivated to try again. This deficit manifests itself in the classroom. Women blame themselves when they receive a bad grade on an exam, whereas men tend to hold the teacher responsible or blame the subject itself (Mann, 1994). Simone de Beauvoir (1952) wrote in *The Second Sex* about the consequences of depriving women of the benefits of sports competition.

> [She] has no faith in a force she has not experienced in her body; she does not dare to be enterprising, to revolt, to invent; doomed to docility, to resignation . . . she regards the existing state of affairs as something fixed. (p. 331)

It is important to recognize that the internalization of social stereotypes and prejudices that devalue women, along with the ensuing reinforcement of these attitudes through victimization, represent the more specific facets of harm resulting from the cultural overemphasis on male achievement at the expense of females. As a consequence, a near standard feature of women's psychological development in this society is that the assimilated self-devaluation tends to create low self-esteem, self-doubt, and reliance on the opinions of others (Hamilton, 1989).

Jean Hamilton (1989) has elaborated.

> The internalized devaluation of self (and the group to which one belongs) is reinforced by threats or [discriminatory] experiences. Psychologically, these experiences come to represent the societal prediction of what [women] can expect, of who we are, and what we deserve, as women: to be used, devalued, and humiliated. A sense of unworthiness may thus become part of the organizing nucleus of women's self-esteem and may contribute to the unconscious background of other experiences of victimization or discrimination. . . . The finding from a variety of survey studies show that women who are victims of sexual harassment often experience symptoms such as feeling frightened, angry, helpless, and guilty along with experiencing physical symptoms such as headaches and difficulty in concentrating. (pp. 39–40).

The emphasis on early education programs as a means to eventually increase the proportions of women scientists fails to recognize that surviving the first great wave of casualties, although necessary, does not guarantee that there will be more women scientists. In the absence of support at the latter stages of career development, the early education programs may in fact ensure a greater number of women casualties—the diametric opposite of the stated goal. The development of programs and support networks at the undergraduate, graduate, postdoctoral, and faculty levels must therefore be an immediate priority.

My research suggests that some of the greatest challenges women face to staying in science are experienced during a 2- to 3-year period encompassing the end of graduate school through the beginning of postdoctoral research. It is not surprising that this is also the period when women have the least amount of personal support. The culture of graduate school has a lot to do with this. It is a time of extreme dependence. By the time a person enters graduate school, and certainly when she begins the postdoctoral period, there is a significant amount of time and emotional investment involved. Moreover, the graduate student's or postdoctoral research associate's (postdoc's) career is largely held in the hands of others (advisors, dissertation committees, and so forth). This is a tension-filled period and many students report feeling as if they are constantly "walking on eggshells," attempting not to anger or disappoint someone with perceived power and who might in some way adversely affect their career. It is a paradox that it is within this framework of extreme dependence and tension that the student is expected to exhibit a strong sense of *independence* and self-direction. Thus, it is understandable that this is also a time when women are uncomfortable seeking outside support and help. The perception of many women graduate students and postdocs is that to seek support is tantamount to revealing a lack of independence, which in turn reinforces the cultural message that they do not belong in science in the first place.

Programs designed to transcend this boundary need to be structured so that participation does not further compromise a woman's self-esteem. Much can be done to remove the stigma of participation if there is regular support and participation by female faculty members and administrators. These programs can cross scientific disciplines and be even more effective if the program has a robust, enthusiastic support among the various departments, one that regularly encourages female students to participate. Arranging time for female students and postdocs to interact with invited seminar speakers who are women will further facilitate the success of these programs. This has the effect of personally exposing women to other women who have achieved success, and it is an important source of support, encouragement, and motivation. These events should be cross-disciplinary and therefore need to be structured so that their focus is on the woman behind the science rather than a specific question and answer period about the intricacies of the speaker's research.

The essay that follows personalizes the need for support programs and networks at the graduate level. The writer successfully survived the first and second casualty waves only to face what turned out to be insurmountable barriers in graduate school—and she faced them alone.

Science and Women: From the Vantage Point of a "Leak in the Pipeline"

_____ *Minna Mahlab* _____

My high school physics experience was probably just like everyone else's: very dry, very boring. Chemistry was the fun class, so I decided I wanted to be a chemist. You got to mix together strange substances, and scribble down odd combinations of numbers and letters that seem more like a secret code than anything else. I expressed this preference on my SAT forms, and received many letters and brochures from engineering and technical schools, but I chose to attend Bryn Mawr College, a small, liberal arts, women's college located in a suburb of Philadelphia. Each graduating class is approximately 300 students; this small size contributes to a strong sense of community.

Despite my lackluster experience in high school, I enrolled in first-year physics and was immediately hooked. What I liked best about college physics was that I was fully engaged in the process. It required bringing together everything I knew—not just facts of science but the convoluted ways of thinking that I used in my literature classes as well. Physics was always a challenge; it was never boring. An adrenaline rush accompanied completing every problem and figuring out every new concept. Equally exciting was explaining it to someone else. My classmates and I worked closely together and I was a tutor or teaching assistant throughout my college career. Explaining difficult ideas to others and guiding them to a level of understanding was something at which I excelled and in which I took great pride. After four very successful years as a physics undergraduate, I decided I had found my goal. I was going to do physics for the rest of my life and teach other people to enjoy it as much as I did.

Slowly, I began to realize that all was not as it seemed. Science does not operate in a social or cultural vacuum. Even at a small institution such as Bryn Mawr, there were inter- and intradepartmental politics with which to deal. At larger schools and industries, it was even worse. I became painfully aware of how few women there are in the field, and how much I stood out for the sole reason that I am a woman. On my first day at one summer position, the student group was given a tour that halted awkwardly at the changing station.[4] The director, who was giving the tour, did not know where the women's changing room was located, and finally just left me outside to wait while the rest of the group went in to be instructed in the proper procedure for putting on and taking off the special garb. When they emerged, the tour continued, and I was told that at some point they would find one of the other women to show me.

On graduating from college, I had the opportunity to travel abroad and participate in a political science program. After a great deal of thought, I deferred my entry into graduate school and joined the program. However, even in this seemingly unrelated academic setting, I quickly availed myself of the opportunity to conduct a research project, and spent much of my free time as a research assistant in the physics department at the institution at which the program was administered. Following completion of the program, I returned to the United States and began doctoral studies in physics at the University of California at San Diego. UCSD is a large research-oriented institution located in La Jolla, California, near San Diego. The physics faculty number about 55, with 4 tenured women, and there are active research groups in many areas of specialty. It was strange to walk into the orientation session the first day and find myself to be 1 of 6 women among 50 classmates. The department chair announced that he was pleased that women were so "well represented" in our class. I thought he was being sarcastic, but I was the only person in the room who laughed.

My graduate school experience started off on the wrong foot when I went to my first faculty advisor session. I was nervous, having performed poorly on the entrance exam, and expressed concern that my preparation was weak in certain areas. I suggested taking a couple of advanced undergraduate courses before jumping into the graduate curricula. The advisor replied, "You know, I've looked over your record, and I think that you can handle this. You can always come in for extra help, if necessary."

Three weeks later, I found myself floundering, struggling to keep my head above water, and failing miserably. I went to see my advisor. "Well," he said, "I didn't really expect anything else. You went to that girls' school, didn't you? I'm sure they could not have adequately trained you there." I was both shocked and offended by his blunt arrogance. Going to a women's college had insured my eventual failure? He continued by informing me that had I tried to major in physics at a "real" school, I would not have succeeded.

I found myself completely at a loss. Having no support network to fall back on, and finding myself unable to catch up and succeed, I fell into the trap of believing him. And once *I* believed I could not do it, I was doomed to fail.

My undergraduate experience left me accustomed to asking questions during lectures, but questions were not encouraged by professors or tolerated by most classmates at UCSD. When I asked for further explanations during a lecture, some of my classmates would grumble and wonder why I was wasting their time. Eventually, I stopped asking questions. I had been accustomed at Bryn Mawr to accessible and encouraging professors and teaching assistants. Although some of the professors were accessible at UCSD, they certainly were not supportive. Eventually I stopped asking for help. And throughout all of this, the idea that if I were not a woman, I would not be failing echoed loudly.

Most of the men in my class did not show that they were confused about the material. Instead, they behaved as though everything was crystal clear. They swaggered around in groups, loudly deriding the difficulty levels of problems that took me hours to solve. They were all succeeding, and I was not. Or so it seemed to me. It was only much later that I learned that many of them were performing at the same level as I was. However, they exuded confidence, and I did not perceive that it was usually false. And when confronted with that confidence, I think that all the years of messages that women could not do physics that I had ignored but absorbed internally finally surfaced and took hold. I failed.

When I considered whether or not trying again would be worthwhile, I struggled with several questions. What would I do differently next time? What mistakes would I try to avoid repeating? As I reflected, I began to wonder if the mistakes were totally mine in the first place.

At first, I enjoyed the notoriety that comes along with studying math and physics in general, and as a woman in particular. Most people report that they "hated physics in high school" and claim that they "don't know how to balance a checkbook." Many questioned my interest in physics, as well as my decision to be a physicist and accepted my career choice with some distaste accompanied by a great deal of awe. However, it did not take long before I tired of feeling different. I soon learned that a graduate student in English is received more graciously at a gathering, or in casual conversation on an airplane, than a graduate student in physics—that is, if she is a woman. Therefore, I sometimes lied about what I did. This was easier than trying to explain my choices.

The greatest outright disapproval I have received is from women in their 50s or older. Physics is an enigma to many of them and it is definitely not the sort of thing that might lure prospective husbands. From the perspective of some of these women, securing a husband is the bottom-line criterion a woman should use in making life choices. To illustrate, as an undergraduate I attended religious services in a community a few towns away from my school. More than once, on learning that I was attending Bryn Mawr, women in the congregation would say, "Oh, very nice. And what are you majoring in, dear? English?" "No, physics and math," I would reply. It was a great way to stop conversation—complete, dead silence usually followed that remark. The responses to my proclamation ranged from a weak, "That's nice, dear," to a blunt "Well, you're certainly not going to find a husband that way."

As I became older, the slant of these comments changed. It was no longer, "Why not switch to something easier," but, "Why aren't you married in addition to whatever nonsense you are involved in." I attended the wedding of a grade school friend after two years of graduate school. She and I had gone to a small private school together; many of the guests were the parents of our other classmates who had known us since the age of five.

"So," they said to me, "We hear you're studying physics." "Very nice, I'm sure." "Isn't this a lovely wedding?" "So tell me, when are you getting married?" "Oh, never mind about school, you can always get your degree on the side."

On the side? A PhD program in physics is not a casual, offhand experience even when you do not have the pressures of a family or relationship. But for me, because I am a woman, it was something I could or should do on the side. I am willing to bet that none of my male classmates had ever heard anything like that. But *my* priorities in life should not include an advanced degree in physics. That should be an afterthought, something in addition to the "real" part of my life.

Perhaps the worst part of my graduate school experience was that I spent so much time and energy questioning myself: my abilities, my knowledge, my self-esteem, my self-confidence. When I try to describe how the culture of physics as a whole made me feel unworthy, I can sense the lack of comprehension, and sometimes the disbelief on the part of listeners. I have no statistics that can convey the isolation women experience in the sciences and present a concrete picture. One of the most disturbing things is that condescending statements made about women typically go unchallenged. They are accepted as a matter of course, part of the daily dialog, and therefore in a bizarre twist they "make sense" to the listener.

I was asked recently if I have given up on physics. I have not. I still want to be a physicist. The problem is, I do not think I can be one in this system.

For example, even after I had passed the first hurdle in graduate school and became part of a research group, there were still problems. My desk was in a large open room right next door to that of a professor. His undergraduate students would regularly poke their heads in and ask where he was. If I told them I did not know and to check with his secretary, they would invariably say, "Well, aren't you the secretary?" There were eight graduate students housed in that room. I never observed any other student being asked if he were the secretary. I am not surprised. Other than me, they were all men. I suppose it is "natural" to assume that the only woman in the room is a secretary—even if she is wearing scruffy jeans and a t-shirt, hunched over a physics text or scanning equations on a computer screen.

Even going to the bathroom was an isolating experience. With the exception of those near the secretary's offices on the first floor, there are no bathrooms for women in the science building at UCSD. Thus, for bathroom breaks, when the guys went down the hall, I had to run down three flights of stairs. At night, in a deserted building, that can be a frightening experience. Men do not often worry about their safety when walking alone from the library or laboratory to the parking lot late at night. Conversely, women must always be aware and on the defensive.

Is it harder for women to succeed in the sciences? Perhaps I cannot give a definitive answer, but I can offer the following story. I will never forget the words of my junior-level quantum mechanics professor at Bryn Mawr—a woman—looking at us wearily after a marathon problem-solving session that ran well into the evening and contemplating the rest of her night. Four hours of dealing with a stressed group of college students did not get her off the hook. She still had to go home and cook dinner for her family. As she was piling her books and notes together, she sighed wearily. "You know, sometimes I wish I had a wife."

Even when recognized, women's achievement is characteristically acknowledged within the context of serendipity rather than ability (Frieze, Whitley, & McHugh, 1982). What is skill for the male is considered luck for the female. This characterization severely undermines women's confidence and fosters an internal belief that we cannot trust our successes. After all, if our achievements are a matter of luck, then the odds are that our luck will change. However, if our accomplishments are a direct result of talent and ability, then each success lays a foundation on which subsequent achievements can be built.

Jacquelynne Eccles, professor of psychology at the University of Michigan, directed a series of studies designed to compare objective measures of students' abilities, as determined by standardized tests, grades in school, and so forth, to the subjective assessments and expectations of their parents. A goal of this research was to determine if a general belief that males have superior mathematics and athletic ability correlated with parents' distorted opinion of their child's competency. Eccles and her team found that parents amplified the ability of sons above, and downplayed the ability of daughters below, what the objective measures indicated. Eccles explained these results:

> If I believe that a girl is not going to do as well, then I am likely to believe she is not as talented as her grades would suggest. And it is that latter belief that is the important one. They know that their daughter is in the 98th percentile on performance. But they explain that by focusing on her hard work rather than her talent. It's very subtle, but it has the impact of undermining her own confidence in her talent. She starts to believe that she is doing well because she is a hard worker rather than because "I am good at this." . . . If parents believe the stereotype, they say to the girl, "It's because you're working hard." And to the boy they say, "You are working hard and you are talented." Over time he will come away with more confidence in his ability. (Mann, 1994, pp. 99–100)

A step in the right direction would be for parents, as well as teachers, to acknowledge a child's talent when it manifests. At the same time, resist the temptation to overdramatize achievements. It sends the wrong message to girls when they are overly praised for achievements that are treated as a matter of course for boys. As Eccles advised, stop recognizing girls' achievements solely in the context of hard work and determination. This characterization sends an inappropriate message to girls that they lack the requisite talent and ability to excel. Instead, hard work and determination should be acknowledged within the context of their *complementing* talent and ability. Finally attach a future to childhood interests and talent. Aptitude in a specific area can usually be applied generally to several career endeavors. For example, an outfielder on a high school girls' softball team had just made a spectacular running grab of a fly ball, making the third out and retiring the sides. As she approached the bench from the field, she was welcomed with pats on her back and compliments such as, "Great catch!" I was substituting for the regular coach, who had been unexpectedly called out of town, and as I congratulated the player I remarked, "You'd make a great physicist!" The entire team was shocked at my seemingly out-of-context statement. However, I explained that the outfielder had actually performed a highly sophisticated set of mathematical calculations that, among other things, accurately projected the trajectory of the ball—estimating its hang time as a function of the ball's momentum and the competing forces of gravity, wind resistance, and humidity—ultimately allowing her to set up and solve the equation that mapped the correct velocity and running angle necessary to meet the ball at the precise point at which it could be caught. All of this without the help of a calculator or pencil and paper! I ended by informing the team that each time they stepped up to bat, or made a play on the field, they solved problems far more challenging than anything present in their school textbooks.

For many of these young women, this was the first time anyone had connected mathematics or science to their daily lives. Whereas they had previously been abstractions, my connection made them real, and it attached a future to a seemingly unrelated talent. By the end of the game, team members were approaching me with questions.

"Do you mean when I'm late for school and run to catch the bus, I'm doing a physics experiment?"

"Absolutely!" I replied. "You need only to learn the language that will allow you to communicate this exceptional ability to others—and that language is mathematics."

I was not able to follow the academic progress of these women, but I would venture to guess that they approached mathematics with a new attitude —one that said, "I can do this!"

Attaching a future to talent is of paramount importance for girls, because the culture directs them to define their self-esteem more by popularity than achievement. As a consequence, simply acknowledging mathematics talent may be insufficient, because a girl might deem other people's assessment of her social skills as far more significant than mathematics ability. Thus, girls may elect not to take mathematics and science courses despite having the talent and ability to successfully negotiate through them. In my opinion, girls need a regular diet of future-oriented connections to their daily lives.

An outcome of not properly supporting female achievement is that large numbers of women enter college with little or no sense of purpose and direction. Among college seniors, women are often more unsure of what their next step will be, a trend also evident with women graduate students and postdoctoral research associates. This should come as no great surprise given that the culture does not promote girls to think in terms of having a professional future. Furthermore, women often bring an alternative outlook to the masculine professional arena, one that is not always welcome. When women join a male-dominated profession, they frequently confront complications that originate as an outcome of conflicts between the conventional roles women have occupied in society and the new functions that they are undertaking within the profession (Coe & Dienst, 1990). Duane Schmidt (1987) provided a classic example:

> Dr. Harper made an appointment with a new attorney. Shortly after he was ushered into the attorney's office, a young woman entered. "Honey, would you get me a cup of coffee?" the doctor asked. "Black. No sugar." "Certainly," she said and left the room.
>
> In minutes, she returned with his coffee, then took the seat behind the attorney's desk.
>
> "You're the attorney?" Dr. Harper gasped. "Oh, I'm so sorry. I thought you were the secretary."
>
> "No problem," she said. "But I think you should know my rate is $100 per hour. That cup of coffee just cost you $25." (p. 37)

We can applaud the courage of the attorney in her response to sexist assumptions, but in the long run she may pay a heavy price for her action. Dr. Harper may ignore his own offensive action and instead focus on her assertiveness—viewing it as a negative quality. In retelling his experience in the attorney's office to others, he may describe her as irrational, combative, stubborn, or even a "man-hater." Although all untrue, the news about her will travel fast and she may find herself effectively "walled out" of her profession.

There are costs to violating social norms. There are also rewards. Girls and women need to be informed so that they can make appropriate choices. Value struggles can result in emotional fatigue as a woman strives to satisfy both the demands of a professional role and social expectations that are tied to her gender. Girls and women often see themselves as being trapped into undesirable "all or nothing" options, and the consequences are lasting. In the process, women fear loss of their femininity and their affectional relationship. And it is a fear that is based on reality. For example, women medical students more often lose their affectional partner through separation or divorce during medical school compared to males (Bowers, 1987). Furthermore, the loss of primary partners reported by several contributors to this volume suggests that the trend is not unique to medical school. Hilary Cosell (1985) commented:

I think we're being terribly misled about how much success women as a group have achieved and about how real that success actually is. I think there may be a bitter day of reckoning for many of us that's not too far off. A day where women will say, "I gave up my personal life, I destroyed my marriage, I didn't have children, I gave up this and I gave up that and what was it for? I still haven't been able to achieve the way men do, in the same arena they do, the way I was told I could." Let's face it: women are no longer disenfranchised, be we don't have anything like the power of the white male corporate establishment. I don't know if we'll ever acquire that kind of power, but if we do, it's not going to be anytime in the near future. (p. 135).

As students, women face challenges of isolation, animosity, and harassment while striving to integrate their professional roles with their identities as women. The pressure becomes particularly intense during graduate school, where the competition for limited resources tends to suppress women from articulating their concerns. Consider the response of a medical student when asked about reporting incidents of discrimination and harassment.

[E]veryone here is paranoid about residencies, and getting good letters of recommendations from clinicians, therefore, they seldom create waves . . . in order for prejudices to be weeded out of the system, some waves have to be created . . . but who will do it and risk a good shot at a residency? (Coe & Dienst, 1990, p. 337)

Women are human. The sense of powerlessness to effect change combined with an increasing weariness from fighting a lone crusade for integrity and respect in a system that judges women more by stereotype than ability eventually takes its toll. It is therefore understandable that a significant number of women in the science career track elect to search for a scientific niche where male competition is low, to seek alternative employment opportunities such as science writing and reporting, to seek teaching positions in which tenure is based on one's effectiveness in educating students rather than fund-raising ability, or to exit the field entirely. In short, they settle for something different from their original dream. Women do this not because they view themselves as lacking in talent and ability, but because they want *relief*. Ann Saterbak provides a prime example of a woman choosing to redirect her career aspirations in the essay that follows.

Around and Around

_____ *Ann Saterbak* _____

"Oh, is your father a chemical engineer?" This is the most frequent response when I tell people that I am pursuing a PhD in chemical engineering. "No," I tell them. Sometimes I become brash and reply, "No, but my mother is." (Just for the record, the second response is untrue. Neither of my parents is a chemical engineer.) However, as I begin my fifth year in graduate school, I enjoy confronting people's expectations.

My story begins with becoming aware that my gender mattered in education. This revelation took place throughout public school and college. During graduate school, my thinking about women in science and engineering evolved through cycles of rage, creativity, and action. I learned that each of these three stages of the cycle is critical for the process to continue. Rage is a common response to injustice. When my heart feels that passion, I act and take risks. The primary enemy of rage is cynicism: to become resigned to the status quo, to give up hope for creative solutions, to allow pessimism to mask anger. The passion of rage must feed the power of creativity. Ideas are generated and creativity blossoms when people come together and identify common concerns and goals. Action requires pushing ideas through concrete, deliberate steps. Without action, there is no change; rage and creativity are extinguished. I believe that my journey through many cycles of rage, creativity, and action has increased my awareness of problems and issues faced by women in science and engineering, and has propelled me toward defining and refining my personal direction. For me, I hope that this process never ends.

My interest in exploring and constructing things was natural and began when I was young. I preferred building the house to playing house. I enjoyed mathematics and science more than reading. My parents were supportive throughout high school and were instrumental in helping me select a university and my intended majors of chemical engineering and biochemistry.

I attended Rice University in Houston, Texas. Rice is a small, private university, traditionally dedicated to undergraduate education. Of the 2700 undergraduates, about 50% major in science or engineering. The graduate enrollment is 1400; most of the departments have active research groups.

I had my first experience as a woman alone in a class my first year. I took a FORTRAN class with more than 50 men and 1 other woman. When she slept in, I was by myself. I knew no one and often sat alone. The homework groups were already established, and I was not part of one. This situation had a surprising impact on me: I wondered if maybe I should not have been there. That uncertainty led to self-doubt and the fear of being judged as technically weak. I perceived a higher risk asking a man for help than asking a woman. I dreaded facing this isolation day after day. I looked with trepidation to my sophomore year, but was relieved to find seven or eight women in my introductory class in chemical engineering.

Around 25 students enrolled in that first chemical engineering course. When I graduated, there were four women and eleven men. I remember those numbers precisely for, by then, that aspect of my environment was important to me. At no time did I feel that any peers in my chemical engineering classes made assumptions about my qualifications or lowered their expectations about my technical ability because of my gender. In these courses, the women generally outscored the men on tests and projects. So any biases the men might have had were quickly dispelled.

I had only one female teacher in all of my science, mathematics, and engineering courses at Rice University. She was a temporary instructor in the Department of Mathematical Sciences. Several undergraduate men in my class heckled her and obviously made her feel uncomfortable. I remember feeling sorry for her. Rice hired its first female faculty member in the Chemical Engineering Department while I was an undergraduate. Even though I never took a course from her, I became better acquainted with her than with most of the male faculty members who served as my teachers. I came to know her because she sought me out and introduced herself when she first arrived.

I first experienced rage at Rice. Anger filled me when I was trapped in one particular professor's office. Whenever I went to ask him a question about homework, he positioned himself between me and the door. He talked endlessly, often invading my personal space. No excuse to leave worked; I virtually had to bolt around him and through the door. He did not talk this way to the men in the class, only to the women. Eventually, I deciphered the pattern, and a male friend accompanied me on subsequent visits to this professor. I learned that if I wore tank tops, shorts, or skirts, he commented on how nice I looked in my outfit. In my handwritten course evaluation at the end of the semester, I discussed my anger and the many uneasy trips to his office for consultation. I also informed another engineering faculty member about my encounters. Several years after I graduated, I learned that his colleagues had discussed this inappropriate behavior with him and that complaints from undergraduate women had subsequently stopped. Aside from this one professor, I never experienced differential treatment based on gender during my time at Rice. However, I did leave Rice with an awareness that some people perceive a *female* chemical engineer as different from a *chemical engineer.*

Although I respected several faculty members for their commitment to teaching and research, I did not really have a role model or mentor. In fact, I do not remember thinking it was important. Now I struggle to find role models. It is not enough for me to respect a person for his or her technical position or expertise. I must understand and respect the personal and professional decisions a person has made along her career path. In this way, a role model provides me with realistic alternatives as I forge my own way. The teaching and mentoring aspects of an academic job were attractive to me. Thus, I set off to obtain a PhD in chemical engineering at the University of Illinois at Urbana-Champaign (UIUC), a state school 150 miles south of Chicago, Illinois, with the intent of pursuing an academic career. The undergraduate enrollment is 26,000; the graduate enrollment is 10,000. I have sensed an unfriendly, cold attitude from the administration and faculty, and this feeling is echoed by friends in a wide range of technical and academic fields. I have not found the University of Illinois to be as receptive to students' opinions and contributions as Rice University. The attitude of "the best will survive and rise to the top" is pervasive and, in my opinion, serves as an excuse for perpetuating the status quo.

Female graduate students in the Chemical Engineering Department make up around 30% of the department. This percentage is high compared to other programs across the United States, but it is misleading. Over the past 7 years, the attrition rate for women has been 20%; the attrition rate for men has been three to four times lower. This statistic reflects students who declared an intent to earn a PhD and did not fail the doctoral qualifying exam. Critics of change argue that because these statistics reflect only 35 women, the pool is too small and the statistics should be discounted. I might believe the argument that the numbers are not meaningful if I had not been a colleague to most of these women. They have not left for random reasons.

The College of Engineering (graduate enrollment of 2200; 13% percent women) does not keep statistics by gender on the paths of graduate students. A group of students and faculty confronted the dean of the College of Engineering with the information that in several departments the attrition rate is much higher for women than for men. The dean responded that, as a whole, the College of Engineering has produced and continues to produce top-notch research and top-notch MS and PhD engineers. In his opinion, even if women were dropping out because of unfair treatment, harassment, or a hostile environment, these problems affected only a small fraction of the college. The dean was not convinced that he should expend his energies or resources on problems affecting a small percentage of students.

The Chemical Engineering Department at the University of Illinois at Urbana-Champaign has never employed in the past, nor does it currently employ, a woman at the instructor-, assistant professor-, associate professor-, or full professor-level. In the chain of command at the UIUC, men hold all of the positions, from my department head to the chancellor. During my second year in graduate school, I began to wonder how many other chemical engineering programs lacked women professors. Was this the norm at other top programs? After a little investigation, I determined that 17 of the top 20 schools had at least one female faculty member. Several departments had as many as three. My posing the question to the department, "Why are there no female professors here?" unleashed hostility, biases, and a dialogue that continues to evolve.

In the fall of my third year, a tenure-track position opened. A group of male and female students organized to form the graduate student branch of the faculty search committee. We identified our primary goal: Locate qualified women and minority candidates and encourage them to apply for this tenure-track position. We brainstormed extensively and developed a list of 10 possible ways to meet this goal. After many faculty search committee meetings and appointments with the department head, we narrowed our focus to one action. The faculty search committee mailed 250 letters to male and female fourth- and fifth-year graduate students at 13 highly respected departments. Of all the women receiving that letter, only one applied for the job. At the beginning, and at the end of this experience, I felt rage. My rage abated while I led the committee through the processes of brainstorming and action. But when a White male received and accepted the offer, I felt powerless. I chalked it up as a good effort; and for the first time, I realized the size of the system I was challenging. Now in my fifth year, the UIUC Chemical Engineering Department is the *sole* representative among the top 20 departments that has not hired a woman into a tenure-track position. Perhaps female faculty candidates avoid this department; I know I would. Maybe they anticipate isolation. Maybe they suspect a hostile environment.

In my opinion, several faculty members at the University of Illinois sustain a hostile environment by making different assumptions about graduate students based on gender. For example, a female graduate student who had clearly stated her intention to pursue an academic career was discussing with her advisor the presence of women in other top-20 departments. This faculty member commented that he believed that only one of the women at all of those schools was actually qualified for the job; the rest, he alleged, had secured positions only because of their gender. The knowledge that his own female graduate student was interested in pursuing an academic career did not alter his biases, nor did it curb his need to express them. In my opinion, this young faculty member could hardly have amassed either the breadth of expertise—ranging from fluid dynamics, to chemical vapor deposition, to polymer dynamics—or the free time to evaluate technically and critically the work of all 30 of these female faculty members. I believe that he expects better science from men than from women.

I feel that most of my male peers think I am as technically competent as any student in the department. However, I sense that they have lower long-term scientific career expectations from their female peers than they do from their male contemporaries. One extreme encounter I had was with an American-born White engineering graduate student who stated that when women have babies, they go crazy and cannot do science anymore. I believe that part of these lowered expectations derives from the observation that women are often the primary caregivers in families and do make career sacrifices.

These stories, plus many more, churned around in my head for countless hours. Again, my anger drove me to creativity. The graduate student branch of the faculty search committee restructured with a diversity of goals: Decrease the attrition rate of women, improve the environment for all students, and facilitate the placement of UIUC graduate students in academic positions. We doubled our list of concrete ideas and compiled 20 action items. The suggestions fell into two broad categories. The first addressed departmental policy: Establish an official procedure for changing advisors after the MS degree is awarded for students pursuing doctoral studies, initiate a mentoring program for women graduate students with women at other universities or in industry, and develop a top-down policy that does not tolerate sexual harassment or gender discrimination. The second category centered on women developing a safety net for other women: Sponsor regular dinners or social events for women in the department and initiate a mentoring program for incoming students to be partnered with older graduate students. In the end, the department head implemented only one suggestion: Increase the diversity of the departmental seminar speakers and allot time on those seminar speaker's schedules to talk with interested graduate students. As graduate students, we initiated potluck dinners for all women in the department. Neither of these steps is huge, but each is a step in the right direction.

I have tried to move away from simple, reactionary rage and to move toward an anger that grows from a continual awareness of an unjust environment. Specific inflammatory instances in my department no longer trigger the cycle of rage, creativity, and action. Rather, I am set to move through creativity and action whenever people are ready to come together to work and as the department head is receptive to listening. For example, a recent BS graduate mailed letters to a major departmental donor and to the faculty in the department. Her letter recounted three stories that she put forth as examples that the department discriminates against female students. For several days, the former department head was clearly uncomfortable with the situation. He scheduled an appointment with me to discuss the "facts" of the letter and possible programs to avoid such occurrences in the future. With the help of a colleague and resources from the journal *Science* (Benditt, 1993, 1994; Culotta, 1993), the Association of American Colleges (Sandler; 1992), and several University of Illinois reports (e.g., *Chancellor's Workshop on Women in Science and Engineering,* 1994; *Final Report of the Committee on the Status of Women Graduate Students,* 1993), we followed up on previous brainstorming sessions and compiled a list of 65 suggestions. We identified seven items that we thought were particularly reasonable and feasible. The department head later admitted that he really did not want to establish any frameworks or structures specifically for women because he feared that in the future he might need to dismantle these structures. I do not know why he was afraid. He did, however, agree to send out a climate survey to former students, establish a procedure to track all students, and distribute the university policy on sexual harassment and gender discrimination to all students. To date, only one of those promises has been fulfilled. A recent industrial grant provided financial resources to the department to tackle some issues, but higher-priority items seem to swamp the human resources.

I have spent time reflecting on how the actions taken to date actually affect the departmental environment. Are our actions curing real problems or are they just bandaging wounds? Really working with these issues is painful, confrontational, and costly. I have challenged the status quo and made waves in my department. I think that my actions have only been bandages. Diversifying the faculty will make an impact; inviting minority seminar speakers is a bandage. Zero tolerance of sexual harassment will cure one wound; distributing the university policy on sexual harassment is a bandage. Tackling and dismantling the tenure system will reshuffle the power structure; hosting potluck dinners is sometimes all I can do.

To affect real change in the academic community, I believe I would have to join the community. Even though my interests and aptitudes have not changed, I am making the decision not to pursue a career in academic research. I want a career in which I can apply my technical skills to solving problems and can function as a mentor to younger women interested in engineering; I *do not* want to be a colleague to many of the men I have encountered. I want to be in an environment that encourages and expects innovation and diversity; I *do not* want a career in which my decision to have a family will be perceived as not being "truly committed to research." I want a career in which I can balance the social, technical, and spiritual aspects of my life. Because I enjoyed my teaching experiences, I will look for job openings at small, teaching colleges. In addition, I will pursue job opportunities in industry. Whatever job I choose, I will endeavor to continue my cycles of rage, creativity, and action to facilitate change.

I want that change to enable a future generation to move away from the painful reality of this final story. While visiting schools as a prospective graduate student, I asked in each department for the number and percentage of female students.

"Oh, we have a lot of women here. About 30% of our graduate students are women," answered one department head.

"Really," I responded, "That's great."

"Well, let me actually count," he replied. With a list of the names of the graduate students in hand, he concluded that fewer than 10% of the students were women. I wonder how he can mistake fewer than 10% for 30%? What is "a lot of women"? To him, maybe one woman constitutes a lot of women. To me, there never are a lot.

As might be suspected, social stereotypes regarding feminine inferiority are amplified to their greatest degree during the graduate school and postdoctoral period, precisely because it is the step directly preceding a fierce competition for a limited number of jobs. Whereas women in science at the earlier stages are stigmatized as a "joke," it now becomes a serious issue, because women might be *stealing* jobs from men. Notice that the representation of stealing jobs is selectively applied to women. Men never speak of stealing jobs from each other. They simply recognize that the most qualified person or the individual able to gain an edge over the others will be selected. Only women *steal*[5] jobs, implying that there is something dishonest about the whole process. Furthermore, *stealing* invokes an image that males are "entitled" to the jobs and that women are robbing them through underhanded means, as this quote from a medical student indicates: "[F]emale residents seem to be those dating male staff" (Coe & Dienst, 1990, p. 337). Comments such as these reveal a belief in the global inferiority of women. As a consequence, it is impossible for the person to conceive of a woman succeeding because she has ability and is qualified. David Coe and Evelyn Dienst (1990) conducted a study at the California College of Podiatric Medicine in which, among other things, medical students were asked what advice they would offer to an incoming female student. The two points most frequently mentioned were to be prepared academically and to study diligently. However, the four additional suggestions presented below perhaps better than anything reveal that stereotypical attitudes regarding the components necessary for women's success have not significantly changed from previous generations.

Male student:	"Do your best at all times, you have to be twice as good to be thought of as half as good. Play the game, it is only 4 years out of your life."
Female student:	"Cut your hair and wear pants. Be twice as smart as any guy."
Male student:	"Wear short skirts and low-cut blouses."
Female student:	"Be beautiful and attract male professors to get better grades." (p. 337)

The year 1992 was proclaimed as "The Year of the Woman," a phrase that was bandied about particularly heavily during the presidential campaign. Since then, each successive year has received a similar designation. I have often watched the people making this proclamation and while shaking my head in bewilderment asked, "I wonder what planet they're living on?" Women essentially repeat the same struggle generation after generation. I close out this chapter with a quote from Judy Mann, a columnist for the *Washington Post* and author of the book *The Difference: Growing Up Female in America* (1994). She has remarked on how this cycle might be broken—that is, if we are serious as a society about valuing women.

One point is beyond question, yet it has been largely ignored by the feminist movement. . . . The point is this: We will never effectively change the way we raise girls unless we also change the way we raise boys, and we will never alter the outcome for most girls until we change the way boys think of girls. We have to give girls strategies for dealing with boys and boys strategies for dealing with girls that are grounded in mutual respect, not fear of humiliation. And we have to appreciate in much greater measure the qualities we associate with girls—the sensitivity and the relations skills that bind a society together—and begin to deemphasize the qualities we associate with boys, such as aggressiveness and violence, qualities that are certainly consuming our society in bloodshed and tearing it apart. Until we do this, until we weigh boys and girls on an equal scale, generations of children will repeat the patterns of adversarial relations between the sexes—a pattern firmly rooted in an imbalance of power between the sexes, a pattern that has gone on so long that it has been called the longest war. Generations of girls will be knocked off the ladder and disabled, repeating the histories of their mothers. Generations will repeat our struggle for equality, until we truly find out what happens to girls. Then we need to implement the profound social changes that are still necessary so that girls can climb the ladder to adulthood without being dislodged, without being silenced and submerged into a male culture. (pp. 15–16).

3

Is It Natural or Processed "Sugar and Spice"

Why, in the Peking Opera, are all the women's roles played by men?
Because only a man knows how a woman is supposed to act.

David Henry Hwang, *Madame Butterfly*

Are there measurable differences between males and females?
Yes. Men die on average 7 years earlier than women. Color blindness, hemophilia, and other gender-linked genetic traits affect 1 woman for every 16 men. Women tend to have a superior sense of smell, taste, hearing, and sight. The list goes on and on.

But wait a minute. Why focus on these things?

Why not?

These statements highlighting female advantage seem awkward because male–female comparisons are typically structured to favor males. This is such a common occurrence that we tend to be somewhat disoriented by variations on the theme. As a result, comparisons favoring females are discounted as "trivial" and are typically countered with statements beginning with, "Yeah, but men are . . ."

But men are what? Smarter? Stronger? Which males compared to which females? Under what set of circumstances? For example, men are generally considered to be superior in sports, but as author and athlete Mariah Burton Nelson (1994) pointed out, this is a dubious standard that is based on a false

44

comparison in which upper-body strength is valued above all other attributes that could be considered.

> Those who claim male sports superiority are not thinking of male gymnasts, who lack the flexibility to use some of the apparatus women use. Or male swimmers, who can't keep up with women over long distances. Or male equestrians, who gallop side by side with—or in the dust of—their female peers. . . . They are not considering how much women and men have in common: the human experience of sport. These same people would never think of comparing Sugar Ray Leonard to Muhammad Ali. One weighed sixty pounds more than the other. Clearly, they deserved to box in different classes. Yet the top female tennis player is often compared to the top male tennis player ("Yeah but she could never beat *him*"), who usually outweighs her by sixty pounds. (pp. 55–56).

At the very least, it can be concluded that male–female comparisons are rarely as straightforward as they are presented. Unfortunately the debate surrounding the validity of these comparisons is so intense that it tends to swamp what I consider to be an even greater issue. Rather than arguing over the existence of male–female differences, a fundamental area of concern at the policy level should be to ask if comparisons alleging that "men are better" form a sound rationale for excluding women from participation in a given endeavor. Turning it around, why have women's presumed status as "more nurturing and better caretakers" *not* been a legitimate reason for preventing men from pursing such fields as nursing and primary school teaching? Indeed, Laura Swaffield (1988) pointed out that despite being a decided minority, men in nursing are paid more and achieve higher status.

It really boils down to the fact that men have traditionally held social power and therefore set the standards and rules under which the comparisons are made. This creates an asymmetry of opportunity in which men (those holding power) are able to take full advantage of the total available resources while simultaneously erecting boundaries that severely impede the progress of women (the disadvantaged group). The existence of the boundaries is not addressed seriously as an issue because it is sufficient for those in power to state that there are none, and the subject is closed.

This paternalistic relationship, in which men assume a parental role and women are perpetually seen as children, manifests itself in other detrimental ways. As the privileged group, men routinely voice unsubstantiated pejorative claims about women that are generally accepted as fact with only anecdotal or no supporting evidence. Consider the following declaration: "Women are too emotional to be good leaders." By itself, this is a testable hypothesis. Parameters of *good leadership* could be defined and experiments constructed to measure the impact that being in touch with one's emotions has on effective leadership under a variety of conditions. This could potentially lead to the identification of a threshold level, defined as *too emotional for good leadership,* and controlled experiments comparing women and men could be initiated. Conclusions could subsequently be drawn judging the degree to which the data collected supports the test hypothesis that women are too emotional to be good leaders. The entire study would then be subject to the scrutiny of the scientific community. Other researchers might decide to launch independent investigations designed to replicate or expand on the initial findings. Should the original conclusions be supported by the replication studies, a picture regarding the relationship between emotions and leadership might begin to emerge. Additional studies could also be initiated with the goal of testing the predictive power of the conclusions drawn from the original data. That is, given a specific set of circumstances and a scientifically measured level of *emotionality,* how well can a person's leadership ability be predicted? Finally, should the original data be replicable and also show predictive power, it might then be reasonable to use it in conjunction with other factors for guiding policy regarding suitable qualifications for leadership positions.

This is an example of how *good science* is conducted. Nevertheless, despite there being virtually no empirical data to support its validity, or the host of inherent assumptions imbedded within it, the declaration that women are too emotional to be good leaders has historically been used to exclude women from leadership roles—including positions in academic and research science. Notice that the burden of proof for the claim does not rest on men. As the parental figure, it is sufficient for them to merely state that it is true and it de facto is true. Rather the responsibility rests on women—the group to whom the statement is directed—to take on the greater challenge of proving that the assertion is *not* true. As a consequence, the asymmetry of opportunity is further reinforced. Women must devote valuable resources toward gathering data focused on the *reactive* goal of dispelling a myth, leaving little time and energy remaining for *proactive* projects. Even if sufficient evidence is gathered to call the claim that women are too emotional to be good leaders into question, women are still faced with the arduous task of getting those in power to listen. Securing their ear proves to be a double-edged sword; the standards for *good science* are suddenly applied and the data gathered subject to intense scrutiny. In the process, women subordinate themselves to the judgement of male paternal figures regarding the integrity of *their* data designed to refute the *men's* original unsubstantiated claim! More often than not, the data and conclusions are criticized, leaving women with little choice but to design new studies that will circumvent the criticisms. The cycle continues.

In the end, disadvantaged groups wanting to use the resources of those holding power are left with two basic choices. The first is to question the validity of the current standard or rebel against it. The second is to create ways of working inside the present system, with the expectation that it will be more accommodating over time. Although different in their fundamental approach, both options share two commonalities. Each requires that large amounts of energy be expended before the actual projects of interest can be undertaken, and they both lead to the same end result—subordination to those holding power. For this reason, women are rarely on an equal professional footing with men, despite the existence of a host of programs designed to ensure parallel treatment, status, and opportunity. At birth we are fitted with a straightjacket constructed of stereotypes and we spend our lives struggling to get free, learning to exist within its confines, or both.

To some, this may sound like a classic example of male bashing, but it is merely a statement of women's reality. Standards for proficiency are typically constructed out of a male model. Women are compared *up* to men; the scope is structured such that we almost always fall short of the mark. The scenario is played over and over. By the time women reach college age many have been so indoctrinated with this propaganda that they are shocked at the notion of pursuing a career in male-dominated fields such as science and engineering. Those women attempting to do so enter the field with an under-privileged status, often harboring an apologetic ("I really don't belong here") attitude. This is reinforced by the surrounding environment. For example, it is not uncommon for professors to use a good performance by a female student in an attempt to shame male students to a higher level, implying that if they were "real men" they would be able to consistently outperform her. The unfortunate message to the female student is that she *should not* be performing better than the male students and that she really *does not* belong in the class in the first place.

The essay contributed that follows illustrates the suffocating effect that the application of social stereotypes about women can have on one's career development.

The Silver Lining

_____ *Katrien J. van der Hoeven* _____

As I pulled out my dusty folders from elementary school, I came to realize where my love of the sciences began. Inside my fifth-grade science materials I came across a folder labeled "Geology" that had the word "rocks" written on the outside several times. It made me smile to remember my first introduction to geology and my growing interest in the sciences. My fifth-grade science teacher was my first introduction to the sciences in a more formal fashion, and she was my first science role model. She treated her students as adults, creating an atmosphere that demanded that we take science seriously. She provided me with enough assurance to convince me that I belonged in the sciences. As a result, when I was faced with opposition later in life, I was able to persevere.

I plunged into the sciences during middle school. I dissected my frog with vigor, created unique experiments with the microscope, and tested my blood type with anticipation. The last year of middle school, I encountered a previously unfamiliar attitude projected from my first male science teacher. He would tell jokes in class that demeaned women. These jokes perpetuated the theme of women belonging in the kitchen, barefoot and pregnant. I was frustrated and angry; I felt cheated. The ability to prove myself as a capable student was in his eyes inhibited by the fact that I was female. Everyone in the class had to work hard, but being a girl, I felt I had to work harder to achieve the same credit as my male counterparts. This teacher began to chip away at my wall of self-confidence. Soon, I began to regret that I had been born female. I felt I had to prove that even though I was a girl, I could still do well in science. Although I have long since left this class, the mandate to "prove myself" has not changed.

During my senior year of high school I confronted more opposition. I was taking two science classes—physics and physical geology (a college-level class)—unusual in high school and even more rare for a female. The teachers of both classes were men.

My physics teacher never seemed comfortable with the class and spoke quietly and timidly. Many male members of the class took advantage of his insecurities and would push their limits further than most teachers would allow. They degraded low achievers and taunted high achievers. Anyone that appeared different was fair game. It should thus come as no surprise that most of their negative attention was focused on the few females in the class. Because this disruptive group had essentially taken over the classroom, the teacher catered to their degrading antics in a seeming attempt to gain their respect. To illustrate, there was an incident in which I experienced difficulties properly phrasing a question. Playing it up for his approving "audience," my teacher snapped, "Kaatje, you remind me of the *Saturday Night Live* skit where Dan Akroyd turns to Jane Curtin and says, 'Jane, you ignorant slut.'"

The class immediately roared with laughter. I was mortified, but insisted on not letting it get to me and so I laughed along with the crowd. However, that comment was another large crack in my wall of self-confidence. After that episode, I did not feel secure raising my hand in class. The teacher's actions sent a message to all of the males in the class that it was open season on women who dared to enter a science classroom, along with the accompanying message to the women in the class that it was wrong for us to be upset by it. I suddenly found myself catapulted back in time to middle school, insecure with my own thoughts and actions.

I left for Colby College in Waterville, Maine, the following fall. Despite sparse encouragement from my high school teachers, I intended to become a geology major. Nevertheless, desire is not always enough. In the back of my mind, I worried that my prospects for success were bleak because of a weak background in mathematics. I shared this concern with my geology laboratory professor. He encouraged me to stick with it, noting that it was not worth giving up a dream just because of one class.

Approximately 32% of the geology majors at Colby are women. Nationwide, however, the percentage is much smaller. Why aren't there more women geology majors? Why aren't there more women scientists? One study followed 2000 girls expressing interest in science through high school and college. Only 20 out of the original 2000 females received a BS degree in the natural sciences (Widnall, 1988). A 1% success rate for women in science? What could be the cause of such a dismal record?

During my junior year, I took notice of the fact that there were no female geology professors, yet a large number of women geology majors at Colby. I became increasingly curious why such a gap exists. I began to question how I ended up in the sciences, considering my past negative experiences. Where do women lose their interest and why? Was I unique in my experiences, or was discouragement of females in science classrooms prevalent everywhere? At what point did women start to lose interest in the sciences? I decided to conduct research addressing these questions. My advisor was extremely helpful. He encouraged me to do a prospective study, not just research previously published reports. He wanted me to have something I could claim as my own and of which I could be proud. The department was also very supportive. For example, the chairperson regularly cut out any articles that he thought might be of interest to me and my project.

According to my research (which was on a limited scale), interest in the sciences is not lost during high school (van der Hoeven & Doss, 1994). I was somewhat relieved to learn that my negative middle and high school experiences were relatively unique, but I was simultaneously concerned that an adequate support network for women during the college years is lacking at most institutions.

Despite frustrating experiences in the sciences, I still felt a continual push to achieve. Although my family was supportive of my interests in all areas, there was a definite emphasis on the sciences at home. My father was a physicist and my mother a computer programmer. They provided living examples of success and active encouragement. I also reflect on that period during the fifth grade when my performance was not judged based on my gender. It helps me to remember that it is possible for women in science to be respected.

I am now about to enter my senior year at Colby. I have a minor in chemistry in addition to my geology major. I hope to pursue volcanology or geochemistry as possible fields of research. I feel a continual desire to keep learning. To be able to go hiking for a weekend and contemplate how the rocks got there, to take a rock hammer and discover the unweathered surfaces of rocks, to look at an outcrop on the side of the road and think of the time that it took to get where it is today are but a few of many things that fuel my love of geology. To me, geology is like a religion; I feel comforted by it, but also look at it in awe. That overwhelming feeling is what drives my momentum. Between the encouraging and discouraging, science has crept inside and become an integral part of me.

———————

Growing up female in most societies is to be assigned *inferior* status—not just in some things, but across the board. Women are, as Simone de Beauvoir (1952) aptly put it, *The Second Sex*. It does not really matter whether a woman considers herself inferior. At some point in her life, and usually multiple times, her gender will have a negative impact on her circumstances. Being reared in a nurturing, egalitarian environment can help a woman to cope with these instances, but it does not insulate her from their occurrence. Feminine inferiority is taken for granted; it is just the way things are. This "reality" is one of the first things that young boys learn. For example, in her groundbreaking work on gender socialization, Raphaela Best (1983) found that boys have a deeply internalized abhorrence of performing housework—a stereotypically female role—as early as the first grade.

> The boys declared independence from housework vocally as well as in their behavior. On one occasion, for example, the first-grade boys made it known that they would never cook or sew or do any other housekeeping chore under any circumstances, even if they starved to death or had to throw away their torn clothing or go without clothes. (pp. 79-80)

Prejudices relating to the inferiority of women are so pervasive and ingrained that males frequently question their masculinity, and in some cases become hostile, when a woman equals or surpasses their performance.[1] In her book *The Stronger Women Get, the More Men Love Football,* Mariah Burton Nelson (1994) shared her own experience with this phenomenon.

> What seems to make [men] the angriest is my observation that men are not better athletes than women are. In no sport are all men better than all women, I point out, and in many sports, women routinely defeat men. Although single-sex competitions are often appropriate, and men do have physical advantages in some sports, women should see themselves as men's peers, I suggest, rather than exclusively competing against women. . . . [M]en don't want to hear any of that. In voices I can only describe as high-pitched and hysterical, they say, "Yeah, but you're never going to see a woman play pro football!" . . . Most men are not 320-pound linebackers. But identified with these hulks, average men take great pleasure in the linebackers' exploits (a revealing term). Football, baseball, basketball, boxing, and hockey are important to men in part *because* they seem to be all-male pursuits, because they seem to be activities that *only men can do.* When women demonstrate excellence in sports like running, tennis, and golf, men take great pains to describe that excellence as less important, less worthy, less of an achievement than male excellence. (pp. 53–54).

As mentioned previously, the paranoid fear of failing to meet perceived standards of male competence—a level that clearly distinguishes them superior to women—is so common among men that professors and coaches regularly use it as a motivational tool. The way women think about themselves is also profoundly influenced by these attitudes. A case in point are contributions by several authors contained in this volume characterizing their aptitude for mathematics and science as unusual or atypical. (They were not like the other girls; they were different.) However, it is important to ask under what standard was the mathematics and science aptitude of these women considered unusual or atypical? A scientifically established norm or a stereotype? It certainly could not be the former because scientific studies, led by the pioneering work of psychologists Eleanor Macoby and Carol Nagy Jacklin (1974), have rather convincingly shown that there is a very small area of difference between the genders when matched samples are compared (see Rhode, 1990; Fausto-Sterling, 1992; Travis & Offir, 1977). In fact, *intragroup* differences (those found within a sample of males or females) are consistently greater than *intergroup* differences (those found between matched samples of females and males).

The salient issue, then, is not one of alleged feminine inferiority but centers on what society values. Specifically, how valued qualities are selectively nurtured among male and female children to *create* differences that are subsequently ascribed as innate and amplified into stereotypes. As several of the contributors to this volume attest, living in a world in which one is judged according to prevailing stereotypes rather than by aptitude, ability, and accomplishment is a crushing experience. Beth Martin provides an example in the essay that follows.

Coming to Terms With Science:

A Woman's Story of Disillusionment

_____ *Beth Martin* _____

Science has always been more than a career aspiration to me; it is a way of thinking. My father, a nuclear engineer, always encouraged a curiosity about the world. He challenged me to think on my own—not just to work through a problem or question, but to look deeply enough into a situation to find new problems and questions not readily apparent. These exercises in critical thinking led to an interest in science classes at school. I was convinced that scientists had a special hot line to the truth. I believed that using the scientific method to examine the world would reveal nature's secrets.

Needless to say, my idolized faith in the omnipotence of science has worn off. I was still in high school when I began to see that science is more a pastiche of haphazard knowledge, a collection of creative insights and solutions, and a political entity than a methodical building of truth about the world. I felt disappointed but was still hopeful that somewhere within the structure of modern science, there exists a core of pure discovery driven by method as well as insight. I was convinced I had that essence of science.

I am 25 years old. I always planned to be in some aspect of science, ranging from space exploration to biomedical research. I earned my baccalaureate in biology from a major research university and have worked for more than 3 years in molecular biology and crop biotechnology. An opportunity to continue my education under one of the leaders of the field is available to me, but I have decided not to pursue this option.

In truth, I have periodically considered getting out of the science career track since my undergraduate years. In the past, I always abandoned this notion in lieu of holding on to the last ounce of hope that I would eventually find a niche in science in which I could thrive and make a contribution. However, the outcome of my efforts to endure through the system has always been the same: an increasing sense of disillusionment and disappointment. These experiences have led me to the inescapable conclusion that finding a science where I can flourish is an impossibility.

When I entered college at Appalachian State University, a small institution in the mountains of North Carolina, I declared a major in biology. Before the year was over, I discovered that I was more comfortable in the nonscience classes I was taking—for instance, philosophy and English. What I was then able to express only as a vague discomfort in the biology classroom and laboratory, I eventually came to recognize as a consequence of what I saw as a sort of boy's club within the biology department. The fact that the department was populated mostly by men at all levels, from undergraduate to professor, may not be enough to explain why I felt alienated. It was not simply the presence of men or absence of women that I found discouraging, it was the culture of science itself and the social assumptions about who scientists *are* that left me feeling like an outsider.

There was no room for exploring the criticism and doubts I was developing toward science while still embedded within the structure of science. Thus,
in my second year at Appalachian State, I created a major that combined
history, philosophy, and sociology of science. I thought by better understanding the problems linked to my growing sense of uneasiness, by exposing
the inequities of the scientific culture, I could ultimately return to science and
do productive work. From that point on, biology, chemistry, and physics
seemed to me more like anthropological fieldwork than training for a career
in science. The critique and study of science came easily because I was
interested and motivated. I continued to take science classes because I believed
that only a shallow analysis of science would result if a factual and conceptual
knowledge of that science was absent. Although I was content with the
academic combination I had found, I noticed that moving between departments did not liberate me from disciplinary restrictions. In fact, I found that
the flow of ideas *between* the sciences and humanities was not just lacking, it
was actively discouraged from both sides.

I encountered resistance within the biology department to my critical
analysis of science. It is ironic that the professors found no apparent contradiction in the fact that they were attempting to quell in me the very same
critical thinking skills valued so highly in science and that they professed as
a goal for their students to achieve. My critical thinking was not exercised in
the *proper context.* I saw this enforcement of disciplinary boundaries as a sign
that the enterprise of science did not welcome critique because its authority
rested on being "beyond critique." To question scientific knowledge would be
to question our existence in the modern world. Alternatively, insights and
comments dealing with science were seen as out of place in nonscience
courses that did not specifically address the study or critique of science.

During my sophomore year, I became sensitive to how markedly our
thought organization and interpretation of everyday events rotate around
defining things by their opposites. For example, logic is characteristically
defined as the absence of emotion. Other commonly accepted binary opposites
include active versus passive, thought versus feeling, and knowledge versus
intuition. In each case the first term is associated with masculine characteristics, the second with feminine. A sweeping generalization typically
results in which women are perceived in terms of culturally ascribed feminine
characteristics. As a consequence, the ability for scientific reasoning is effectively eliminated from the concept *feminine* (e.g., Haraway, 1991; Keller,
1985), the two are antinomic. The social entrenchment of these dichotomies

is in part responsible for the professional neglect that women in science, as well as women in most other male-dominated fields, encounter.

Famous women in science such as my personal heroine, the Nobel laureate Barbara McClintock, are usually described as being *abnormal* in some way. They have mystical qualities; they are loners; they do not raise a family or have husbands. They are often disliked by their professional peers, misunderstood, and ignored. They are viewed as lacking *femininity,* and it is precisely because of this lack that they are able to be *good scientists.* Famous male scientists are sometimes depicted as eccentric, but they are still considered "normal" men. Breaking this tradition, fighting the system, facing the resistance, and changing assumptions struck me as a worthy challenge.

I transferred to the University of Illinois in Urbana-Champaign at the beginning of my third year as an undergraduate. The biology program impressed me and I saw a fresh start for my attempt to bring a feminist consciousness to scientific practice. A critical analysis of science seemed to be something that I could pursue in my spare time, and a degree in science was more practical from a career standpoint. Thus, I decided that I would be among the new guard of the have-it-all women scientists.

Soon after enrolling in the biology program at the University of Illinois, I got a job as a part-time laboratory assistant in a crop engineering and biotechnology laboratory in town. I worked exclusively with women during my two-year tenure there, including my immediate boss and the another scientist with whom we worked closely. Our interactions were cooperative. We were working to solve a problem together. There was no competition. I was treated with respect as a junior professional. My questions about the research, regardless of how naive, were either answered or I was encouraged to investigate the answer myself and share it with the group. My suggestions for the project were addressed seriously. If they were not practical, I was told why. If they were considered interesting, I was often encouraged to pursue them.

I attribute this wonderful environment both to this special group of people and also to the fact that we were all women. The qualities that made me so comfortable, and that made the laboratory successful and productive, are in my experience more common within female groups than among males. Cooperation was the rule.

When this company was taken over by a conglomerate, leaving a pool of out-of-work experienced laboratory assistants (mostly women), I was fortunate to secure a position as a technician in one of the university laboratories researching corn tissue culture and genetic manipulation of immature corn pollen for production of new inbred corn lines. I was awarded my baccalaureate shortly after, and continued to work in this laboratory for two more years.

I was consistently mistreated by the researcher who employed me. He refused me any sign of respect, resisted my attempts to contribute to the project, and undermined my efforts by withholding information. To him, I was nothing but cheap labor. It is not that he did not *expect* me to contribute to the project, he did not want me and thus did not *allow* me to contribute—not a rare situation within university laboratories, but intolerable just the same.[2] Nevertheless, I persevered. Although I am still appreciated mostly as cheap labor, this professor eventually grew to treat me as a junior colleague, and I am viewed as a peer by the graduate students and postdocs in our group. I have the opportunity to start graduate training with this professor, but a loud voice inside me warns that I would be facing years of frustration in graduate school only to face equal discouragement as I enter the professional field. I no longer believe that I can help bring a revolution to science. I have soured on the idea of spending the rest of my life either fighting the system or acquiescing to it while simultaneously repressing my anger and frustration.

What happened to cause me to renounce the career for which I trained? I have already shared what I do not like about science—the general characteristics of modern science that seemed heroic and exciting as a child but now strike me as amoral at best. I can also articulate some of the explicit, if subtle, behaviors I have encountered throughout my undergraduate education and work experience in science. None of the bias I have encountered is unusual or illegal. I would have taken action through the channels provided if that were the case. It was simply the persistent, subtle biases and discouragements that have made me want to separate myself from a research science career.

One factor I have experienced that commonly leads to the alienation of female students in the sciences is the persistent neglect of women in the classroom. Females in science classrooms are treated as *extras*. It is generally assumed that we are just taking classes for fun and could not possibly be as serious about learning as our male counterparts. After all, aren't women just in college to find good husband candidates and be conferred with the coveted "Mrs. degree"? At best we are cast as being in college for purposes of establishing the basic skills necessary to get a job as a laboratory technician or assistant to a *real* (i.e., male) researcher or physician. There is a tendency to ignore women in class, and we are not expected to do remarkably well. Perhaps the professors who adopt this attitude believe that they are doing women a favor by protecting us from potentially humiliating episodes in the classroom, occasions in which our presumed ignorance would be exposed. When a professor with this attitude is encountered, making yourself seen and heard can conceivably cause them to rethink their assumptions about you. Speak up in class. Talk to the professor after class. Ask good questions and perform well on exams. Being ignored is discouraging. But the other end of the spectrum, to have praise melodramatically heaped on you each time a stated objective for a course is met, can be equally damaging to your self-confidence. Recognition of work well done is one thing, but the persistent attention to *any* achievement implies that an outstanding performance was unexpected and in essence enigmatic. For example, I once had a computer science teacher who, by praising me to the heavens on my completion of writing a successful program, made me feel as if my achievement was quite unusual. The fellow sitting next to me finished his program in about the same time but received no special praise because, I assume, he was expected to be able to complete the task. It was as if the teacher was saying to me and to the rest of the class, "See!? She did it even though she's a girl!" I could only surmise that I simply was not expected to do as well as my male counterparts.

Why is anyone concerned about how many women practice science and what sort of contributions they make? If scientific discovery is driven by creative and well-trained researchers and everyone benefits from the basic research that in turn supports medical and technical advances, then it is everyone who suffers from the systematic exclusion of more than half of the population from scientific careers. But maybe scientific discovery is driven by money and for profit, and not everyone benefits from discoveries in basic research or from the medical and technological advances.

Can the presence of more women in science make a difference in biased and amoral applications of knowledge? Yes and no. Women already have made a difference in medical research. The inclusion of women in drug testing and significant research specific to diseases common to women are encouraging, but they are also a fairly new phenomenon. Furthermore, a woman scientist is, after all, just a scientist. Her laboratory runs off of funding, and research is always geared toward the interests of the granting agencies. If anything, women researchers have fewer options for choosing funds that would allow socially responsible research than male scientists have, both because the funding system is male dominated as well as profit oriented. My feelings are that a male scientist would be more likely to obtain funding for an unusual or risky research project. He would be considered innovative, socially concerned, and probably be praised for his desire to explore new questions. Conversely, a woman submitting the same proposal would more than likely be seen as a money-wasting rogue, pursuing a personal agenda with no overall benefit to science.

An optimistic part of me (the part that kept me in science until now) does believe that more women in high-level policy and research positions would make a difference in the direction of research, the types of questions asked, and the applications of the results. But more women working as lower-level foot soldiers in research laboratories will only reinforce the perception that women are technicians but not scientists, hands and not brains.

My plans for the future rotate around science. I intend to complete a program for science writing, a program designed to turn disenchanted scientists into translators of scientific research. I will not be conducting laboratory research, but I will be reporting on and explaining research. I will get to be around science but I will belong to a community of writers. I do not know if I will miss being in the laboratory, but I know I will not miss the isolation and alienation, the feeling of never quite belonging.

The application of social stereotypes affects how women with an affinity for science view themselves in two primary ways. Not only are girls bombarded by external messages implying that they *cannot* be successful at science and mathematics, the stereotype confronts them internally with the notion that they *should not* be successful in these areas of inquiry. To do so is to be less of a female and this makes most girls uncomfortable. In their classic essay, researchers Elizabeth Fennema and Penelope Peterson (1985) stated that gender-role congruency—the process of aligning one's behavior to match perceived social expectations—is the prime factor contributing to the disassociation of girls from mathematics and science. They found that girls do not value success in mathematics and science largely because they believe that others will harbor negative opinions about them if they perform well, a factor that intensifies between the sixth and eighth grades. Expanding on this idea, Sherman (1976) pointed out that the spheres of femininity and competence do not necessarily overlap, and in some cases are viewed as mutually exclusive. For example, if a woman is considered intellectually competent, her femininity will be doubted. Conversely, if she is viewed as feminine, her intellectual ability will be questioned. Sherman further noted that the outcome of achievement and competence is gender dependent. For men, it brings social and financial rewards with accompanying respect; for women it brings stigmatization. Under these circumstances there is little incentive for females to achieve and show competence. Indeed, it appears that many actively *choose* not to, directly contradicting the notion that lackluster achievement and mediocre competence are *innate* feminine qualities.

Similar to the concept of internalized homophobia—a process by which lesbian, gay, and bisexual individuals internalize negative social messages and stereotypes about homosexuality—women are subject to an internalized, socially imposed "gynephobia." The result is a lingering sense of self-doubt. Among other things, this tends to lead women to make inaccurate assessments of their capabilities. For example, rather than concluding that a failure to successfully solve a mathematics problem is simply a result of not properly understanding a fundamental concept—a situation that can be corrected relatively easily—at some point girls and women often ascribe these difficulties to a *fundamental quality of being female,*, something that cannot be corrected. This offers women no hope. Despite its absurdity, this conclusion is arrived at by girls in school every day. It is rational for them given a social context in which girls receive a scarcity of information opposing such a conclusion and a plethora of input reinforcing it. Girls exist in an environment in which they learn that sooner or later the "handicap" of being female will catch up to and ultimately overcome them.

So, is it natural or processed sugar and spice? The answer depends on to whom the question is posed. Men's responses tend to be skewed toward *natural* explanations—natural, of course, equated with inferiority. Women's assessments tend to lean more toward *processed* explanations. Remember, however, that until women can *prove* that it is processed, that we are socialized to be feminine rather than competent (which is deemed to be mutually exclusive), the paternalistic assumption that women are naturally inferior prevails and is consequently internalized by both females and males. For example, Cole (1981) identified attitudes concerning abilities and roles as a major barrier to women's achievement.

> The belief that women are less competent than men at science, whatever the validity of this belief, contributes to women's ambivalence toward work and reduced motivation and commitment to scientific careers. (p. 386)

Psychologist Lucia Gilbert added that even when women reject the prevailing social attitude and embark on a professional career, they tend to judge themselves as performing less well than their male contemporaries, even when they are, in fact, performing as well, if not better. This is supported by several studies. For example, in an investigation in which junior faculty at two major universities were asked to rate their professional status relative to their peers, Widom and Burke (1978) found that men overall viewed themselves as above average in number of publications and exhibited a reasonably accurate appraisal of their relative standing. In contrast, women inaccurately assessed themselves as lower in relative standing to their peers than actually was true. In a separate study, psychologist Kay Deaux (1979) compared women and men holding entry-level management positions and found that men more favorably rated their overall performance, saw themselves as having superior ability and intelligence, and more frequently attributed ability as the primary factor responsible for their success.

The belief that women are performing at a lower level than their male peers seems to be nearly universal even when there is evidence to suggest the contrary. In comparably matched groups according to educational level, skill, and experience, men are consistently rated higher than women in job qualifications and other related areas (Deaux & Emswiller, 1974; Etaugh & Kasley, 1981). Looking at gender disparities in academia, Bayer and Austin (1975) found that women receive less recognition and prestige for contributions made and are viewed as less knowledgeable and having lower levels of expertise compared to their male counterparts.

Given this environment, it should come as no surprise that women often enter scientific and other professional fields harboring a deep sense of self-doubt. Professors are frustrated and perplexed when it is encountered, because on the surface, there appears to be no reason for it. Unfortunately, this is often translated into yet another negative stereotype: Women are low in self-esteem and self-confidence. However, Lenny (1977) proposed that rather than being globally low in self-confidence, women are discriminative. Their self-evaluations are for the most part based on the gender composition of the group, nature of the achievement domain, and the gender-appropriateness of the task. It is interesting to note that women tend to more frequently give inaccurate appraisals of their performance and ability as the number of males in the comparison group increases. This is a particularly important finding for women in science and engineering fields, in which the male to female ratio sometimes exceeds 30 to 1. Women also tend to appraise their ability and performance more accurately when the achievement domain is cooperative rather than competitive. Finally, favorable appraisals are directly correlated to the perceived gender-appropriateness of the task. As Bernard (1976a) noted, the social mandate for women is that we should all desire the same goal:

marriage and children. To want otherwise or to elevate other goals to an equal level of primacy is perceived as acting contrary to a woman's nature.

How do we begin to address such a formidable set of boundaries and challenges? The scientific community must collectively raise its level of consciousness so that sexist and other discriminatory practices that previously were considered to be part of the social order but that place women at a distinct disadvantage relative to men can be recognized and addressed. Academic institutions and industries must also make the commitment that the application of traditional social stereotypes demeaning to women will not be tolerated. Whenever they are asserted, the individual making them should be challenged, *their* character placed into question, rather than the women to whom the stereotypical claims are directed. Finally, as I maintain throughout this volume, we must listen to the voices of women in science. They can best pinpoint the problem areas and provide ideas for solutions to transcend boundaries. Kimberly Groat Olsen rounds out this chapter by addressing the effects of social stereotypes on self-esteem and how these factors can impact career decisions.

Women, Science, and Self-Esteem

_____ *Kimberly Groat Olsen* _____

Dr. Kimberly Groat. Is it so wrong for me to admit that this is a designation I have wanted to hear for the past 7 years? I admit working for a title may seem a bit pretentious, but for a long time I really thought a doctoral degree was out of my reach. And when I finally receive that degree, it will be a result of my overcoming a great many obstacles, not only from the world around me, but also from within.

For now I am Mrs. Kimberly Groat Olsen, a fourth-year graduate student at Indiana University in Bloomington, Indiana. Bloomington is a small college town about an hour south of Indianapolis, just large enough to accommodate the 20,000 or so undergraduates that invade every fall, but still small enough to allow one to feel comfortable saying hello to strangers passed on the street. I came to Bloomington by way of Memphis, Tennessee, where I attended both high school and college. I graduated from Rhodes College, a small Presbyterian liberal arts college, in the spring of 1991. That was where my path to the field of chemistry began.

Being in a small department of only 6 professors and 20 chemistry majors afforded me a lot of personal attention from my professors. There was a lot of encouragement and praise, and I was told that I could, and indeed would, move on to a graduate degree. My parents and sisters have always demanded my best efforts in academics, and their motivation to excel has been a strong influence on my life. When I finally reached the beginning of my undergraduate senior year, my advisor called me in to his office and discussed various graduate programs with me. The future was staring me directly in the face; I had to choose. My frightened subconscious was telling me to get a technician's position, but the pressure to live up to the expectations of my professors and family was bearing down on me.

It is not that I did not want to proceed to the next level. Indeed, I always wanted to prove my analytical abilities to myself and to others by achieving the PhD. But when one sees the images of women in television and advertising, it is hard not to drown in a pool of insecurity. For example, who can forget the portrayal a few years back of a "complete" woman presented in the television commercial for an inexpensive perfume? She was able to (a) bring home the bacon (career), (b) fry it in a pan (domestic expertise), and (c) never let her romantic partner forget that he was a man (sensuality). All of this, and she was physically attractive and had a great singing voice! I grew up with the feeling that women were to be all-powerful, wonderful, career-oriented superwives and mothers who freelanced as runway models. And yet, I was never instilled with the confidence that I could achieve even one tenth of that image. All of this insecurity, despite the fact that I had a very loving family, a wonderful base of friends, and had succeeded in many areas. Indeed, I recently read in our Sunday paper that most boys and girls enter kindergarten with healthy self-images, but by the sixth grade roughly 80% of the girls have suffered a significant drop in self-esteem. I seemed to be a member of this majority contingent. In the end, I sent out 13 graduate applications, afraid that all but one or two would reject me.

I was petrified that I would fail immediately in graduate school. Instead, I have soared. Once I focused on my major and minor fields (analytical and physical chemistry) I really felt at home. The chemistry graduate department at IU is an extremely active one, with 47 professors and more than 200 graduate students. Within the department, I was fortunate to find a research group that was, and still is, uncommon. My advisor is an assistant professor who worked under Dr. Marye Anne Fox for his postdoctoral research, and our group is made up of four females and one male. Needless to say, the emphasis on female involvement in this professor's work has been significant, but atypical in the scientific community.

Although there are several female instructors and technicians, the department lacks a single woman in a senior-level faculty or administrative position. Despite this imbalance, I can attest to the fact that I have neither felt pressure nor bias from the faculty at this institution because of my gender. Rather, I feel that I have been pushed to be the best scientist I can be by all of the professors I have encountered. However, I am aware of serious obstacles encountered by women students in other fields and divisions. The cases most often center around the lack of respect that female students receive within their groups. These problems usually surface in peer-to-peer interactions, not between student and advisor, and can escalate to crises that entangle entire research groups. I have faced minor infractions of this sort, and to that extent I have been a victim of discrimination. For example, I was sitting with several of my friends, all male, discussing research, and a question about magnetic resonance imaging was bounced around the group. Several people gave educated guesses, and when I attempted to voice my opinion, the "guys" all looked at me, chuckled, and one person joked about me getting all "anal" again. (I was the only *anal*ytical chemistry major present at the time.) It was not meant as an insult; as a matter of fact, these gentlemen were my friends. And yet, without stating it outright, my opinion was ignored. I have observed this behavior by men for years, and have coined it, Little Sister syndrome (LSS). I am an intelligent, rational scientist, yet so many men choose to treat me like their little sister rather than deal with me on a peer level. LSS is rampant within academia, with women unconsciously playing the dependent role in many research groups. The problem becomes a crisis when a woman in a research group has a strong, dominant personality and refuses to defer to powerful males in the group. At this point, I have observed a lot of men blaming the woman, saying that she is domineering and bossy.

This underscores my central belief that self-esteem plays a crucial role in women's success in scientific endeavors. We have been told that we can become the best scientists in the world, yet we still feel the need to play the role of little sister. If we do not, and instead act confident and assertive, we are often rebuked or ostracized. This places women in a quandary regarding what role they are expected to play in life. The result is often self-doubt and a hesitancy to study subjects traditionally dominated by men, such as mathematics and science.

When I was young, my mother (who grew up in prewar Japan) told me stories about her math drills in elementary and middle school. The teacher made the entire class stand up and would ask questions one by one, until the students made mistakes and were told to sit down. Inevitably, my mother and a young boy in the class would be the only ones left standing. The teacher would pose questions to both of them for what seemed like an eternity, until my mother *chose* to back down and purposely miss one. The unfortunate reality for my mother was that a female could not be top in the class. This false dramatization of male superiority was played out over and over. Thank goodness I do not have to live in such a world, but I still do have to live with the "women aren't as good at math" comments. So the question becomes how do I deal with the stereotypes being forced on me, and how can I change them?

In my own naive way, I would like to think I can change the world single-handedly, and this probably contributes to my desire to be a professor in the future. I would like to serve as a role model for future female students as well as try to show them that understanding chemistry is within their reach. And yet I find myself guilty of some of the mistakes others are accused of making. In a recent introductory-level laboratory that I taught, I found myself prodding the male students to think more for themselves, while slowly working with females and eventually leading them to the answer. Perhaps this was all rooted in the fact that most of the males were fairly boisterous and the females were for the most part quiet and almost hesitant to ask for assistance. Nevertheless, by challenging the males to think analytically, I encouraged the development of problem-solving skills. In contrast, my well-intentioned attempt to "help" the females was actually me spoon-feeding the concepts to them, which probably ultimately hurt their chances of grasping the overall picture.

One curious observation I made during this class was that there were a few females that I pushed to excel. I realized that these women were a lot like me, and in many cases, a lot like the men. They were outgoing, usually buddied up to the males in the class, and outwardly seemed fairly self-confident. One of these students was at the top of the class, and she and her male laboratory partner would always finish the experiments quickly and with little difficulty. Once, however, a particularly challenging experiment caused some problems for this pair, and when she attempted to help explain the concept behind the exercise to her partner, he dismissed her answer and asked another male for assistance. After observing the entire exchange, I went over to the woman and asked if there was anything wrong, because she was visibly flustered. From that point on, she was never quite the same in laboratory. She did not seem as assertive, and despite a rotation of laboratory partners the following week, she never seemed as excited about the class. Although this student's performance level remained high, her enthusiasm had been smothered. This is not to say that the male student had a definite prejudice against women, but even the appearance of prejudice caused damage to the woman's student's self-worth.

It is important to understand that social prejudice relating to the assumed inferiority of females does not give women just cause to lay down our intellectual arms and return to the days of submissive silence. Nevertheless, I feel that gender discrimination is still affecting the stature and upward mobility of women within the scientific community, and the only way to fight it is to change the way we, as women, view ourselves. As a consequence, it is crucial that women in the sciences take an active role in mentoring younger female students who might not have the self-assuredness to push forward in their educational careers. Peer groups such as the American Chemical Society Women Chemist's Committee and the Association of Women in Science also hold key roles in acting as motivators to young women. Female teachers, instructors, and professors, who have perhaps some of the most vital inter-actions with young women, have pivotal roles to play in developing self-es-teem. To be a professor, I will need the belief in myself to stand in front of a class and feel that I am the best possible teacher and motivator for my students. I must have the self-confidence to trust in my intellect, and know that I can help the class to achieve. I hope to stand among other women chemists as living examples that it is possible for a woman to succeed. We must send a strong message to female students that they are capable of excelling, not only in sciences, but also in the humanities, in politics, indeed, in any field they wish to pursue. Women are demonstrating to men that the stereotypes about mathematics and science are not true, and that we *do* have a significant contribution to make to the sciences, both in research and in academics.

4

Searching for a Needle in a Field of Haystacks

I'll bet every one of us can identify a person who helped us get over the hump, stay in the profession, and really get excited about it. Two or three people in my career—both men and women—have done that for me. Those of us who are more senior should be mentors. (quoted in Geppert, 1995, p. 42)

> —Dr. Julie Shimer, vice president of the technical staff and director of advanced custom technologies at Motorola

My journey into science followed a somewhat unconventional path. Contrasting several of the other contributors to this volume, I did not have a special person in my past who fueled an interest in scientific inquiry. I did not have a parent who was a physician or a scientist. In fact, I cannot recall ever seeing either of my parents reading a book. I had no special toys nor events in my early years to start the ball rolling and spark an interest in science. Instead, I was one of those "disadvantaged" inner-city children on which the news media and politicians like to focus but for whom few practical opportunities exist. Unlike many of my esteemed scientific colleagues, I showed no special promise as a student, never participated in any science fairs, and never received any special academic honors or awards. In fact, my performance as a student was abysmal. When I finally graduated high school at the age of 19, I read at about a sixth-grade level and could only perform the simplest of mathematics calculations.

As young people, my friends and I envisioned two basic options for making an exit out of inner-city life. Neither involved education. The first was to marry our way out, and I had many acquaintances who spoke expectantly of finding someone who could give them a "real life." The second was to become a star in the entertainment industry, and I spent my days dreaming of having a hit record of mega proportions.

On graduating high school, I set out naively but determined to fulfill my dream, and pursued a career in professional music. I soon realized, however, that my goal was much easier to achieve in dreamland than it was in the real world, particularly when I lacked the skill to compose a coherent letter. Therefore, instead of performing at concert halls filled with adoring fans, I found myself performing for an audience of customers to the tune of "Burger with cheese; extra pickles, hold the onions." I was a bitter young woman, spending most of my time blaming outside influences for my situation.

I might have remained an hourly minimum wage worker had it not been for a brief trip to the hospital. My patient status rendered me a captive audience, affording me the opportunity to observe hospital routine. As a result, I became fascinated with medical science. On the day prior to my release, I mentioned to a group of the nursing staff that I would like to work at a hospital. At the time, I was thinking in terms of being a member of the food service staff. However, one woman encouraged me to set my sights higher and to become a nurse. Through her, I learned of a 2-year program offered by Truman College, a community college part of the City Colleges of Chicago. Nursing seemed like a good career *for a woman.* The high visibility of women in nursing instilled within me a sense of confidence that I could succeed in the field as well. Thus, after my discharge from the hospital, I enthusiastically embarked on the quest to become a nurse.

The hospital experience expanded my horizons and opened up new and exciting possibilities. I was inspired. It is interesting to note that I never examined my motivation for becoming a nurse, nor did I inquire what a nursing career entails. Nursing offered me a way out of my situation and I seized the opportunity. At the time, everything else seemed like a minor detail. Of course, other prospects were available as well. For example, another member of the hospital staff encouraged me to study medicine. However, this career seemed completely out of reach. I encountered no male nurses nor any female medical doctors during my stay at the hospital. For me, the lines of demarcation were clearly drawn. Women were nurses; men were medical doctors. I viewed a career as a medical doctor as beyond my capability. Conversely, success seemed clearly within my grasp for nursing, largely because I was surrounded by evidence that women do in fact succeed. Thus, despite initially being turned down for admission in the Truman College Nursing Program because of severe educational deficits, I still held great hopes for becoming a nurse. I viewed no obstacle as insurmountable. They were merely challenges to overcome en route to achieving my goal. A few years of adult remedial education took care of my academic weaknesses and I eventually gained entrance to the nursing program. However, I soon realized that it was not nursing per se that generated my enthusiasm; rather it was the science that is a part of nursing, and relating those concepts to others, that fueled my passion. I transferred to Northeastern Illinois University, a 4-year commuter institution on the Northwest side of Chicago, and began my journey into biological science.

In nursing school, a majority of my student colleagues and professors were women. The course work was challenging, and the environment was cooperative. We all shared a common goal and genuinely wanted each other to succeed. My experiences in basic science were quite different. A majority of my classmates and professors were male, and there were few examples of women succeeding around me. Furthermore, the environment was competitive rather than cooperative. I was alone. However, the greatest difference that I experienced in the two programs was not external but internal, focusing on how I viewed myself. Although I faced a host of challenges, I never questioned that I could be a nurse. Conversely, despite succeeding spectacularly, I regularly questioned my ability to be a scientist.

Although opinions vary regarding the importance of female role models in sustaining a long-term interest and enthusiasm for science among female students, most agree that a lack of female visibility in the sciences has a strong negative impact on both the number of women choosing science as a career, as well as those aspiring for advanced degrees and leadership levels in science. We are few in number and are often relegated to behind-the-scenes work. Nevertheless, sheer visibility is also inadequate. For example, if our role in science is typically cast as being subordinate—the hands but not the brains— then I maintain that visibility could actually have a negative impact. Therefore, I would go one step further to propose that it is not just female visibility in science that is crucial, but even more important is the acknowledgment of the value of women's contributions by the scientific community and by society at large.

Women's contributions to science tend to be either glossed over or are absent entirely in textbooks, lectures, and discussions. Thus, women often travel through science careers without a clear sense of history and connection science. For example, *Biochemistry* by Lubert Stryer (1995) is a popular textbook used widely in universities and medical schools. Stryer expertly weaves the technical aspects of biochemistry with accounts of important discoveries that advanced the field and the people who made them. Thus, the book reads like an exciting story: "The Complete History of Biochemistry." However, depending on the gender of the reader, the interpretation of the story might be quite different. Male students are exposed to a rich history, with 320 men cited as performing the cutting-edge research that led to important biochemical discoveries. In fact, I maintain that it would be difficult for a male student to read Stryer's textbook and *not* be motivated, envisioning himself as a future member of the fraternity of scientists. Female students reading Stryer are presented with quite a different picture. The scant total of eight women listed are cited as making major contributions to biochemistry.

- 1917: *Agnes Pockels* performed experiments contributing to the discovery that oil spread on water forms a layer a single molecule in thickness.

- 1952: *Martha Chase* and Alfred Hershey demonstrated that viruses infect cells by attaching to the host cell membrane and "injecting" their DNA into the interior, providing experimental evidence that DNA is the genetic material.

- 1953: *Rosalind Franklin* and Maurice Wilkins's examination of x-ray diffraction patterns of DNA provided the groundwork for the elucidation of the DNA double helix by JamesWatson and Francis Crick.

- 1955: *Marianne Grunberg-Manago* and Severo Ochoa discovered the enzyme Polynucleotide phosphorylase, which catalyzes the synthesis of polyribonucleotides from ribonucleoside diphosphates—a discovery that contributed to the elucidation of the genetic code.

- 1956: *Dorothy Hodgkin* crystallized and elucidated the complex structure of Cobalamin (Vitamin B-12).

- 1967: *Ruth Benesch* in collaboration with her husband Reinhold Benesch discovered that 2,3 biphosphoglycerate (BPG) binds to hemoglobin and significantly lowers its affinity for oxygen, which is essential in enabling hemoglobin to unload oxygen in tissue capillaries.

- 1969: *Paula DeLucia* and John Cairns isolated a mutant of the bacterium *Escherichia coli,*, named polA1, that was the groundbreaking work that led to the discovery of two additional DNA polymerases and the elucidation of the mechanism of DNA synthesis and repair.

- 1969: *Mary Lou Pardue* and Joseph Gall developed the technique DNA in situ hybridization, enabling specific DNA sequences to be located and visualized on chromosomes.

Although these contributions are certainly significant, they are like elusive needles in the 1064-page haystack of Stryer's text. The inescapable message that women receive is that science is a male enterprise—97.5% of the important contributions to biochemistry cited in Stryer's textbook have been made by men. It would be difficult for a woman student reading Stryer to envision herself as a member of the *fraternity* of scientists. Her reaction instead might be to question whether there is a place at all for her in science.

My criticism is not that Stryer chose to disproportionately highlight the scientific contributions of men over women. It is impossible to deny that men have historically held positions of scientific leadership. Rather I use Stryer as an example to highlight my concern that the educational system is structured such that students, female and male alike, receive the message that women only rarely make important contributions to science. This is absolutely not true. Most individuals directing a research laboratory employing technicians and mentoring graduate students and postdoctoral research associates can attest to the fact that women regularly make significant contributions to their overall program.

Scientific textbooks typically ascribe important discoveries to the directors of laboratories. Among those in the scientific community, it is generally understood that the principal investigator's name is actually used inclusively, representing the totality of individuals working in the laboratory that made contributions leading to a given scientific discovery. A significant number of these behind-the-scenes people are typically women. However, their contributions are rendered invisible by this convention. Moreover, a student reading a textbook may not be aware that such a convention exists. Therefore, the problem is not a lack of women contributing, it is a lack of women reaching the level of directing long-range research projects that generate the type of scientific recognition necessary to be included in textbooks such as that of Stryer.

Despite the impression one might have from reading scientific textbooks, women's participation in science has neither been rare, nor is it a recent phenomenon. In fact, women have participated in scientific discovery throughout history. This is the message that is lacking and must be communicated. Men in science have a history in which they can locate themselves. Women also have a history. It just needs to be told—not just once, but repeatedly. In this context, successful women in science might, or might not, be looked on as role models by those aspiring for scientific careers. What is fundamental is that women be visible and their contributions acknowledged by the academy. This enables girls to see women as active and valued participants in the scientific process at all levels.

Role models spark interest and generate enthusiasm. I was a teenager when Muhammad Ali (with the help of announcer Howard Cosell) electrified the sports world. I vividly remember the matches that he fought—not because I necessarily saw them myself but because the boys in my neighborhood immediately after each of his bouts erected makeshift training areas and enthusiastically worked toward following in his footsteps. Ali served as a platform on which the boys launched their dreams. Of course, few of the millions of males who experienced an adrenalin rush when they watched Ali fight, and ran outside to "train" afterward, actually did follow in his footsteps. However, this is not the yardstick by which his influence should be measured. Ali's success and charismatic personality infused confidence in millions of young men—confidence that they could "be somebody."

Visible women in science represent concrete examples to those aspiring for science careers that it is possible for women to succeed. However, just as Ali's influence on young men was not limited to the boxing ring, successful and visible women in science can generate an infusion of confidence in millions of young women—confidence that they too can "be somebody." Visible women in science can often provide sufficient incentive for a person struggling to persevere in her own career endeavor against what seem to be insurmountable odds. The converse of this also tends to be true. For example, Hirshberger and Itkins (1978) found that male graduate students are more likely to complete their graduate degrees than are female students, despite the ability difference between them for the most part favoring women. One explanation for this trend is that males face the rigors of graduate school within the context of a built-in support system, whereas women characteristically struggle in isolation. The textbooks are filled with examples of men making valued scientific contributions, and men nearly always outnumber female faculty and students in science and engineering departments at coeducational institutions. In short, male students are surrounded by an atmosphere of hope. Although individual students may not think consciously about it, the support system is present and it is strong.

The importance of role models tends to be trivialized by men in science, many claiming to have never had a role model. However, those making this assertion miss the point. They are like the executive who always takes a private elevator 20 flights to a top-floor conference room and then wonders why other members of the staff, who must take the stairs, arrive significantly later than he does and are not nearly as energetic. The executive has no appreciation for what he has! Men in science characteristically have a similar lack of appreciation. The point is that men in science are surrounded by an infrastructure and culture that supports their success. The fact that many are unable to pinpoint a particular aspect of it as significantly affecting their career does not negate the existence of such a system. Instead, it highlights how much supporting male success is embedded within the fabric of science. Lucia Gilbert (1983) painted the scenario women face trying to achieve within this system.

> The psychological burden of disapproval, indifference, and discomfort that women experience in their graduate training and professional settings may undermine their commitment to professional careers, dampen their spirits and energy, and contribute to self-fulfilling prophecies about not being able to make it in a "man's world." Further confounding this situation is the external reality, provided by our societal norms, that women can "drop out" with few, if any, negative social sanctions. In fact, this "out" provided by society may contribute significantly to conflicts women experience within their student or work roles, potentially resulting in their prematurely putting their career goals aside or lowering their sights because they think they cannot succeed. (p. 9)

Several studies have documented the relationship between female students' achievement profiles and their reports of having female professors as role models (Gilbert, Gallessich, & Evans, 1983; Goldstein, 1979). Elizabeth Tidball (1973) stated that women seek out role models who are likely to affirm them as professionals, in an atmosphere in which their career goals are supported and encouraged. The fact that women identify female role models when many more male models are available highlights the significance women attribute to a relationship with a same-gender role model and what women deem essential to the process. With this in mind, more programs modeled after Project WISE (see Katkin, this volume) that create a support system for women as they move through a science career track will be crucial for meeting the goal of increasing women's participation in science at all levels.

Although Nobel laureates such as Marie Curie, Barbara McClintock, or Christiane Nusslein-Vohlard might serve as role models for hundreds of aspiring women, their influence—albeit potentially strong—is indirect. Mentors, however, directly shape and guide a student's career. They are essential in science, particularly at the graduate level and above. In fact it could be accurately stated that without mentors, an aspiring scientist would have *no* career. Mentors are so fundamental to a person's success that scientists are often referred to in terms of their *pedigree*—a blanket term for the mentors they have served under and past institutional ties.

A successful mentoring association requires that both parties be mature. The relationship is asymmetrical in terms of power, the mentor holding most, whereas the student enters the affiliation highly dependent and with a fragile ego. The student must be willing to listen and accept guidance. The mentor must act with the student's best interests in mind—which is usually moving them from a state of dependence to one of independence. The following essay describes such a relationship and its positive influence on a student's career.

The Roots of a Woman

_____ Laura J. Gaines _____

With a gloved hand she holds the rat's ventral skin taut and deftly slices a lengthwise cut with a scalpel. I watch as the mass of intestine and other internal organs are exposed and listen as she begins to sing the opening verse to "Me and Bobby McGee," a song made popular by the late Janis Joplin, with a forced raspiness and lowered voice. She does not miss a cadence as she replaces the scalpel in a beaker of sterile media and picks up a pair of tweezers and small scissors from a second beaker. Snipping out one ovary, she drops it in the media, then moves to snip out the other. I hold my breath while I decapitate the next rat and bleed it over a beaker of water. My stomach tightens. I am working too slowly and she has to wait for me. Tilting her head back and pointing her blue paper face mask upward, she belts out the finale to the song. She understands that this part of the experiment is difficult for me and sings to keep my mind off of sacrificing the rats. Even though I am slowing down her work, she remains patient, gently reminding me that we are using this information to help improve women's health.

This researcher first opened the doors of science for me through her informal women's network. She had asked a student employee if they could recommend a woman for an open position at the National Institute of Environmental Health Sciences (NIEHS), a branch of the National Institutes of

Health. At the time, "network" was not part of my vocabulary, but it was this informal woman-to-woman network that pulled me into my first research position and introduced me to the woman who would become my mentor.

The position at NIEHS provided an opportunity to immerse myself in the world of women's health issues. The research served as the material for my undergraduate thesis and played an integral part in my acceptance into a graduate program. However, these were not my reasons for working at NIEHS. At the time, I was a junior at the University of North Carolina at Chapel Hill, struggling to regain my focus after two faltering years in college. In the middle of changing my major for the fourth time, I was rapidly losing confidence in my ability to meet the entrance requirements for medical school and realize my lifelong dream of becoming a medical doctor. When my friend suggested that I apply for the research job, I agreed in a last-ditch attempt to salvage this dream. It was not that science sparked my interest so much that I wanted to spend my entire summer inside a stuffy laboratory dissecting rats and working with radioactivity. Instead, I knew it would look good on my medical school application.

As my mentor, this woman helped me by simply believing in me. Her infinite patience, support, and personal drive catalyzed changes in my own ambition and self-discipline, and ultimately empowered me with the courage to pursue my dream. She profoundly influenced the course that the past 3 years have taken and also my future path.

By all accounts this woman was an exceptional mentor. However, what made her truly unique was that she graciously nurtured my development as a scientist while simultaneously tolerating lack of support and often blatant discrimination from our supervisor. For example, rather than provide her with the guidance that she needed, our supervisor would take her limited weekly supply of ovarian cells to use for his own experiments. His experiments, he said, needed to be published immediately. Hers could wait. He neither bothered to fully understand her research nor ask directed, critical questions until he had to deliver a lecture on her material. During a presentation to scientists at the Environmental Protection Agency (EPA), which my mentor and I attended, our supervisor lamented that no one at NIEHS was studying reproductive toxins on the female system. I almost fell out of my chair. This was precisely the focus of my mentor's research! It was then that I fully understood that my mentor's work did not exist in his eyes. She was invisible. However, instead of being overcome with bitterness, this mentor channeled these frustrations into an enthusiasm for teaching me. Her anger and her experiences challenged me to confront my illusions of a system that I wished to be purely scientific and apolitical. Her encouragement and tenacity inspired me to work through this system and to attempt to change it, just as she changed part of it for me.

Prior to working at NIEHS, I considered myself a feminist. I thought I understood discrimination in the workplace. I did not. I missed the simple acts of bias and discrimination that so powerfully push people away. I had a determined, proud, angry, sensitive mentor who revolutionized my view of women in science. She explained to me how women are kept out, recounting stories of sexism and ostracism from her veterinary residency where she was one of two women. She cut out a large black and white picture of Bernadine Healy,[1] framed it with blue marker and taped it to the wall above her chair, just to make a point. The scientific community will not tolerate outspoken women.

Laboratory chiefs often do not provide the same quality of support to females as they freely give to males. I witnessed her struggle to obtain advice and guidance as a new researcher. Because our supervisor would not accept his responsibility to provide critical input on her research, yet at the same time exercised complete control over the project, my mentor was in a constant state of limbo. She facilitated her progress by seeking out assistance from other scientists who respected her intellectual ability. In return, she used her veterinary skills to help interpret their experimental data.

Other women in the laboratory also faced discrimination. A case in point was our supervisor's laboratory technician. The only African American woman in an otherwise all-White laboratory, she was frustrated by her lack of autonomy. This resolute mother of two, who held a master's degree in science (biology), approached the supervisor for advice on selecting a PhD program. He discouraged her, suggesting that she would make more money selling Amway products. In his view, her only concerns were financial. He did not take the time nor the interest to correctly understand that her motivation to pursue doctoral studies centered on respect and intellectual freedom.

My mentor's steadfastness to endure in the face of hardship and barriers to success enabled her to overcome obstacles and fueled a determination to open doors for other women. She became a teacher and guide for many women, such as Gina, an African American woman who worked in the Animal Handling Facility. She held a bachelor of science degree in biology and was an intelligent, diligent worker. Although my mentor demanded a great deal from Gina, she continually praised her work. As I watched my mentor interact with this woman, I began to understand the power of a woman helping another woman.

My mentor repeatedly recommended Gina to our supervisor for job openings in the upstairs research laboratories. After several such requests, he finally granted Gina an interview. As with his laboratory technician, however, she arrived at the interview only to be advised to join the Amway sales team. After that, my mentor finally went to our supervisor's boss to level a complaint regarding his behavior toward both Gina and his laboratory technician. She had not taken this action on her own behalf because she did not consider her discrimination to be documentable. However, even in these extreme cases, my mentor debated whether or not to report him, doing so only after an intense personal struggle. There was always the possibility that instead of helping, she would make matters worse for the two women, and ultimately be labeled a "troublemaker" herself. In the end, she decided that the incidents could not be ignored. The supervisor was verbally reprimanded in response to her report, which merely resulted in him waiting until after official work hours to ask the next young woman to join Amway. Three years later, Gina is still in the basement. My mentor is trying to get her another interview elsewhere.

For the most part, my mentor acted as a buffer and effectively prevented me from directly facing much of this discrimination. Reaching unwavering branches around me, she sheltered me from the brutal climate of prejudice and ruthless competition. She protected me while I struggled upward through my insecurities, becoming sturdy enough to stand on my own. Her support meant that I did not have to face difficult situations alone. By her either directly addressing the problem with the person in question or simply believing my story and getting angry along with me, I always felt someone was available to validate my perspective.

After completing a few months of part-time work, I was stocking the tissue culture room one day where my supervisor was also running an experiment. He did not know me on a personal level. In an attempt to make conversation, he began recounting a news program he had seen the night before. This program documented the current women's movement. He scoffed that the women's movement—a movement he qualified as one that he generally supported—was being led "by a bunch of lesbians." Telling me that he supported feminism only when it was not led "by a bunch lesbians" implied that he approved of feminism as long as it did not threaten him. His statement suggested an unwillingness to empower women or genuinely accept change (much less work personally for change) unless it was within the context of *his* limited comfort zone. This seemingly minor encounter represented one of the first instances in which I understood that it is not the outwardly violent acts that prevent entire groups of people from rising up through the system. It is the everyday comments and attitudes that beat down individuals. I was shocked, both by his statement and his blatancy. I did not realize that within scientific circles those in power so easily share their prejudices, especially with someone like myself who was only a student. I was beginning to realize that in order to move upward through science, I could not be the kind of feminist who threatened him. I could not speak out against his "good old boys network." I could not support women of color moving up in science. I could not be any sexuality I wanted to be. I could not voice my belief system if it differed from his. I could not ask for support.

By guiding and encouraging me, my mentor transformed her negative encounters into positive experiences for me. Conducting experiments was not enough. I was more than a pair of hands to her. She wanted me to understand the hypotheses and rationale behind our experiments. She took extra time to explain the reasoning behind our approach, the endpoint we were testing, or why we modified the conditions, always asking for my input. By using *we* each time she referred to the research, she gave me ownership of the work, though I felt that it was more than I deserved. She gave me a stake in the experiments and fostered a growing sense of pride in me.

Soon after beginning the position at NIEHS, I misinterpreted her directions and inadvertently nullified 5 weeks' worth of her experiments. She was angry, but did not take it out on me. Instead, she made sure that I learned from the mistake and moved forward from there. Her support and perspective made a significant difference in my self-assurance, which fueled my determination and ambition. At a time when I was just beginning to regain my confidence academically and reorder my priorities, she forced me to articulate my thoughts. She made me defend our research in front of other people. Gradually, she convinced me to assert myself. When someone asked what I planned to do after graduation, she would not let me say that I might, or was trying to, go to medical school. "You *will* go. You *will* be a physician."[2]

Regardless of her gender, she was a truly outstanding mentor. Her individual qualities, as well as her willingness to invest time and effort in me, are characteristics of any outstanding mentor. However, my time at NIEHS was an especially valuable learning experience because I watched a woman negotiate a system set against her. She responded to the exclusionary actions of her peers and superiors by opening the doors within the system for other women. Each time she was pushed away, she resolved to fight harder.

My mentor filled a role that my formal science education could not provide. As an undergraduate at UNC, I did not have strong female leadership in my science classes. As a premedical student, I took 14 suggested or required premed classes in biology, chemistry, and physics. I had women as professors for only two classes, both of which were in the Biology Department. I switched into the School of Public Health's Department of Environmental Science and Engineering (DESE) to major in Environmental Science and Policy. Out of 27 faculty members in the department who were tenured or on the tenure track, only 3 were women. Eighteen men were full professors; one woman was a full professor. The six division chairs within DESE and the Dean of the School of Public Health were men. No one on the faculty was a person of color. The personal role models for young women scientists are almost exclusively men. Although my scientific training was good, these men did not teach me to address the social inconsistencies between gender and race.

The discrimination that my mentor faced did not deter me from going to medical school. On the contrary, she motivated my determination to enter a system that I intended to change from the inside, just as she had changed part of the system for me. When I worked with my mentor, however, I did not speak out frequently. I was still absorbing her experiences and seeking out my own, assimilating new ideas into my evolving belief system. I am now finishing my first year at Eastern Virginia Medical School in Norfolk, Virginia. For the first time, I feel vulnerable to the prejudiced attitudes around me. Here at school, in this small, contained environment where *multiculturalism* is considered a bad word, I do stand up for my beliefs. The people who hear me can easily influence my future. I worry about the potential negative impact that they can have on my career in 3 years when I apply to residency programs. My mentor tried to teach me to choose my battles wisely. She told me that there are times to fight out loud and times to fight silently. You pick your battles by the ones you can win, because there is too much to fight against to waste energy on a futile struggle. I have learned to stand up for what I believe in because it is important to me. I try not to expect anything in return.

Medical school is a forbidding place to make changes. There is little room for diversity—for alternative methods of healing, for the spirit, for creativity, for social change. There is a strong emphasis on conformity. If you do not fit in, medical school will crush your spirit. I have felt mine begin to crumble. As a society, we are not training compassionate healers. Instead, we are training physicians to thrive on competition and self-interest, not cooperation. We are indoctrinating students into the hierarchy that places the white-coated male at the top. I sit through lectures riddled with sexist comments and conversations revolving around racism and homophobia. I struggle to find others who share my vision. I wonder if I have the wisdom to change this system. Sometimes I wonder if I have the stamina to make it through. To speak out against prejudiced policies and attitudes in this isolated environment places a great deal of pressure on me. In order to be taken seriously in my attempts to initiate change, I realize that my academic achievements must be above the standard.

As I continue through school, I still seek and need my mentor's encouragement and wisdom. She is still unselfishly there for me. I am grateful to the women before me who have already fought a way through. I am thankful for women like my mentor who, in the middle of their struggle, turn to help the women behind them.

Levinson (1978) outlined the key role that mentors play in professional development. As teachers they act to enhance skills and guide intellectual progress. As sponsors, they exert influence to promote career entry and advancement. Kanter (1977) further emphasized that mentors act as advocates for those under their guidance and can often negotiate around established procedures and policies. Therefore, mentors generate *power.* They help people to believe in themselves, facilitating a vision that their overall goals are attainable. Kanter stressed that mentors are absolutely essential for women, given that the deck is stacked against their success from the beginning. Unfortunately, the mentor process is largely unavailable to women, thus amplifying their disadvantage.

Mentoring is predominantly a male phenomenon for the following reasons:

- Leadership positions in the scientific community are typically held by men. Men accordingly are more often afforded the opportunity to act as mentors.

- Males tend to be more assertive in opening the dialogue that leads to establishing mentoring relationships.

- Cross-gender mentoring relationships have a potential to become sexual or carry sexual overtones. In this case, the threat of innuendo alone can effectively deter the formation of a cross-gender mentoring affiliation.

Men in power explain that they tend to choose other males, rather than females, for mentoring relationships because women are too alluring, too timid, or both. This represents a classic illustration of what Caplan and Nelson (1973) called a *person–blame interpretation of a social problem.* Accountability for the problem is ascribed to qualities alleged to reside within the individual, in this instance women as a group, whereas pertinent situational or organizational factors external to the individual are completely dismissed.

Simply acting more assertive in establishing mentoring relationships is clearly not the answer, because women doing so risk having their intentions viewed by the male as having sexual implications, as Lucia Gilbert (1983) noted.

> Women, in fact, learn early in their careers that the quickest way to be "deskilled" by a male is through eroticism. She talks seriously about work-related tasks, and the employer or colleague comments on her lovely smile. Women quickly develop strategies to deflect or side-step male attempts to make the interaction sexual— with the hope that eventually they will be taken seriously as professional women. It's rare indeed for a young professional male to have to spend time and energy counteracting potential sexual overtures from his colleagues! Yet such behavior on the part of males towards female colleagues is often considered *as part of the social order*, rather than as a harmful structural defect. (p. 10)

Indeed, one of the biggest structural barriers that women face is that they cannot simply be scientists. For example, men can *be* engineers. Moreover, men can be *average* engineers. However, women must always do something *extra* in order to create a safe professional environment or gain respectability and validity. As a consequence, a common belief held by women is that they cannot be average and succeed in the sciences. We receive the covert message that we are trespassers on male territory and that we must prove our right to be there. The result is a belief that we must be spectacular just to be considered average. In numerous arenas, this is also a reality. Therefore, many women select themselves out of the sciences because they are unable to meet per-ceived standards of perfection—standards that they asymmetrically apply.

We rarely, if ever, hear phrases such as *male engineers, male scientists, male physicists,* and so on. The gender is never mentioned when references are made to men, implying that this is something that men naturally do. An analogous phenomenon occurs in the athletic community. For example, at Indiana University, the men's basketball team is simply known as "The Hoosiers," whereas the women's basketball team is known as "The Lady Hoosiers." The sciences are only genderized for women, signifying that it is out of the ordinary for women to be scientists. It is not an endeavor that is *natural* for women to pursue. We are *female* or *women engineers, women geneticists, female physicists,* and so on. Our status is enigmatic, unusual, requiring an explanation. Thus, women face isolation in science careers not only because of a paucity of women in the field, but also because women are cast as atypical—in many instances our status as women is subject to question, or we are expected to conceal our status as women in order to succeed.

Women in graduate school often relate that they learn very quickly on entering a program to appear as gender neutral as possible. They are not expected to appear or behave like men, but neither are they supposed to emphasize that they are women. There is no stated policy, nor are they taken aside and specifically informed. It is just part of the culture of the program— something that is learned by example. In a research environment, women showing evidence of spending time on their appearance are regularly cast as being not dedicated and are consequently not taken seriously. A woman's talent as a scientist and the degree to which she excels are completely overshadowed by the fact that she is emphasizing that she is a female. Pregnancy is the most extreme example, because it is both visible and cannot be changed on a daily basis to more closely match department mores. Women scientists are often discounted, and in some cases ostracized, by colleagues when they become pregnant. My interpretation is that this is a mandate for women to be invisible, and reinforces the notion that we do not belong in science. A more subtle message of this cultural taboo is that it is women's responsibility to take care of men. The general fear is that women not conforming to a gender-neutral image will stand out and serve as a potential distraction to men, those who are doing the "real" work. The lesson is that women who insist on being scientists must be invisible, because our visibility might undermine the careers of men. It is interesting to note that little attention is given to the fact that being relentlessly hounded by men can also adversely affect a woman's career. Either way, our presence is cast as a problem that must be effectively managed and women are placed in a position in which we must conceal our identity as women if we are to succeed in science. Thus, a paradox exists for women in science. We are conspicuous, yet at the same time we are rendered invisible. Women cannot just *be* scientists, nor can women just *be* women. At the same time that women are expected to hide their gender, or at least render it insignificant, women exist in a system that constantly focuses on the fact that they *are* women and that they do not belong.

The following essay offers a personal account that explains how structural boundaries to success and a lack of visible women in science can adversely affect a woman's career.

Piecewise Discontinuous Function:

Experiences in Engineering

_____ *Marybeth Lima* _____

I am currently a doctoral student studying agricultural engineering at the Ohio State University, which is located in Columbus, Ohio, and is home to approximately 40,000 undergraduate and 10,000 graduate students. My baccalaureate was conferred in agricultural engineering from the Ohio State University in 1988. Because of previous research work I conducted at Oak Ridge National Laboratory as an undergraduate, I was admitted directly to the doctoral program at Cornell University in the Department of Biological and Agricultural Engineering. Located in Ithaca, New York, Cornell is home to 12,000 undergraduate and 6000 graduate students. I experienced some conflict with my major advisor at Cornell, which caused me to leave the doctoral program in 1991, after almost 2 years of study. I returned to the Ohio State University to complete my PhD in agricultural engineering in 1992. My goal is to be a professor.

Agricultural engineering is a diverse field, encompassing the design of agricultural buildings, equipment and electrical systems, the study of soil and water ecology, and food engineering. In the past 10 years, there has been an increasing move toward biological engineering, an effort to design and develop processes using biological principles. This, and the people-based approach of agricultural engineering is what prompted me to go into the field. My parents were also instrumental in my career choice.

In 1985, I walked into my first course for undergraduate students majoring in agricultural engineering and found myself the only woman in a class of 23. I found for the most part that the students in the class simply did not know how to interact with me; most were nice and did not try to make my classroom experience difficult. Many times I received an, "Uh, excuse me," after a crude comment had been made in class; I seemed to hinder my classmate's behavior.

I was isolated from my classmates until the senior year of the program, when a woman student switched into agricultural engineering from another major. We began studying together, and it was not until this point that I realized how much I had been struggling to work on my own. I began to see how much the "two heads are better than one" strategy could really pay off. In a group setting, students have the opportunity to struggle with homework problems both individually as well as together; an elusive concept for one person may be crystal clear to another.

Stereotypes of women abound everywhere, and engineering is no exception:

- If I kept quiet, I was invisible in the classroom.
- If I opened my mouth, I was considered aggressive.
- If I complained, I was considered a troublemaker.

I strived to maintain a clear voice while according respect to my colleagues and professors. I think that some people saw me this way, but many others saw me as *trouble.*

I became very discouraged with agricultural engineering at this point. I shared with my advisor that I was seriously contemplating switching out of the major. He encouraged me to stick it out a little longer, and to add incentive asked me if I was interested in a job. Dr. Karen Mancl had just been hired, the first woman in the history of the Agricultural Engineering Department at Ohio State.[3] My advisor's strong recommendation proved to be instrumental in me being offered a position as her student assistant. In Dr. Mancl I found my first mentor, something I consider to be extremely important as a woman in a male-dominated field. She was my first link to a successful woman in this field, and she had been through the sort of things I was experiencing—and had made it. Her empathy and advice were the main reasons I stayed in agricultural engineering. I also appreciated the effort of my advisor to facilitate this situation. Despite being awkward—not knowing quite how to deal with me (a woman) either—he did his best to support my success in the field. An unfortunate thing about Dr. Mancl's job was her appointment in research and extension, making her invisible to most students because she did not teach any classes. She has tenure at Ohio State today, but still remains largely invisible to students.

I graduated from Ohio State in 1988, and continued working in the Agricultural Engineering Department until I began graduate school the following year. Cornell was a big change in the right direction. There were 6 women graduate students including myself during my first year (out of 55), and another 6 during my second. Among the undergraduates 50% were women. Most of the professors I worked with were relatively young, and I had very positive experiences with them because they seemed comfortable working with women. I did not feel that I had to prove my competence; it was assumed. I was free to speak my mind without being interrupted, and I felt that everyone listened to what I had to say. For these reasons, Cornell was like a breath of fresh air for me.

Unfortunately, a conflict with my advisor during my second year at Cornell precipitated a transfer back to Ohio State. A professor I had worked with there as an undergraduate accepted me as a graduate student. He did so with a reprimand that he did not know what happened at Cornell, nor did he want to know. I was to keep in mind that he expected exemplary work from me in every respect, including personal relationships.

I am grateful to my present major advisor for taking a chance on me. At the same time, I have experienced a lot of anxiety because of his warnings. I have felt a lot of pressure to make sure my grades are extra high, to impress on him that I am a competent and hard worker, and especially to interact with others very carefully so that I am not interpreted as having a problem with personal relationships. If a male student is accused of having problems with personal relationships, I believe it is dismissed a lot more quickly than with a woman. Women are supposed to be good at personal relationships. Also, a male with personal problems is seen as misunderstood, whereas a woman with personal problems is seen as too weak or too strong, depending on the situation. If a woman student falls into a bad situation with a major advisor in graduate school, the system is stacked against her. If one professor in a network of professors condemns this student, she may not be able to work with anyone. Further, most women in science have limited networking opportunities. Unless she has built up previous contacts, a run-in with a major advisor could very well end her career.

Despite the pressure I feel to prove myself as a graduate student, I believe that I am in an excellent position now. I am comfortable with the working relationship I have with my current major advisor, am very focused on my work, and am in an extremely supportive environment. My fellow classmates take me seriously, and I feel no barriers working with them in classes. I was elected president of the Agricultural Engineering Graduate Student Council by my peers—90% of whom are men. I am free to bring any concerns I have to the department chairperson without feeling that he does not know how to interact with me because I am female. Most important, I have another mentor, whose presence has contributed to my comfort and confidence more than anything else. I am fortunate to have Dr. Sue Nokes—also a contributor to this volume—serving on my graduate committee. Not only is she brilliant, she is empathetic and supportive. We share our frustrations and victories, concerns and goals, and a common vision in which women are fully integrated into all ranks of engineering.

It is encouraging to have this positive experience at the same place in which I experienced some difficulty years ago. I have tangible evidence that things are improving for women in science. However, women are still under-represented; 2 of the 16 professors in the Department of Agricultural Engineering are women, and only 1 is in a tenure-track position. Three out of 30 graduate students are women, and in June 1994, the first woman PhD graduated from our department. Thanks to strong recruiting and retaining efforts put forth by Dr. Nokes (with some assistance from me), the number of undergraduate women majoring in agricultural engineering has risen from one student 3 years ago to it present level of 22, or about 25% of the undergraduates.

At times I am still overwhelmed; I see those subtle (and sometimes not so subtle) forms of sexism so clearly it is almost as if someone coated them with fluorescent paint. However, I can balance this feeling with the knowledge that I am continuing to move forward, not only as a role model but as a messenger to those around me. I know that every article I write, every supportive conversation I hold with a woman student having trouble, every recruiting effort I make, every student I mentor, and every seminar I organize to bring multiculturalism to my colleagues is helping. I am part of making a difference. Just as those ahead of me are making a difference in my life, I am making a difference in the lives of those behind me. This knowledge is one of the things that spurs me on. I feel a great sense of connection and responsibility to women in academia.

How things work and why they work have always fascinated me. My investigation into these questions naturally led me to pursue science and engineering as a career. However, I also feel that I personally have a lot to offer science and engineering. Science is based on a so-called neutral standpoint. Yet, this neutral standpoint has been responsible for justifying the "biological inferiority of women and Blacks," through craniology in the nineteenth century. It is also responsible for the Stanford Binet Intelligence Quotient (IQ) test of the twentieth century, which is criticized as being biased so that White males achieve the highest scores. In the 1940s, my Portuguese father was found to have an IQ of 70; he is now a world-famous researcher in pharmacokinetics. Science is an institution, much like any other functioning force in the United States. Thus, adhering to the belief in the neutrality of scientific endeavor would seem to be a naive position. Neutrality is based on politics, the state of society, and the scientist's own biases, whether they are aware of them or not. Politics slowed money for AIDS research to a virtual standstill in the early 1980s. As a result, we lost precious research time and countless lives (Shilts, 1987). To be truly effective scientists, we should be aware of our relationship to society.

I have seen two attitudes among scientists that disturb me. One is that "hard" sciences such as physics and chemistry are superior avenues to the truth compared to "soft" sciences such as psychology and sociology. This attitude causes many scientists to conduct their research—their search for the truth—wearing blinders. Other disciplines are often judged as beneath them, and in some cases "unscientific." Their interactions tend to be mostly with those in their field under the guise of an open, objective inquiry, whereas in reality they conduct their "neutral" research in an environment of intellectual separatism. This is a dangerous attitude. I believe that everything comes together on some level. Scientists do not have to be only scientists; they can also be artists, economists, and historians. In fact, an understanding of these areas is crucial for a scientist to determine how her work fits into the fabric of society. As scientists, we should not simply put our heads in the sand and concentrate on our little specialty. This type of mentality was used to build the atomic bomb.

A second attitude among scientists that disturbs me involves the battle over intellectual territory and a reticence to collaborate. If, for example, an engineer studies biology, she is breaking the unwritten but very real rule of impinging on the biologists' turf. By reinforcing the separateness of our fields, we lose entire dimensions of understanding. Further, progress in one area can be stifled if all those working in that field have the same training. Many times collaborative work results in greater creativity and productivity. In science, I think we should be moving toward an interconnected whole, not fractured parts.

As an engineer on the verge of earning a PhD, I bring an awareness of my own biases and an awareness of the relationship between science and politics into my research. As a professor, I will call attention to these biases to my students, and push them to explore themselves in order to determine their own biases. And I will share my own philosophy of science, which is to improve the state of the world today and to effect true change: a philosophy that respects and not exploits the earth and her inhabitants; one that is based on a holistic approach and not a so-called neutral one; one that is based on interdependence, not capitalistic dependence; and one that based on peace and not war. In short, I want to give science a soul.

———————————

Another area in which mentoring effects career development is by providing introduction and access to outside contacts in the scientific community. The student gains legitimacy by attaching herself to the mentor's reputation. Kaufman (1978) asserted that because mentoring is predominately a male phenomenon, women are often isolated from informal collegial connections, and such isolation, whether by choice or by exclusion, renders them at a professional disadvantage. The term *stag effect* has been coined by Bernard (1976b) to describe the structural segregation of women professionals. It represents the outcome of a system of exclusionary conventions, procedures, attitudes, customs, and other social traditions, that essentially guard the male turf from the encroachment of women. As a consequence, female professionals may not be given adequate support in their professional development, may receive less recognition for their accomplishments, or may be actively shunned by male colleagues all together. Eleanor Baum, dean of Engineering at Cooper Union in New York City and president of the American Society of Engineering Education, shares her experience.

> [A] very discouraging thing was that when I passed the doctoral qualifying exam, people had the attitude that I was taking a place that a man really needed. I didn't need it because I would [supposedly] have a husband to support me. (quoted in Geppert, 1995, p. 42)

When women are sparse in the classroom, either as students or professors, they are often viewed as *tokens* and thus subject to greater scrutiny, including being more critically evaluated. In the process, women's achievements are often viewed as coming from the outside (e.g., standards are lowered so that women can "appear" to excel; professors are alleged to grade women more generously; women students are portrayed as having sexual relations with the faculty and administration; and women's success is cast as pure luck that cannot be repeated). The number of women in professional and academic positions, coupled with the character and breadth of networking and support structures among women in these settings, are critical components for coun-

tering potential negative consequences associated with the structural exclusion from colleagues and of inhibitions placed on participation in organizational and professional undertakings.

A study of women in science conducted by sociologists Kathryn B. Ward
of Southern Illinois University and Linda Grant of the University of Georgia
found that mentors are largely unavailable to women (Grant & Ward, 1996).
Those women able to establish mentoring affiliations do so later in their
careers than their male counterparts. The consequence of the lack of mentoring for women scientists is evidenced early in their careers, particularly in
terms of securing grants and publishing their research (Gibbons, 1992a).

A creative solution for transcending the boundary characterized by a lack
of mentors for women is to expand the search through the use of electronic
mail. Most academic institutions are connected to the Internet and provide an
easy accessible directory of electronic mail addresses of faculty and students.
A woman in science can comb through the literature for someone whose work
she respects and can subsequently contact that person through electronic mail.
There are also several e-mail networks that can provide support. One of these
is the Systers Network for women computer scientists administered by Anita
Borg of Digital Equipment Corporation's Western Research Laboratory in
Palo Alto, California. The network provides a unique opportunity for women
at various points along the computer science career track to connect with other
women, particularly those with more experience, for support and advice
(Gibbons, 1992b). There are many electronic mail lists specifically directed
to women in assorted scientific subdisciplines. Easy access to most can be
obtained through the World Wide Web; or you may contact the systems
administrator at your institution for assistance.

Although same-gender mentors and role models can have a significant
positive impact on the career development of women in science, it is important
for women to understand that anyone, female or male, can be an effective
mentor or role model. My own career is a good example. I had three excellent
mentors and all have been men: Dr. Jules Lerner at Northeastern Illinois
University, Dr. Thomas Kaufman at Indiana University, and Dr. Dean Hamer
at the National Institutes of Health. In fact, one of the greatest cautions that
women in science give to other women coming up in the field is to not fall
into the trap of holding the expectation that every woman they encounter will
be supportive and every man will be unsupportive. As this volume illustrates,
women often must endure extreme hardships and self-sacrifice to secure a
position in science and to earn the respect of colleagues. Under these circum-

stances, it should come as little surprise that some would hold to the belief that the *only* way for women to survive in science is to keep a stiff upper lip and plow your way through. Thus, it is sometimes the case that the most distant and critical reactions that women in science experience are from other women in the field. These are often interpreted as hostile, resulting in deep feelings of betrayal on the part of the woman in need. They enter science with the presumption that other women should be empathetic to their plight. However, rather than promoting a hostile agenda, the sometimes harsh responses they receive from senior women in science are more typically attempts to help the student face reality and to be prepared for the inevitable challenges women face in the field.

Dr. Sue Nokes addressed the lack of mentors available for women in her career by forming a reciprocal mentoring relationship with her husband as they both traversed through their graduate and professional careers. She has also served as a mentor to Marybeth Lima, contributor of the previous essay. In the final essay of the chapter, Dr. Nokes cites an often overlooked characteristic of mentoring: It benefits the mentor as well as the student.

Because I Did Not Know I Was Different

_____ Sue E. Nokes _____

I was born in 1960, the fourth of six children. My eldest siblings were twin girls, then a boy, then myself, and finally two more girls. We were all 1 to 3 years apart, and we paired off almost immediately. It may be significant that I was paired by birth order with the only boy in my family, and as such I spent more time with my brother than with any of my sisters. By default, I also spent more time with my father, because Dad would put my brother to work and I would usually tag along. Through this I gained exposure to traditionally "male" projects such as rewiring our house, tearing down the old shed, and fixing the cars. Even though I did not directly participate much in the activities, this practical education—typically passed down from father to son—later helped me through engineering school. Despite my being a by-stander, my questions were answered, enabling me to think through what I was not encouraged to touch.

My parents are well-educated; my father was a veterinarian and my mother has a Master of Arts degree and taught health and physical education at the University of Akron. As far back as I can remember, they just expected me to get all A's in school, and I never doubted that I could. Their confidence boosted mine, and I knew that I could accomplish what I set my mind to do.

Two childhood events stand out in my memory that were early predictors of my present career. The first occurred at about 7 years old when I "designed" a water-powered car. I even prepared rough drawings. However, my dad was not impressed, because without realizing it, I had violated the first law of thermodynamics. My car had no external source of energy—only water that turned a paddle-wheel connected to the rear axle causing the wheels to spin. Although I had a lot of other features designed correctly, it did not occur to me at the time that there had to be a pump to recycle the water for the car to run. According to my design, the water just magically circulated past the paddle wheel. It all made sense to me. The second event occurred when I was about 8 and involved dissecting an ear of corn. I wanted to find out how the kernels were held onto the ear. I remember painstakingly removing each piece of the ear and diagraming it. The exercise seems a little trivial now, but I was really excited by the experiment. In fact, some of the reasons I went into research as an adult can be traced back to these first investigations.

I attended the Ohio State University (OSU), primarily because I was a resident of Ohio and tuition was low. I started in the Nursing Department, mainly because the only college-educated jobs available for women that I was aware of were in nursing or teaching. My mother encouraged me to be a physician, mostly out of concerns centering on my future ability to support myself. But I did not want to attend college for so long. Little did I know at the time that I would eventually end up attending graduate school and earning a PhD.

Because nursing school is competitive, applicants were asked to write an essay focused on our alternative career choice should we not be admitted into the program. I did some checking and found agricultural engineering. Growing up in a rural community I was familiar with agriculture. My interest was piqued, and I enthusiastically investigated the major. I was already disappointed with nursing because the academic advisors discouraged me from taking more mathematics, which I really enjoyed. The prospect of integrating my love for mathematics and science into a future career was both motivating and exciting. I spoke with an academic advisor, who was herself an engineer, but she discouraged me from changing my major. She asked if I was aware of all the difficult mathematics and physics courses I would have to take. Despite my records clearly indicating that I had taken all of the college preparatory mathematics courses offered at my high school and had managed to be valedictorian of my graduating class, she still lacked confidence in my ability to handle engineering. I assume that she had found the engineering curriculum difficult, and she thought she was doing me a favor by warning me. Fortunately, I had confidence in my abilities, and, ignoring her advice, changed my major from nursing to agricultural engineering. I also chose a different academic advisor. I wonder how many women are discouraged from attempting science and engineering majors for no good reason. If I was discouraged from attempting engineering, what happens to women who are not at the top of their high school classes?

I quickly felt at home in agricultural engineering and did well in my courses. The students and faculty within the department treated me fairly. For the most part, I was listened to and my ideas were valued, although I vividly remember a time when a professor made an issue of my gender in class. I had received the highest grade on his exam. Nevertheless, on sharing my accomplishment with the entire class, he stated that I was book smart but had no common sense. I was too young and intimidated to respond. His statement implied that I could not make the transition from the theoretical knowledge mastered in the classroom to the practical application of theory necessary for success in the outside world. It was a powerful statement that focused on a concrete quality that presumably could not be changed, the lack of common sense, and thus offered me no hope. The message came through loud and clear: Women lack common sense and therefore cannot be successful engineers. My accomplishment was effectively nullified. Furthermore, this denouncement was not made in a vacuum. Instead, it was a public statement made by a person with authority. Thus, it carried validity and helped to reinforce any existing biases against women in engineering held by others in the room.

During my senior year I applied to do a senior honors project in engineering, mainly because a scholarship was provided. This was my first taste of research, and I was successful at it. Therefore, when OSU offered me a fellowship to pursue a Master of Science degree, I accepted.

On successfully completing my master's thesis, I accepted a job in the automotive industry, fully expecting to be treated fairly and shown respect. I was excited and motivated, and had a strong desire to make a contribution to the engineering profession. Unfortunately, my first day on the job revealed this was not going to be the case; my boss informed me that I was in his group solely because I was the last person available.[4] We had just been introduced and already my enthusiasm was drained. I assume he did not value me because of my gender, because nothing else in my record could explain his treatment. Unlike my male colleagues, I was presumed incompetent until I could consistently demonstrate otherwise.

I started this job the same day as a new male engineer. He was given more work than he could finish, whereas I was assigned nothing. I helped him complete his work to avoid being completely bored. However, my supervisor's condescending treatment continued. I went to the library one day to research a problem that test engineers were having on a part for which our group was responsible. My boss saw me reading the material, and he asked what I was doing. When I told him he told me that I was paid the same salary whether I was busy or just sitting there, so I should just sit. He subsequently had his telephone transferred to my desk so that I could answer his calls, and regularly asked me to make photocopies for projects with which I had no connection. In a separate incident, this supervisor called me into his office one day to discuss a project. I understandably took a notepad with me. He looked across his desk at me, remarked that I would make a good secretary, and asked if I wanted to be one. This angered me. I told him that I did not obtain a master's degree in engineering to become his secretary. I then went to personnel and asked to be transferred. Six months later, when no transfer was in sight, I changed jobs.

My next position was with the Department of Defense as a civilian employee. It was a nice change. I had work to do and my accomplishments were recognized. During my tenure in this position, I was afforded an opportunity to work with scientists from a research laboratory. The experience sparked an enthusiastic interest in research. By the end of my first year I had decided to return to school and pursue a doctorate in engineering with a focus on biologically based research.

My husband is also an agricultural engineer. He was a classmate during my undergraduate days. I heard almost from the first day I transferred into engineering that women only major in engineering to obtain an *Mrs. degree*. I was always entertained by this myth because there are many easier ways of meeting men than laboring through calculus and physics. Despite its absurdity, the blanket application of this and other stereotypes about woman occur in engineering programs every day. Therefore, when he first asked me out, I informed my husband that it was my policy not to date people in my class.

Sensitive to the stereotype, he responded in protest, "It's not like we're getting married or anything." We have since happily retracted our statements.

I realized early in our relationship that Steve was more attuned to the challenges facing women in traditionally male fields than any man I had ever met. For example, very early in our relationship we were discussing characteristics we wanted in a spouse. He described his ideal spouse as a professional woman. I had never met a man who actually wanted his wife to work. Most of the men I knew either needed their wife to work for economic reasons, or put up with their wife working but did not like it. Steve understood the intrinsic value of being intellectually stimulated and how working would enable his spouse to be a better wife and mother because she would be more balanced. Steve also enjoyed being able to discuss technical things with me. Unlike many of his male contemporaries, he did not find that threatening. Steve regularly asked for my opinion and genuinely respected the answers I gave. He correctly understood how bringing children to a professional function would adversely affect our colleagues' opinions of me, whereas their opinions of him would be unchanged or even improved. We were married after completing our master's degrees.

The department at North Carolina State University where Steve and I chose to conduct our dissertation research had not graduated many women at the PhD level; I think there was just one before me. In addition, there were no female faculty located in our building. Although I was treated very well, it took much longer for me to develop working relationships with the faculty and other graduate students than it did Steve. For the most part, they were at ease approaching and getting to know him, but they did not seem comfortable interacting with me. Faculty and graduate students met informally on a regular basis to play basketball—an activity in which I was not comfortable participating. A lot of socializing that helped to establish and solidify professional relationships occurred on the basketball court. I missed out on this valuable networking resource. However, after about 6 months I felt accepted into the group of graduate students and my experience improved.

Steve and I chose to become parents when I completed my course work and was admitted to doctoral candidacy. The timing of this decision worked out well. Because we were both conducting research, our schedules were flexible and we could take turns caring for our daughter. Steve worked at the university from 6 in the morning until noon, and I worked from noon until 6 in the evening. Contrary to the commonly held belief that family impedes one's ability to conduct productive research, we completed our degrees faster than other graduate students. As a direct outgrowth of having a child, we learned to be more focused in our work and efficient with our time. Thus, family had an overall positive affect on our graduate experience. We defended our dissertations within 2 days of each other. Next came the job hunt.

Because we both held PhDs in biological and agricultural engineering, we were looking for two academic positions at the same institution. Biological and agricultural engineering departments are typically located only at land grant institutions, and usually this means about one department per state. Thus our choices were limited. We were each capable of individually securing a position, but two positions in one location that fit our technical specialties proved to be difficult. Nevertheless, we decided early in the job search that we would not accept one job; we would wait for two jobs, at least until we ran out of money. We had both been employed previously when the other was not working, and we knew that this was not an acceptable situation for us. Thus, our strategy was to accept job offers contingent on our spouse finding suitable employment within a certain time frame. If this did not occur, the offering department was released of their commitment. Although our strategy was well planned, we could not find two suitable tenure-track positions. We finally accepted two temporary positions back in Columbus, Ohio, which were supported by a large research grant that had funding for 5 years.

During my 5-year tenure at the Ohio State University, I worked as a senior research associate and later as a research scientist. I had the opportunity to observe many situations involving women in research and women as engineering students. I was the only female in my department involved in resident instruction, and it was assumed when I joined that I would work on recruiting women students. Fortunately I enjoy this role, because no one asked if I was interested in accepting the responsibility. When I started in the department, there were 2 female undergraduates (out of about 100 total students) and 2 female graduate students (out of about 50 total). The department chair suggested that I organize occasional luncheons for the women students with the hope that they would provide needed support for these students. He and I continued this every quarter. For the last one that I helped to plan, we had about 35 women students to invite. Although we made every attempt to avoid controversy, to the extreme of paying for these luncheons personally, we were still subject to many negative comments criticizing the unfairness of inviting women only.[5] Nevertheless, I sensed a very positive atmosphere when I attended the luncheons. They provide a forum in which women can relax and share their experiences. For most of the participants, the luncheons represent the only instance in their academic careers where women constitute a majority.

When I first returned to Ohio State as a senior research associate, Marybeth Lima, a cocontributor to this volume, approached me looking for a job. Like me, she had graduated from OSU with a BSc in Agricultural Engineering, but because I predated her by 6 years, our time at OSU had not overlapped. I hired her as a research assistant, and after a year she enrolled in Ohio State's PhD program. It has been very interesting serving on her graduate committee. I had not fully realized how different I was treated as a female researcher until I started working with Marybeth. Discussing technical ideas with her is quite a different experience compared to similar encounters with male faculty or graduate students. I had served on other graduate committees where the students were male, and I found it rather frustrating because the students did not really listen to my opinions. Working with Marybeth enabled me for the first time to gain an appreciation for what it must be like for men in science. My opinions were valued and all ideas were weighed carefully. I had become so accustomed to having my ideas discarded by both students and colleagues that I expected it as a matter of course.

In her contribution to this book, Marybeth discusses the positive influence I have had on her as a mentor. However, it is my view that her presence inspired me at least as much as I have supported her. It is encouraging to have someone who believes in you, and when I first returned to work at OSU, Marybeth was one of the few people I felt had this confidence in me. Thus, I want to stress that mentoring relationships are reciprocal. Although it does require a strong commitment, in my experience the benefits that I have derived from mentoring Marybeth far outweighed any sacrifices that I have made.

In working with women students, I think my most valuable contribution is to repeatedly tell them that I truly believe that they will be good engineers. I use "when" generously to preface statements and "if" sparingly. "*When* you finish this course." "*When* you start your first engineering job." Many of the women in undergraduate engineering programs were excellent students in high school, and are encountering C's or D's for the first time. Although this reality shock is a common experience for engineering students regardless of gender, the male students seem to take it in stride. Conversely, women tend to interpret the drop in grades as evidence that they are not suited for engineering. Historically, the women remaining in engineering, especially for graduate degrees, have thus tended to be exceptionally talented students. This causes a potential problem when these women act as mentors for younger women, because the students perceive that their performance should recapitulate, or in some cases exceed, that of their mentors. This is how they define being "average," and they do not often seek or listen to outside opinions on the subject. I have had more than one student ask if I ever received a C. This places me in a difficult position, because I genuinely believe that C students can become excellent engineers. If I truthfully share with them that my academic record contains no C grades, they interpret their performance as falling short of the mark for what it takes to be a good engineer. It is exceedingly difficult to convince them otherwise. One of the tactics that helped to alleviate this problem was to invite women alumni to our lunches and provide an opportunity to interact with the students. This provided the chance for students to share time with a diverse group of engineers and allowed them to see that many different types of people become successful engineers.

A compounding factor that many women face is having family members who doubt their ability to become successful engineers. I have had several students tell me that their parents either regularly suggest alternate majors (typically more traditionally female careers), or when that first C or D shows up on a grade card, the parents immediately question that their daughter is in the right major. I suspect that parents of male students are thrilled that their child chose engineering, are more tolerant of a few C's, and are far more optimistic and supportive regarding their son's potential for success.[6]

I am both amazed and frustrated that all of the classic, yet subtle, discrimination tactics directed toward women are still alive and well. For example, I am regularly interrupted by men when speaking at meetings without them giving any thought to the fact that they are being discourteous. However, they never interrupt each other. Male colleagues will frequently not make eye contact when they are talking to me. I can suggest something in a supposedly open forum and what I say receives no comment whatsoever. However, a suggestion offered by a male always elicits several comments. It is as if I am invisible, or worse yet, do not exist at all. I cannot count the number of times people ask me what my background is, yet they do not ask an unfamiliar male similar questions. I have been asked if I am a graduate student or a secretary on numerous occasions. Men are not confronted with these alienating and insulting experiences. Men are assumed to be experts and in positions of leadership *unless* proven otherwise. Conversely, women are presumed to be novices and in positions of subservience *until* they can prove otherwise. Even then, women are viewed with skepticism and proving otherwise characteristically means being placed in a position in which a woman must demonstrate her competence day after day to the same people.

Students mimic the population at large. They refer to the male professors by their earned title of "Dr.," and to me as "Ms. Nokes" or "Sue." It is rare that I am addressed as "Dr. Nokes." There are constant subtle messages, mainly from male students, but occasionally from female students also, that I am strange to them and out of place.

In December 1994, I was still in a temporary position at OSU, and I received a call from a colleague at the University of Kentucky telling me that his department had two positions available and he wanted to know if Steve and I would consider applying for them. At first we were reluctant to consider relocating because Steve's job had become permanent, and I was applying for a tenure-track position open at OSU. However, I had the opportunity to meet several University of Kentucky faculty during a national meeting. After the meeting, I received a second telephone call asking us to apply for their positions. I had been impressed by the faculty I had met and I agreed to apply and see what the University of Kentucky had to offer. Steve and I were braced for the usual onslaught of questions concerning husband-and-wife faculty— but to our surprise there were none. The interview process was handled wonderfully. I did not change my name when I married; therefore, a majority of the people reviewing our materials were unaware that we are married. The department chair had the philosophy that if we were both the choice of our respective search committees, then we would be offered the jobs. This removed the stigma that one of us was offered the job solely to attract the other one to the university. We are the third or fourth couple hired in the College of Engineering here, and the second or third couple in the College of Agriculture (because our department crosses colleges). It was a difficult decision to leave OSU, but the culture at the University of Kentucky seemed so much more supportive of new faculty in general, and of women faculty in particular, that we decided to move. At the time of this writing, we have been at the University of Kentucky for 2 months. Six new women engineering faculty started this year, joining five others already in place. I have found this group of faculty to be extremely supportive, and we meet regularly to discuss problems and opportunities.

In 1995, the University of Kentucky hired its first female chancellor, and it is exciting to have the opportunity to interact with a female senior administrator. Time will tell what the future holds, but I am extremely optimistic about my career at the University of Kentucky because I feel I have been given the freedom and support to develop my own research and teaching areas.

Even though progress for women in science and engineering has been slow, I am optimistic for the future. I interact with many bright, articulate women students who will have careers in engineering. I predict that they will have a positive impact on the profession. However, I sadly do not see much hope for major changes in the subtle discrimination problems that I, and other contributors to this volume, have voiced until more people outside of science become sensitive to the issue. At the time of writing this essay, our daughter Hannah was 6 years old and had just finished kindergarten. In 10 short months she had "learned" that girls can write well and boys are good at math. I discussed gender sensitivity with her teacher, who assured me that she did not stereotype students by gender. But the next minute she informed me that Hannah was good at desk work "because girls like to do that kind of thing." I believe that Hannah's home environment will counterbalance the "education" on gender that she is receiving in school, but few families genuinely believe that women succeed in science and view it as a rewarding career for their daughters.

I sometimes have mixed feelings about educating young women to be engineers and then releasing them into a world that probably will not acknowledge the talents that they bring to the job. I believe that we need to educate our students to understand gender bias, and equip them with tools to navigate in an unequal world. Traditional engineering education does not address these issues. Maybe I would have stayed with the automotive industry if I had possessed such skills. More women may choose to stay in science or engineering if they are better equipped to deal with discrimination and accompanying feelings of alienation and isolation. It is only by retaining women in science and engineering careers, while simultaneously educating the public and those in supervisory or administrative positions regarding the issues that women face, that equality will become a reality.

5

Just Where Is "Our Place"?

As long as the earth is inhabited with human beings, their sex will bring with it the basic division of labor. It will always be the men who make the history. Women are destined for another role, if not a less important one: to bring into the world the fathers of this history. (quoted in Cutler & Canellakis, 1989, pp. 1782–1783)

—Dr. Renata Tybova, Institute of Microbiology in Prague, whose research interests focus on the transport of ions across biological membranes

One morning while working at my laboratory bench as a graduate student, I overheard a conversation between two male professors. News had come that a female colleague at another institution had announced plans to be married. Rather than express happiness for her, each frowned in disapproval. They both agreed that marriage was a foolish decision and that for all practical purposes her career was over. However, both of these professors were married and had children. I wondered why marriage should mean the abrupt end of her career when it obviously did not have the same deleterious effect on theirs? Furthermore, even if it did mean the end of her career, why should it matter so much to them?

I have watched this scenario played over and over throughout my tenure as a scientist. The outcome is invariably the same. On announcing a pregnancy or plans to wed, a woman is instantly branded as *undedicated* and *nonproductive.* Her record of accomplishments and the fact that she may be a highly respected scientist are completely negated by this single choice in her life. It is as if she has committed an act of treason and her punishment is lifetime banishment from the scientific community. Colleagues begin to speak about her research in the past tense, despite the fact that she may be actively working on a daily basis! The lesson for a budding female scientist comes through loud and clear. If you want to have the support and respect of your colleagues, do not get married or pregnant.

I have always been puzzled by this reaction toward women scientists. There is no a priori reason to suspect that a woman's interest in science, quality of research, or overall productivity would decrease significantly as a result of marriage or a pregnancy. It is true that her life would more than likely change. Priorities would probably be shifted to some degree. The overall quantity of time she spends in the laboratory might even decrease. However, this does not necessarily translate into a sudden loss in ability to conduct productive scientific research. Indeed, it is the opposite that often occurs, as Dr. Sue Nokes points out in her essay in chapter 4 (this volume). Dr. Nokes and her husband married and had a child while they were both graduate students, and this resulted in a marked increase in efficiency for both Dr. Nokes and her husband. Although they logged fewer hours in the laboratory than their unmarried colleagues, they nonetheless successfully completed their dissertation research projects sooner. Mere time in the laboratory does not automatically translate into scientific productivity. This notwithstanding, despite little supporting evidence, the scientific community in general seems to subscribe to the superstition that some mysterious force overcomes a woman once she is married or pregnant that instantly renders her unable to think critically and conduct research. This is an incredibly absurd conclusion that is further compounded by the fact that it is made by scientists supposedly trained not to make such immature errors in logic.

The double standard surrounding marriage is firmly grounded and nearly universal. Winter (1983) reported that a primary difference between successful male and female professionals is family status—women tend to be single or divorced with no children, and men tend to be married and have children. This reciprocal relationship linking gender and marital status to career success is striking. Even more curious is that it seems to be unique to professional positions that are male dominated and in which competition is strong. For example, this double standard is only weakly applied, or not applied at all, in so-called blue-collar positions, particularly if the workforce is unionized. It is absent in service positions such as among fast-food restaurant workers and department store cashiers. In addition, the so-called feminized professions such as nursing do not universally apply this double standard. However, it *is* in place for management-level positions at hospitals, fast-food restaurants, and factories. For example, a pregnant woman employed as a cashier at a national department store chain may receive full maternity-leave benefits and, after delivering her baby, return to essentially the same job that she left. The pregnant manager of the same store—although technically receiving the same maternity benefits—may return to a position of less responsibility and learn that the upper-management staff no longer considers her "promotable."

Some may argue that the cashier is easily replaceable, whereas the manager is not. Hence, this example is comparing apples and oranges. However, in the current job market, it could be countered that *both* are easily replaceable. Consider that the two positions are fundamentally more similar than they are different. The cashier and the manager are both expected to report to work promptly and as scheduled. Although the manager may have more responsibility, each has a set of duties that they are required to perform competently and efficiently. In short, they are both expected to be responsible and productive. There are major differences, however, in the way that the two pregnant women are viewed by others. For the cashier, delivering a baby is not seen as a career-ending move. When she returns to work, the cashier's ability to make decisions and be productive is not subject to question. The same set of expectations exist for her after the delivery of her child as were in place prior to the announcement of her pregnancy. Nevertheless, the same cannot be said for the manager, where the expectations of upper management tend to be significantly lowered. It will be automatically assumed that she is no longer interested in a career. Moreover, she will be viewed as less competent to do her job than before, as if some rudimentary change has occurred in her overall capabilities. However, it appears that the greatest change lies not in the woman but in the attitudes of others. It is the negative attitudes and lowered expectations that can ultimately have a negative impact on women returning to work following a pregnancy rather than the added demands of rearing a child.

Why are marriage and pregnancy viewed differently for female cashiers compared to managers, for laboratory technicians compared to postdoctoral research associates? A common response is that managers and postdoctoral research associates are being trained for positions of responsibility and therefore greater scrutiny of their personal decisions by upper management is justified. This explanation might seem reasonable were it not for the fact that it is asymmetrically applied to women and virtually never to men. Marriage and a family place additional obligations on *both* male and female professionals. In fact it is just as plausible to assume that a man might devote less time and energy to work following a marriage or the birth of a child as it is for his female counterpart. However, it is only considered to be problematic for the woman. This asymmetrically applied standard can be explained if one remembers from the discussion in chapter 3 that the group in power has the ability to establish the rules under which comparisons and evaluations are made. Thus, it is merely sufficient for the power establishment to state that marriage and pregnancy are incompatible with career development for women and it is essentially accepted as fact—that is, until women can *disprove* the assertion to the satisfaction of those in power. The greater scrutiny of women in professional positions can therefore be understood by recognizing that male interest and competition is low for cashier and laboratory technician positions, whereas it is high for management and tenure-track scientist positions. The professional positions *matter* to the power establishment, whereas the other so-called subordinate levels of employment do not.

Marriage and a family are seen as a career-*enhancing* move for men while at once a career-*ending* one for women. This is the reality in which women professionals—particularly those in science and engineering fields, where large quantities of laboratory time are expected—must exist and strive to succeed. It is a formidable barrier. A contributing factor may be that there is an assumed role conflict for married women in careers that is absent for men. Bernard (1976a) suggested that social belief systems that focus on motherhood as a woman's central role have a profound effect on women's achievement, noting that in dual-working families the female spouse continues to assume most of the home and parental role responsibilities. Because women have child care and household obligations in addition to those associated with their careers, they are likely to feel guilty if those chores are not attended to in a high-quality manner. Thus, the demands of parenting continue to have a far greater impact on the achievements and career paths of women than their male counterparts. Men assume they will combine a career and a family without undue difficulty; women assume that combining a career and a family is nearly impossible—a feat only to be achieved by a "superwoman." In addition, single women may not be excluded from this source of stress. They may be considered unusual by their colleagues and must face difficult decisions about whether to marry or to have children (Davidson & Cooper, 1987). Social expectations are also placed on women to assume a majority of the responsibility for nurturing an intimate relationship. Combine all of this with a career outside the home and it is easy to see that the time demands alone are foreboding. *Exhausting lives* is the term used by Bloom (1986) to describe this difficult balancing act for women. As a consequence, women may experience more stress than men in managing the family–work roles. However, there is also the stress associated with switching from the role required at the office—tough, no-nonsense, autonomous, and neutered—to the personal sphere, which includes being tender, compliant, dependent, and sensual (Morrison, White, & Van Velsor, 1992). Hilary Cosell (1985) questioned whether this strict compartmentalization is achievable and desirable.

> I am not really sure that it is possible for most of us to fuse the personal and professional into one smooth, charming, comfortable, and competent whole—doing everything our mothers did, and everything our fathers did as well. (p. 188)

The polar nature of these two roles suggests that they cannot be effectively maintained over time and that one will eventually take prominence over the other. For women, it is nearly universally assumed that she will choose family over career. Indeed, her character is usually suspect if she does not make this choice. As mentioned in chapter 3, the social mandate for women is that we should all desire the same goal: marriage and children. To desire otherwise or to elevate other goals to an equal level of primacy is perceived as acting contrary to a woman's nature (Bernard, 1976a). Thus, women in careers are stigmatized as unstable and unreliable; they are acting contrary to their "nature." Regardless of how talented a woman might be, it is generally surmised that the marriage and family "handicap" will eventually overtake her.

Married women with successful careers face a different dilemma. They typically have a supportive spouse, relieving the pressure for them to assume the home role, or are financially able to hire out the family responsibilities to private contractors. However, remember that a successful professional career is generally seen as contrary to a woman's "nature." The presumption that women should *not* be able to successfully manage career and family over time is so strong that women able to do so are subject to a host of innuendos regarding their gender and sexuality—insinuations that also typically extend to her spouse. Given these pressures, it should come as no surprise that many women in professional positions are unmarried and childless.

In the essay that follows, Janet Vorvick shares the prejudice that she confronts as a graduate student and mother. She emphasizes that the most difficult part of the balancing act is not finding time to study while also giving quality time to her child, but rather it is negotiating through the stereotypical views of her colleagues.

The Making of an Honorary Male

_____ *Janet Vorvick* _____

"We're very happy to have you here. You won't be different from us, will you?"

I have been an alternative student from the start. For more than 3 years I was enrolled for just one computer science class each term at the local university, Portland State University (PSU). Entertainment was my motivation for the course work—I like to learn. Instructors were very happy to have me in their classes. I was devoted, hardworking, enthusiastic, and successful.

"How can we improve the quality of our graduate students?" I was asked one day by a professor.

"You're asking the wrong person," I replied. "I'm not one of the graduate students."

The professor was noticeably surprised. He not only encouraged me to apply to the graduate program, but also arranged a research assistantship for me. The faculty and administration at PSU were happy to have me in their program.

I have been happy to be there, too. But I seem to keep surprising people by being different. I am different in that I'm a woman. (We have the typical 1 to 9 ratio of women to men in our program.) I am also different because I am the primary caretaker of a small child. Other factors may account for my being different, too. Humanity is diverse, after all.

Pleased with my new status, I attended a meeting of graduate students. It was an afternoon gathering—and in the afternoon I am accompanied by my child. Though unaccustomed to the presence of a 4-year-old, the faculty and students at the meeting seemed to take it well. Some were surprised that I sat with my child on the floor and divided my attention between him and the proceedings. However, they need not have been surprised, for *divided attention* is the definition of a mother–graduate student. Fortunately (for children), it works.

My child has accompanied me to rescheduled classes, meetings with my advisor, as well as meetings with other faculty members. Reactions indicate that his presence is unexpected. A few have objected (all male), most do not comment, and a few have brought out toys (women and men).

The moment I joined the ranks of graduate students, a subtle change in expectations occurred. People kept asking me (and continue to do so), "When will you finish?" *I don't know when I'll finish!* People also ask me, "What classes are you taking next term?" *I haven't planned that far ahead!* I am in the program because I was invited. I like studying computer science. Someday I will graduate!

In this manner, I am different from male students. Male students tend to be here to earn a degree. Female students tend to be here for the experiences involved. A female classmate of mine is from India and has a master's degree in another field. Her reason for studying computer science?

"In India," she explains, "I can't just go sign up for these classes."

Being at this university is valuable to her as an experience, not solely as a step toward a degree.

And what will the faculty members think of me if I am not hurrying toward graduation? Well, money is harder to get. I was offered a graduate assistantship my first and second terms. The third term I turned down a similar offer because the money comes with the requirement that I be a full-time student. I chose—for that term—not to be so busy. But I asked for money again another term. I was told that once a student turns down this kind of assistantship, she probably will not be at the top of the list for money again. Why, I wonder? Because she is not dedicated? Because she is not serious about getting a degree? This system is set up for students who pursue an assistantship, work like crazy while they have it, earn a degree in 2 years (or less) and move on. I do not fit the pattern.

Still, they cannot ignore me—I am a star student! When someone was needed to teach an introductory FORTRAN class, I was awarded a teaching assistantship. That term I worked like crazy (I mean I worked like a crazy person). But that is not how I show my dedication. My dedication can be seen in my persistent presence. Term after term, I am there at the university learning and contributing.

I have noticed that the women in the computer science program at Portland State are generally more capable than the men. What accounts for this excess of ability? I believe that women who are as mediocre as the men in the program do not persist in their studies. Highly successful women are compensated by their academic laurels for the difficulties of studying in a field traditionally dominated by men. My child might be in day care and my floors are not vacuumed, my sisters do not get birthday gifts from me and my legs are unshaved, but at least I can say that I am a terrific success in my artificial intelligence class! Imagine a woman who has diverged from traditional female role expectations by choosing to pursue a degree that has nothing to do with helping children or caring for people and then has to admit that she is not very good at her chosen field! A fair number of the men in our program are not very good at computer science, but it does not seem to stop them. I look forward to the day when women can be average—that is, as mediocre as the men.

Being a star student does not change the fact that I am uncomfortable in my position at PSU. I might be more at ease if I were naturally inclined to conform to the feminine stereotype. Even in a computer science class I would be acceptable if I would just keep quiet and defer to authority. Unfortunately (or perhaps fortunately in the long run), I do not want to take a backseat. Seldom has an instructor objected to my assertiveness, but I do not feel like a "nice lady" when I speak up. In fact, I have had to give up on the hope of being a nice lady (nice girl?). My choices at home and at school leave me feeling bold, decisive, strong, and able. Yet a part of me still wishes the neighbors would say, "She's such a nice lady."

Here is my problem: Even when I am not at school, I interact with others in an atypical way—atypical, that is, in the sense that I do not always conform to social expectations surrounding my gender. One day I was sitting on the lawn chatting with the other moms as our children played in the sunshine. Three of the children were driving around in plastic cars. Noticing that each child was riding in a car that was not his own, I commented, "I wonder how many ways three boys can be arranged in three cars with each child driving a car that is not his own?" The neighbor ladies laughed. They teased me about my mind. A few minutes later the husband of one of these ladies arrived home and joined us. I remembered that he has a background in mathematics. Therefore, I asked him the question.

"Six ways," he replied decisively.

"No," I corrected. "There are indeed six ways to put the three children in the three cars, but only two of them have each child in a car that is not his own." Well. He went in the house.

Stereotypes quiver and crumble when I speak. Who benefits? Smart women benefit when they encounter this man who is my neighbor. Because of me, he is better prepared to engage in an intellectual conversation with a woman. Another beneficiary: my female classmates. They see behaviors modeled by me that they may seldom have seen before. My students benefit, too. When I teach computer science courses at a nearby community college, I have the opportunity to be the authority. Most of my students are men. I encourage them to challenge me in class if they believe I am in error. Usually I am right! When I am, I get to play the part of a competent, confident female in their lives.

And now for a confession: I sometimes go to the computer science office just to chat with the office staff about clothes. I ask them if my skirt is too long. We discuss laundering rayon. These conversations are such a relief. No posturing, no carefully chosen words.

Such is not the case in my conversations with faculty members. Though there are three females on the faculty here, I never see them. My advisor is male. The people using the copy machine are male. My instructors are (almost exclusively) male. The people blocking the halls with their conversations are male. With these people I converse carefully. I never mention children or clothes. I never qualify my words with, "in my opinion," or, "it seems to me." I hold my ground. I adopt their of-course-I-know-all-about-it tone. I stand like them, blocking the hall every bit as well as they do.

These conversations are tiring, though rewarding. Honorary masculinity is bestowed on me and I get to hear the interesting technical ideas I would otherwise miss. Self-esteem is bolstered by this professional interaction. Recognizing the cost, I do it willingly.

What is the price I pay for an exciting career in computer science? I expend energy introducing PSU to the issues of working mothers. I sabotage my feelings of feminine adequacy by talking like a man. I pay by absorbing teasing from the neighbors and puzzlement from my advisor. I am not happy about it at all—my male classmates do not have all of this extra stuff to deal with. But the option of giving up my studies is not decisively attractive. So I keep typing instead of tidying, and programming instead of preening. And one day, my now 6-year-old will come to commencement exercises when I have earned my degree.

The problem as I see it is not that some women choose to shortcut or postpone a career in lieu of focusing on family responsibilities; instead it is the universal application of the double standard. Specifically, that it is impossible for women to maintain a career and a family over time, and as a consequence *all* women will eventually choose family over career. A woman making an active choice not to marry or raise a family faces a professional environment in which speculations are regularly made about her sexual orientation, and she is either pitied, when in fact she may be perfectly comfortable with her decision, or she is subject to scorn and cast as selfish and self-centered. Women such as Janet Vorvick face a different challenge. Not only are they seen as self-centered, they are viewed as directly harming their children by their "selfish" choice. In many circles, it is still common to question a woman's love for her family if she has a career. Her choice of maintaining a career and family is seen as pathological.

Several studies have demonstrated the positive effects of employment on women (Barnett & Baruch, 1985; Baruch & Barnett, 1986; Kessler & McRae, 1982). Moreover, the advantages seem to increase as the status of the occupation or position increase (Baruch & Barnett, 1986). Contrary to the commonly held belief that employed women with children are overwrought with guilt, the data suggest that work provides women with greater satisfaction, self-esteem, and *less* conflict. This is perhaps achieved through the challenges, sense of accomplishment, and social ties afforded by employment. This finding explodes the assumption that the additional strain connected with employment outside the home will result in greater stress for women. Although it is true that certain jobs, particularly those with little autonomy and high demands, which are often held by women, may create stress for the individuals occupying them, in general work has positive effects on women. This is not to suggest that the unique conditions experienced by working women outlined in this volume are not important or without consequence. Instead, it suggests that the image of a tension-free life for "nonworking" women may have been more a myth than fact. Furthermore, it focuses the problem of women exiting careers where it belongs—on lack of support within the system and perceived limits on career advancement, rather than women collectively heeding the call of the "maternal instinct." Managing a scientific career and family is not only theoretically possible for women, it is successfully accomplished every day, as the recent letter to *Science* signed by 65 eminent women scientists attests.

"Women in biomedicine: Still slugging it out" notes very real problems facing women who work in a predominantly male environment in research science. However, we disagree with the article's assertion that success-minded young women would "be well advised to forget about babies." This notion, which persists despite studies to the contrary [Cole & Zuckerman, 1993], contributes unnecessarily to the anxiety that women experience throughout their scientific training. It is regrettable that many women do not have nearby senior colleagues whose examples would challenge this myth.

We write as women scientists who have children and who have also been successful in our research careers, as judged by criteria such as tenure, positions on review panels and editorial boards, teaching awards, and scientific honors. We are a diverse group in terms of the age at which we had children, the paths our careers have taken, and our marital and financial status. We can all testify that combining parenthood with a professional career is not easy; that it requires two major (and sometimes conflicting) commitments of mind, heart, and time; but it can be done, and the rewards of doing so are great.

Our intent in this letter is not to tell people what they should do on such a personal matter. But to women—and men—who decide that they wish to be both parents and scientists, we want to offer the encouragement that it is possible to do so. (quoted in Long & Zakian, 1994, pp. 1357–1358).

I am not at all suggesting that marriage and children are an easy road for women in science. Rather my goal is to dispel the myth that marriage and a career are mutually exclusive for women. The fact that the women signing this letter to *Science* are successfully managing scientific careers, marriage, and families should provide hope for other women that the challenges are not insurmountable.

The stereotype that characterizes women exiting scientific careers to the heed the call of the maternal instinct exists largely because *career versus family conflicts* is a blanket category used within the academy to account for the low representation of women in most scientific fields. As I stated in chapter 1, it is a method by which the scientific community, as well as the society at large, can absolve itself of any responsibility for a woman's career derailment. Once this blanket category is invoked, all conversation about the woman and her career stops. Conspicuously absent is an examination of the nature of the alleged conflicts women in science careers face. Rather it is simply assumed that the female "handicap" has ultimately overcome her—that she has left science to assume her "proper role" in society.

As Laurie Tompkins points out in the essay that follows, the dual-scientific-career family is often a source of tremendous stress for women. Doctoral-level scientific positions are scarce. It is rare for a couple to locate openings in the same geographic area, and even more uncommon at the same institution, that match each member's respective area of expertise and needs. When sacrifices are necessitated, it is usually assumed that the woman in the relationship will make them. This convention is so deeply ingrained in our culture that it is common for a man not to even consult his female partner about career options and potential sacrifices. More often than not the male thinks solely in terms of establishing his own career. His partner is expected to tag along and forge something out of the scraps—a situation that often creates feelings of deep resentment and that sometimes spells the end of the relationship.

Being a Scientist:
One Woman's Experience

_____ *Laurie Tompkins* _____

I was born in 1950, my parents' first and only child. When I was 6 years old, my parents were divorced, and my mother and I moved to Poughkeepsie, a small city in upstate New York. Following graduation from a suburban high school in 1968, I went to Swarthmore College, a small (1400 students), coeducational liberal arts institution near Philadelphia. I graduated from Swarthmore with a BA in zoology in 1972. My graduate study was conducted at Princeton University, a relatively small (5000 undergraduates) Ivy League school in central New Jersey, where I was conferred with a PhD by the Department of Biology in 1977. I then conducted postdoctoral research in the laboratory of Dr. Jeffrey Hall at Brandeis University, a private institution outside of Boston. In 1981, I was hired as an assistant professor in the Department of Biology at Temple University, a large (28,000 undergraduates), state-related commuter school in Philadelphia. Except for the spring semester of 1988, when I was on sabbatical leave at the University of Hawaii, I have been at Temple ever since. I was tenured and promoted to associate professor in 1986, and subsequently promoted to full professor in 1992.

Why did I become a scientist? I did not have any relatives who were physicians or scientists, nor was I encouraged to pursue a career in science by anyone in my family. Indeed, my mother would have been much happier if I had obtained a job teaching high school after graduating from college rather than, as she put it, wasting my time going to graduate school and eventually becoming an overeducated university professor who did something totally unrelated to the "real world." With regard to the impact of my precollege education on my interest in science, some of the mathematics and science courses that I took in high school were enjoyable. In particular, I liked my ninth-grade earth science class and the advanced placement courses in calculus and biology that I took during my senior year of high school. Although these courses were fun, none of them thrilled me to the extent that I declared that I wanted to be a scientist or a mathematician.

My attitude toward science changed dramatically during my first year of college. Introductory genetics was very different from the science courses that I had taken in high school. Dr. John Jenkins gave well-organized and enthusiastic lectures. He encouraged students to ask questions during and after class. Moreover, "Dr. J." conducted research and was obviously excited about it; some of the class laboratory exercises were directly related to his work, and he talked about his research and that of his contemporaries when he lectured. Thus, Dr. J. conveyed to the students in the class the idea that genetics was an exciting, rapidly changing field in which a young investigator could make a real contribution. After taking the course, I was excited about conducting research, rather than simply reading about it in books. Dr. J. encouraged my interest. I worked in his laboratory during the summer after my first year. In subsequent summers I conducted research at the Jackson Laboratory in Maine and a research laboratory at the Pennsylvania Hospital in Philadelphia. These experiences were invaluable; simply put, conducting independent research projects as an undergraduate was what convinced me that I wanted to be a scientist.

In addition to encouraging my interest in research, Dr. J. made another major contribution to my scientific career: He encouraged me to apply for the biology honors program. As a result, during my junior and senior years I was a member of a small group who took seminars in which we discussed journal articles, rather than taking lecture courses. The real significance of this experience for me was that one of the papers discussed described an elegant technique for isolating behavioral mutants in the common fruit fly *Drosophila melanogaster.* After reading the paper, I was hooked. I wanted to conduct that type of research.

Not knowing how to go about fulfilling my dream, I followed Dr. J's suggestion that I go to a good graduate school where there were several investigators working with *Drosophila.* Hence, I ended up in the Biology Department at Princeton, one of 8 women and 36 men in the PhD program. When I started graduate school, no one on the faculty was conducting behavioral genetics research. I therefore joined the laboratory of Dr. Tom Sanders, a new assistant professor who was studying genes on the *Drosophila* Y chromosome that affect male fertility. By the end of my first year of graduate school, after having run literally hundreds of polyacrylamide gels to identify the products of genes that other people had characterized, I was bored. Fortunately, I got lucky. Tom, faced with the necessity of designing a research project for an undergraduate in the laboratory, solicited suggestions from a faculty colleague, Dr. Vince Dethier, who studied feeding behavior in blow-flies. Vince suggested that the undergraduate isolate mutations that affected the responses of *Drosophila* to chemical stimuli. The student successfully isolated several mutant strains for her undergraduate research project. I was able to persuade Tom to allow me take over the project after the student graduated and moved on; characterization of the "taste" mutants became my doctoral dissertation research.

Dr. Chip Quinn, who was hired as an assistant professor when I was a third-year graduate student, studied mutations that affected learning and memory in *Drosophila*. When I was not actually conducting an experiment, I spent most of my time hanging out in his laboratory. Chip treated me like one of his own graduate students; he helped me design experiments, got excited when I obtained interesting results, and occasionally chided me for laziness, sloppy thinking, or some such failing. In addition to serving as a surrogate research advisor, Chip was a role model. The fact that he had been hired by Princeton, and had obtained funding from the NIH, was what convinced me that it was possible to earn a living by characterizing genes that affect *Drosophila* behavior.

After finishing my doctoral research at Princeton, I briefly behaved like a "traditional" woman: I moved to Tennessee to join my husband, who had started postdoctoral research at Oak Ridge National Laboratory. Going to Tennessee meant putting my dreams on hold, because no one there conducted behavioral genetics research. To avoid boredom and earn some money, I made arrangements to work in a *Drosophila* laboratory at Oak Ridge, but I was not particularly interested in the research. The situation—having worked so hard to forge a career in science only to place my aspirations on hold at a critical juncture in sacrifice for my husband's interests—left me full of anxiety and restless. Not surprisingly, given my unhappiness and my husband's reluctance to talk about the situation, our marriage began to deteriorate. The breakup of our marriage did have one desirable consequence: Once it became clear to both of us that a separation was inevitable, I was free to think seriously about what I wanted to do in my next life. I decided that I wanted to conduct postdoctoral research in a laboratory that specialized in *Drosophila* behavioral genetics. I went to Jeff Hall's laboratory at Brandeis University to learn how to analyze sex mosaics[1] as a means of identifying cells that are affected by particular mutations. My postdoc was an incredible learning experience: I developed proficiency at mosaic analysis and became familiar with several arcane aspects of *Drosophila* sexual behavior. As a bonus, I learned how to conduct sophisticated genetic analysis, neuroanatomy, and some pheromone chemistry.

When I look back on my postdoctoral years, I am grateful to Jeff Hall for paying my salary and for insisting that everyone who worked in his laboratory learn a variety of techniques. The latter proved to be invaluable, because possessing an unusual combination of skills was what brought me to the attention of the faculty search committee at Temple University. Nonetheless, working in Jeff's laboratory was somewhat stressful in that he rarely came out of his office; when he did, he spent most of his time talking to the men in the laboratory or, alternatively, scolding everybody for minor infractions. Indeed, I would have been miserable in Jeff's laboratory had it not been for the presence of two remarkable women at Brandeis. Dr. Kalpana White, a newly hired assistant professor whose laboratory was next to Jeff's, made me feel welcome immediately by taking me home to dinner the first night I was at Brandeis. After that, I spent lots of time in her laboratory and in her kitchen. Besides making my life pleasant by simply being my friend, Kalpana treated me as a colleague; she talked about the work going on her laboratory, told me how she felt about competition and funding, and even asked me for advice about how to handle reviewers' comments and "problem children" in her laboratory. Thus, for the first time in my life, I had a picture of what being a faculty member was all about. The other woman in my life was Dr. Alice Fulton, a postdoc who worked in the cell biology laboratory downstairs. When we became friends, Alice and I quickly discovered that we had something in common: strained relationships with our respective postdoctoral mentors. Alice and I spent lots of time complaining to each other and trading tips on how to cope with the situation. When we began to look for faculty positions, Alice and I became each other's worst critics: We scrutinized each other's curricula vitae, cover letters, and slides for presentations; gave each other advice about what to wear on job interviews; and took turns consoling each other when the inevitable rejection letters came in the mail.

Overall, I do not think that the road has been exceptionally difficult for me; I have had lots of opportunities and some lucky breaks. For the most part, the problems that I have faced have not been female specific. Only a few times in my adult life have I felt as though I was discriminated against because I am a woman. Although unpleasant, none of the situations were so devastating that I thought about giving up science. However, the problems encountered by some of my female colleagues *have* caused them to reassess their commitment to science—difficulties finding jobs despite being qualified; bad relationships with department chairs, supervisors, or other senior personnel; the stress of balancing work with family life. For the most part, these either have not been major obstacles for me or were not problems for long.

Based on my experience and that of my female colleagues with whom I have discussed these issues, what advice would I give to a young woman who was considering a career in science?

First, I would tell the young woman to avail herself of any opportunity, in college or even earlier, to conduct independent research so that she can determine for herself whether she likes doing research and is good at it. I can personally attest to the influence of undergraduate research programs on young women's career choices: Although only one of the seven female undergraduates who have worked in my laboratory in the past 5 years wanted to be a scientist before she started, four of those women are now in PhD or MD/PhD programs.

Second, I would tell the young woman to initiate discussions with scientists in general, and female scientists in particular, about their day-to-day lives and their strategies for coping with the stresses of the profession. She should talk to as many scientists as possible, because each of us has specific problems and concerns as well as unique strategies for dealing with them.

Third, I would tell the young woman that being a scientist is in many respects a deeply satisfying endeavor. In what other profession can a woman use her brain daily, discover new things about the natural world, and get paid for it—all without wearing pantyhose or a business suit? However, being a scientist is more difficult now than it was when I first started out: Faculty and industry positions, at the postdoctoral level and above, are harder to obtain, as is funding for research. Moreover, in academia at least, faculty members are asked to do more and more with less and less.

Fourth, if the young woman still had a burning desire for a career in science, I would tell her to do everything possible to maximize her probability of getting a job. First and foremost, I would tell her to avoid overspecialization: The long-term goal of her graduate and postdoctoral training should be acquiring the background necessary to identify interesting problems and the expertise necessary to attack them on several levels. With regard to her postdoctoral research, specifically, I would tell the young woman that potential employers weigh a job candidate's postdoctoral work most heavily when considering the person's credentials. She should choose the best laboratory possible for her postdoc, even if it means accepting a relatively low stipend or moving to a less desirable part of the country (or abroad). I would also advise her to postpone pregnancy or, alternatively, to complete her family before starting a postdoctoral position so that she can concentrate on research during that time.

Fifth, I would urge the young woman to think about whether she really wants what most graduate students and postdocs think they want: an industry position or a tenure-track faculty appointment at a prestigious research-oriented university. If she has family responsibilities, or simply has "a life" outside of work, she may be happier working at a college or a university that is not exclusively research oriented (what I will call a nontraditional institution), where she probably will not be expected to work 16 hours a day, 7 days a week, to get tenure; nor will the pressure to publish several papers a year or obtain grant support be as intense as it is at a top-ranked research-oriented university. Contrary to popular belief, it is possible to do publishable, fundable research at a nontraditional institution. Many colleges and universities have modern equipment, grants to support undergraduate research, and modest sums for supplies. Furthermore, many of the nontraditional universities nonetheless attract reasonably good graduate students. Indeed, the best-kept secret about working at a nontraditional institution is that the head of the laboratory can do bench work herself, rather than spending all of her time sitting in an office, writing grant applications to support a laboratory full of technicians, graduate students, and postdocs![2] If the young woman does choose to go this route, she should be prepared for criticism from people who think that women in male-dominated professions should always aim for the top, and she may have to come to terms with her own feelings about this issue. Nonetheless, based on my own experience, and that of many of my colleagues and former students, I can recommend a faculty position in a nontraditional setting for any scientist, male or female, who wants to have a satisfying professional life but is not willing to sacrifice his or her personal life to this end.

The extra stuff that women in science face on the career front is often compounded by a domestic environment in which they receive little or no support from loved ones, and in some cases confront deliberate attempts to sabotage their careers. Commenting on this situation, Choate (1986) noted that many women are "bailing out" of the managerial ranks not because they find domestic life more appealing but rather because of difficulties coordinating family responsibilities with career demands, thwarted ambitions, lack of support and mentors, and inflexibility of company policies. If academia and industry remain reticent to address these issues, they will continue to lose valuable resources. For example, although many institutions promote family values as part of their overall policy, many women with newborn children return to work much earlier than they want to because they fear the negative impact extended leave might have on their careers. Furthermore, although some institutions have experimented with providing day care (or subsidizing private day care) that could be used by employees, most have made no effort to assist families in this important area.

The essay that follows emphasizes that women typically do not exit science careers, or significantly alter their career plans, because of a general dislike of science or difficulties in mastering the material. More often than not, they are tired of mounting an endless crusade against the extra stuff.

One Woman's Life in Science

Suzanne E. Franks

I grew up in a small blue-collar town in southwestern Pennsylvania populated with second-and third-generation immigrant families. My grandfathers had begun work in the coal mines at age 12. My father was a coal miner who never finished high school; my mother, a housewife who spent her life placing the needs of her family far above her own. Both of them saw education as the means of escape from the blue-collar life. "Do something where you don't have to do shift work," my father always advised. I felt compelled to choose a practical college major and anticipated 4 years of undergraduate school leading to steady employment thereafter.

Engineering was suggested by my mother. She and my father had helped, and supported, two of her brothers during their education as engineers, and saw them as having successfully escaped the blue-collar world for a better life. I was always good at mathematics in school, so I had the prerequisite skills for engineering. Finally, I wanted to do something that I perceived as difficult and unusual, especially for a woman; I wanted to be and feel impressive.

Behind the question of why I chose engineering as a career lies another, more difficult question: Why college at all, for me? I grew up in a very traditionally gendered household, where men and boys went to work, washed the cars, and took out the trash. Women and girls cared for babies and others, cooked, cleaned, and managed the daily dirt of family life. My parents could have aspired for me to make a good marriage match, or to find employment immediately after high school, such as secretarial work.

Two things that conspired against this were my parents' views on education, and my position as the fifth out of a total of six children in the family. For my parents, a college education was not just an education, nor even just something that led to a better job, but far more important, the way to move up to a better social class. They wanted this for all their children. My four older siblings failed to fulfill our parents' dream for various reasons. Thus, by the time I entered college, the pressure that I felt to be a success and source of pride for my parents was enormous. I think it is fair to say that in some way I needed to go to college and succeed for everyone in my family.

In the fall of 1980, I entered the Pennsylvania State University, a large public university in central Pennsylvania with about 35,000 students. It was overwhelming, after being in a high school graduating class of about 75 students, to find myself among 350 other students in a calculus class. My intelligence could not compensate that quickly for my inadequate high school preparation, and I, who was supposedly good at mathematics, got a D that first term. I wanted to quit engineering; I felt like a failure. My advisor urged me to go on in the calculus sequence and showed no understanding of my fears.

My mother simply said, "Well, why don't you just take that calculus class again?"

I explained how I would be all out of sequence and would lose time, words my advisor had previously said. She pointed out that there was no use in going forward if I did not understand what I was doing, and said I could go a summer term to catch up. I fortunately took my mother's advice and I earned an A in every mathematics class I took after that.

During those early college years, I encountered an interesting phenomenon that affected my view of myself as a woman. Many times, after my beginning an interesting conversation with a guy at a party, he would ask the fateful question, "What's your major?" I soon discovered that the reply "engineering" was the kiss of death. It literally caused boys to walk away from me, sometimes with comments like, "Oh, I guess you're too smart for me to talk to." The only boys who weren't scared away were generally other engineering students. Therefore, by default my college relationships were exclusively from that group. As a consequence, I began to feel defeminized by being in engineering, and to feel that my inability to attract a member of the opposite sex who was not an engineering student was a reflection of some lack in my womanhood. To be an engineering major was to be less of a woman, but not quite a man.

I had an opportunity to become acquainted with some students and professors in the Department of Nuclear Engineering through a work-study job. That made the huge university seem more manageable, and splitting atoms seemed exciting. So I declared a major in nuclear engineering, and thought I was on the way to a job at a nuclear power plant somewhere after graduation. I envisioned myself in an apartment, on my own in a large city. There would be friends, and fun things to do, the money to buy nice things, and lots of dates. The future seemed attainable and set.

At the end of my sophomore year, I began dating a fellow engineering student 8 years older than me. Gordon liked my being smart. And he liked talking with me about nonengineering things: ideas, politics, architecture, literature, and movies. Gordon became ambitious for me. He thought I should be in his major—the honors engineering major, engineering science—and he thought I should go to graduate school and conduct research, not take what he described as a routine and unchallenging job at a power plant. My second brother worked as an operator at a coal-fired power plant. There did not seem to me to be much difference between splitting atoms or burning coal to make electricity. I came to feel, through Gordon's influence, that nuclear engineering was leading me to a glorified version of my brother's job. Therefore, it was not special, difficult, and unusual enough to satisfy all the things driving me.

No professor at Penn State ever showed the interest in my career that Gordon displayed. He was the person who made me think of having a career, rather than a job. I fell in love. Gordon seemed capable of recognizing and loving all the contradictory parts of me. He saw me as both intelligent and as an attractive woman. He wanted me to reach for more than I had thought possible. Thus, I changed majors, and I planned on graduate school.

Gordon and I were engaged to be married during our senior year. I received some congratulations, but mostly people all around me reacted in surprising and painful ways. The head of the Nuclear Engineering Department expressed his disappointment.

"I thought you were going to amount to something, " he said. "And now you're acting like every other woman. Everyone knows that when women get married, they lose interest in their careers."

Male classmates expressed confusion over my insistence on graduate school and marriage; if I wanted a career, why get married, and if I wanted children, how could I possibly think of going to graduate school? Many of them were planning to marry, but saw no conflict with marriage and their career aspirations.

My mother resigned herself to what she saw as my marrying far too early, though I was only 1 year younger than my older sister had been when she got married. She expressed her fears that the marriage would keep me from accomplishing the things that I wanted, even as she acknowledged that Gordon had been the source of these new goals of mine. She, too, had trouble imagining a career and a married life for a woman. Although marriage for my sister had been a form of success to my mother, for me it seemed to spell failure.

While finishing my senior year and research project, I took on the major portion of planning for the wedding. Gordon was not as interested in it as I was—and besides, he was very busy with *his* research project. I typed my senior thesis, and his as well, because he was so busy. It seemed natural; I was a better typist than he was, and women always typed for men anyway. I won an award for the best senior thesis in my department, and subsequently received news of my acceptance into the graduate program in nuclear engineering at the Massachusetts Institute of Technology (MIT).

Gordon was not accepted into the program to which he applied at MIT. Therefore, I compromised and decided to attend graduate school at another university where we had both been accepted. On learning the reason for my refusal, the Nuclear Engineering Department at MIT did an extraordinary thing. They offered Gordon admission as well, along with a promise that he could pursue his own research interests in the department, and that if he was not satisfied with the level of intellectual support, he could switch departments later on. For better or worse, we accepted their offer. We married in June of 1984, and went to MIT in the fall. Once again the future felt knowable and set. I was going to conduct important, exciting research. Moreover, I was going to have a happy married life with a man who respected and loved me. Later there would be a house, children, and a tenured professorship at a good university.

MIT was very difficult for both of us, but more so for Gordon. He was forever busy with classes and research that demanded all of his time and attention. The cleaning, shopping, cooking, and laundry still needed to be done—so I did them. After all, he was so much busier than I was, and I rationalized that I could do those things more quickly and efficiently. Gordon lost himself in work; I almost never saw him. My thesis advisor criticized me for my time spent away from the laboratory.

"Science doesn't stop at five on Fridays," he chided. I don't know who cooked his meals, or washed his clothes. Nevertheless, he communicated to me the impression that to be a good scientist, science had to be the most important thing in your life. By attending to the details of daily life, I was failing to meet this standard.

I was part of a subprogram in the Nuclear Engineering Department, consisting of about 10 students interested in medical imaging. There was one other woman in this group. She suggested that we band together to help each other out, because we were women in a man's world. To my shame, I rejected her. I felt like I was passing successfully as a man, and she was asking me to remind the world that I was *just* a woman, and therefore inferior. I developed an intense dislike for her. The other male students reproached me and suggested that I had an obligation as the only other woman to help her out, because she was having trouble. None of them suggested, or even considered, that as her fellow classmates, they might have a similar obligation.

Gordon did not feel at home in the Nuclear Engineering Department, and quickly discovered that the promises of research flexibility and the option to easily switch departments if he desired were empty. Conversely, I had found research that I liked and about which I was very excited. This created a lot of tension between us. I felt very distressed about my success, and about my responsibility for his being there in the first place. I wanted to succeed, but I also wanted to be liked.

In August of 1985, my father died suddenly of a massive heart attack. I was devastated. I could concentrate neither on my classes nor research. I told my advisor that I wanted to drop one class because I was having trouble coping with everything. His only response was to state that sometimes when you feel like you cannot work, you just have to work harder. I lost all joy in everything connected with MIT. Gordon had been miserable for some time. I finally proposed that we leave and start over somewhere else. I am not sure whether I would have suggested we leave if Gordon had been happy, or whether he would have agreed to leave for my benefit at his expense. At any rate, we decided to get master's degrees and go somewhere else for our doctorates.

My advisor was immediately disappointed. In his world, a master's degree was a consolation prize for those unable to shoulder the rigors of PhD work. He kept saying over and over, "But you're good enough to finish," and never seemed to reach any understanding of my reasons for leaving. He insisted on writing up my results for publication, claiming that he could do a better job than I. As a consequence, my work was never published.

Gordon was still busily focused on graduate school. Therefore, I took on the major portion of the responsibility for applying to graduate programs and arranging visits to the various schools expressing interest in us. It never occurred to me that I was much too busy to be doing all of this for both of us. My mother's potent lifelong example of putting the needs of others before herself was apparently at work in me. We were accepted at several good schools. My last choice on the list, the school that I least wanted to attend, was Duke University, in Durham, North Carolina. Gordon's first choice was North Carolina State University, in nearby Raleigh. He tried to convince me that I could be happy at Duke, and we did not seriously consider a compromise whereby we each might attend a midchoice school. I had so much guilt for his unhappiness at MIT that I felt he deserved to have his first choice, even if it meant my taking my last choice, at a school that seemed only marginally interested in having me. Thus, we chose to go to North Carolina.

We still had to complete our master's degrees. In addition, there was the task of locating an apartment in North Carolina and moving to arrange. I completed my thesis a few weeks before Gordon. Thus, I arranged our move, did all of the packing, and in my *spare time* typed his thesis for him. All of this while still continuing to perform the totality of daily living tasks such as grocery shopping, cooking, and cleaning during those months. I arrived in North Carolina in the fall of 1986 exhausted, bitter, resentful, still grieving for my father, and I began to regret leaving MIT.

One day, after one of my classes, a woman approached me and introduced herself as an engineering graduate student from another department. I was horrified. She was visibly pregnant. It seemed embarrassing. She was being so openly, so visibly female, that it frightened me. Somehow I overcame my fears; I did better by her than I did by my female colleague at MIT, and we became friends. We helped each other to negotiate a lot of the horrors of being women in the very male world of engineering graduate school. Her advisor at one point threatened to cut off her research fellowship, because the mere fact of her pregnancy proved to him that she was not dedicated to her work. Only the intercession of her department head staved off that disaster. She had a very difficult time with this advisor throughout the rest of her graduate career, and she continued to have trouble afterward in the job market. Her experiences certainly put a chill on my thoughts of having a baby while in school, and indeed she strongly advised me against it.

I had a friend, but I was still depressed and confused about why my marriage was not working out as I had hoped it would, why I was so unhappy with school, and why I now found it almost impossible to accomplish anything at all. One day, while scanning the student newspaper, I saw an advertisement for a graduate seminar called the History of Feminist Thought, sponsored by the Department of Women's Studies. The course description made me think that I would find the answer to a lot of important questions in that class. I was too terrified to contact the department before the class started; I was somehow afraid that they would reject me, perhaps as I had rejected my female classmate at MIT. Hence, I just showed up on the first day of class and announced that I wanted to participate, much to the consternation of the instructor. Dr. Jean O'Barr, the director of the women's studies program at Duke, let me sit in that first day, but mentioned that she wanted to speak with me later regarding my participation.

During our meeting, she outlined the difficulties I might experience in the class. She advised that I would be asked to consider things that I had not encountered in my science education, noting that the questions addressed would not have the "hard" answers characteristic of an equation or engineering problem. In desperation—for I feared she was saying I could not participate—I babbled about the Heisenberg uncertainty principle in quantum mechanics, and how this prepared me to think in the ways she was saying were needed. Whatever she saw in me during that interview convinced her to give me a chance, and the opportunity forever changed my life.

I attended the History of Feminist Thought graduate seminar and grew as a person, finding some of the answers, or explanations, for which I was looking. My continued involvement with women's studies has provided further insight. That semester I was also preparing for my qualifying examination, a rigorous oral test before a faculty committee, which if passed would admit me to doctoral candidacy. The friends that I made in the History of Feminist Thought seminar, and the things I was learning, helped me make sense of, and endure, what transpired during this ordeal. Before the start of the examination, one of the professors on my committee wanted to know what I was doing wasting my time in a course focusing on the history of feminist thought; what did that have to do with engineering? This same professor did not address me by name or even look at me while asking questions during the examination. Instead, he looked off to the side and prefaced his questions with, "Perhaps the *lady* could tell us why . . . ," spoken in a disparaging tone. My qualifying examination lasted 4.5 hours, beyond the legal limit set by university guidelines. Under other circumstances, I might have experienced a sense of relief and joy on learning that I had passed. However, I felt only bitter and humiliated. The support of my friends from women's studies was crucial in helping me to get over this and go on.

Soon after my admission to doctoral candidacy, the department appointed a new director of graduate studies. It was well known, though no one would state it on record, that the director of graduate studies believed that women did not belong in engineering and had expressed a desire to convince all women in the department to transfer elsewhere. Despite evidence to the contrary, he said that I did not have a sufficient background in mathematics to be successful in graduate engineering, and that if I wanted a PhD, I should switch to a major in life science where I would be "more comfortable." I was required to have his signature on my registration form for every semester, and each encounter was an opportunity for badgering. During one such meeting in the departmental office, he announced in the presence of several other students, professors, and secretaries, that the dissertation would be the biggest emotional crisis of my life, that I would have a nervous breakdown when I tried to write it, and would fail to finish.

If I had not received the support and encouragement of women's studies professors and other women graduate students involved with the program, I believe that I would have quit graduate school—or at least floundered until I was finally asked to leave. There is no question in my mind that the efforts and caring of those women made the difference. They wanted me to succeed. They believed that I could and gave me the emotional and practical support that helped me to believe it too.

The tensions of graduate school in general, and science in particular, are draining, and to have both partners in a relationship going through them together is horrendous. I kept feeling responsible for making it all work, even as my involvement in women's studies was leading me to question whether that was possible or even desirable for one partner to attempt. Gordon and I both began to feel that career success for the other came at a cost to the self. This feeling intensified as the end of our dissertations approached and the job search began.

Most postgraduate jobs are found, or at least contacts are made, through the help of an advisor and their connections in the profession. Gordon's advisor was doing this for him. My advisor, in keeping with his laissez-faire attitude throughout my graduate career, did nothing for me. Fortunately, one of my committee members made a contact for me with a friend at the University of New Mexico, and I was offered a job. However, despite the fact that opportunities existed for Gordon there as well, he flatly indicated that he had no interest in going to New Mexico. That was it: End of discussion. It seemed impossible to both accept the position and keep my marriage. Thus, I turned it down, rationalizing my disappointment by stating that it did not matter because I really was not that interested in the job anyway. But the truth is, I could not allow myself to want any job badly enough for it to be in conflict with Gordon, because I feared it would destroy our marriage completely. I never asked myself what kind of a marriage I was saving. I simply acquiesced and let him choose first.

Gordon had been offered a very prestigious position in Zurich, Switzerland. I was happy for him and full of anxiety for myself. He suggested that I take a year off while he worked at this job and then we could come back to the States together and look for jobs. I knew it would be incredibly difficult to find a job with 1 year of unemployment following my degree. He would never have agreed to do something similar; for example, to remain unemployed for a year while I worked in New Mexico. It was not enough for Gordon that we both find decent jobs in the same geographical location. He wanted the ideal job and was not about to allow my career to stand in his way. Thus, in the tradition of both of our mothers, I was expected to find a way to fit my career around his goals if I wanted the marriage to continue.

The ambition that he had earlier encouraged in me was now a threat to our relationship, because it conflicted with his own. I searched for a way to hang on to both my career and my marriage. On my own, I contacted the head of a good laboratory in Heidelberg, Germany, and was offered a position with him. It was a 4-hour train commute between Zurich and Heidelberg. Thus, I suggested to Gordon that we take these jobs, live apart, and see each other on the weekends. His resistance was strong, but I talked him into it. I had found a temporary solution to our career conflicts that offered a chance to save our marriage.

There yet remained the dissertations to finish, and the dreaded doctoral dissertation defense to be survived. The night before my dissertation defense, one of my committee members called to tell me that he had major problems with my dissertation and that I would have a lot to prove to him at my defense. He generally stated that my writing style was terrible, not scientific at all, and that my dissertation was too "left-brain." This 5-minute phone call left me in utter panic, and I cried hysterically. My friend, one of the postdocs in my laboratory, talked me through my anxiety. He told me that I had done good work and that I would know more about my dissertation research than anyone else in the room. He encouraged me to go into my defense with the confidence of that knowledge and not let the committee scare me. His effort provided me the support necessary to go ahead with my dissertation defense.

The following morning, my committee assembled and we chatted a bit. As was customary, they asked me to leave the room for a short period prior to starting the defense. I stood in the hall for about 15 or 20 minutes, my apprehension growing again. Finally they let me back in and I began my defense; my voice was shaky and I suddenly could not remember what I wanted to say. I stopped. I looked at the faces of my committee members and read their expressions of mild disgust, as if to say, "This is what we expected." My advisor would not make eye contact with me. I thought, "This is it; I do it or die." I took a drink of water, remembered my friend's words of the evening before, and I got *angry*. I thought, how dare they sandbag me at this last minute! Most of them probably do not even understand my work. I plunged into my talk with no further misstep. The committee members asked a few good questions, and a lot of dumb ones. My anger grew the more I talked and this had a surprising calming affect on me. I performed at a peak I would not have thought possible the night before.

Their discussion went on for some time after my presentation, but when they called me back into the room a second time, I had passed. Later my advisor told me why they had deliberated for so long before my presentation. Some of the committee members had not wanted to allow me to defend my dissertation at all. Some of them complained that I was not an engineer and that I had not done engineering work. The left-brain dissertation criticism was repeated. Apparently they had not seen enough equations in the text. At this critical juncture, my advisor went to bat for me. He chastised the committee members for allowing me to get this far and then wanting to deny me the chance to even defend. He warned that they would see more and more students like me doing interdisciplinary research, because that was the way the world was moving. He said it was not the place of committee members to deny students the right to do such research, but rather their responsibility to find ways to examine such students.

My friends and colleagues gathered that evening to celebrate with me. Gordon was conspicuously absent. He had not even come to wait with me during the agonizing moments that I stood outside alone in the hall while my committee deliberated. He was still working on his dissertation and would not take off even half an hour to spend with me that day. I did not see him at all.

I had typed his senior and master's theses, cooked, cleaned, and washed for him. I had dangerously compromised my career at various steps for him, and he could not, or would not, be there to support me and to share my triumph. Furthermore, he did not want me to share in celebration after his defense. Rather, Gordon wanted me to spend every waking moment on the required revisions to my dissertation until it was finished, so that I would not hold up the departure to his job. His committee, who admired his work and wanted to see him a success, passed him after only a short exam, with no revisions.

The next 2 years were characterized by highs and lows. Although these were the best of my years in science, it was also the time during which my marriage finally died. I was awarded a 3-year research contract to work with Dr. William E. Hull at the German Cancer Research Center in Heidelberg, Germany. I have never met a scientist whom I admire more than Dr. Hull. His work is of the most impeccable standard, and he pushed me to perform up to my potential. Some researchers treat their postdocs as a piece of laboratory equipment purchased for its ability to churn out results. Contrary to this mindset, Dr. Hull believed that postdocs need training and attention in order to do their best work and achieve at the highest level. He saw it as his responsibility to provide that training and attention. I worked with him—not for him—and he taught me to find joy in my work again.

It is interesting to note that two of his three closest collaborators were women researchers who directed their own laboratories. He made it possible for me to spend a month working in the laboratory of one of these women, and she too made a profound impression on me.

In the total of my 11 years of higher education, I encountered only one female engineering professor. It was in a course I took my senior year at Penn State. She did not have tenure at the time that I took her class. As far as I am aware, she was the only female faculty member in any of the departments to which I belonged. One could say that the ratio of male to female faculty in my engineering education approached infinity. Given this background, one might begin to understand how important the month in the laboratory of Dr. Hadassa Degani was for me. She was my first up-close and sustained look at a successful woman scientist. She attracted and nurtured many women students, and I spent a month in the company of these bright and hard-working women. Dr. Degani told me that she felt a commitment to nurturing women students because they were at a disadvantage compared with men, who had plenty of role models and support for their efforts. She acknowledged that there were whispers at the conferences she attended about "Hadassa and her girls," but that no one could criticize the quality of work turned out by "those girls." She urged me to remain determined and committed to my work, and she told me I would be a success.

I came back from my month in her laboratory full of ideas and a renewed motivation to work hard. It began to seem so easy. Living alone during the week, in the absence of competing interests to place above my own, enabled me to devote a great deal of time in the laboratory. I started doing the best work of my life, and I loved it.

On the weekends, Gordon and I alternated commuting to visit each other, though I soon started going to Zurich more often than he came to Heidelberg. He liked Switzerland more than Germany and wanted to spend as much time there as possible. After completing his 1-year appointment in Switzerland, he expected that he could transfer to a collaborator's laboratory in Heidelberg. Therefore, it seemed reasonable to take advantage of Switzerland while we had the opportunity. Our relationship improved slightly during that first year. It seemed that the separation had been good for both of us. I anticipated 2 more happy years in Germany, full of good work and the excitement of European life, shared with my husband.

When Gordon finally joined me in Germany, it was a disaster. The new laboratory in Heidelberg was not to his liking, nor did he like his boss. Gordon did not want to work long hours anymore because of his dissatisfactions. Therefore, he did not want me to work late either. I was entering the most productive phase of my career, and suddenly there was another person's needs that I could again place above my own. I struggled to create a balance for us. However, because I was so happy and fulfilled with my work, it became increasingly difficult to ignore how much compromise was being asked of me.

Gordon began a campaign to convince me that we should return to the United States at the end of 2 years rather than 3. He did not like his job, and he wanted me to give up the last year of the job I loved to accompany him back to the United States. Furthermore, he did not want to go just anywhere in the United States. He planned on returning to work with his advisor at North Carolina State, and he expected that I would find a job somewhere in that area. I despaired, because none of the good research groups in my field were located in central North Carolina.

As I look back, it amazes me how much I was willing to sacrifice for my marriage, and for how long, when my partner was willing to give so little. At this juncture, I could not compromise so completely any longer. I was willing to go back to the United States a year early, but not at a high cost to my career. I was offered three jobs. One was with a prestigious group in Philadelphia. The second alternative was at the University of Virginia in the laboratory of a woman professor that would have meant a change in research direction, but would have provided me with valuable mentoring and support. The third was with a researcher in North Carolina who had no funding or adequate equipment for my research but where I could work for "free" and define my own direction. It was this last "job" that Gordon urged me to take. As a compromise, I suggested the job at the University of Virginia and the prospect of a weekend marriage again. His reply was that if he was going to waste his time commuting on weekends to see me, he did not want to drive to Virginia. If I were in Philadelphia, he could at least get some work done while he was on the plane. It was at this point that I knew the marriage was over for me—though it took several additional months to finally die. The position in Virginia was given to someone else while I hesitated, trying to work things out with Gordon. And so I went to Philadelphia and got divorced.

The grief over my failed marriage, and the loss of my last year in the job I had loved, made it difficult for me to work confidently at the start of my new position. Moreover, for the first time in my adult life, I was forced to think about what I wanted to do with no one else's needs to guide or distract me. It was terribly frightening. A woman colleague who had also spent time in Dr. Hull's laboratory helped me through the first year. She and I reminisced about Heidelberg, the laboratory, and my work—which coincidentally had been a continuation of hers. She talked with me, as well as listened to my grief and sadness. It was a tremendous support through a very difficult time.

Dr. Hull had encouraged, and come to rely on, independent direction in my work. We had an equal and collaborative working relationship. In my new group, my immediate supervisor respected that ability in me, but the head of the research group did not. I have had many conflicts with him because of his managerial style. He finds it acceptable to yell at, and belittle, the members of his group as a means of venting his frustrations and coercing subordinates to his will. The administration finds it acceptable to allow this behavior to continue—despite an official institute policy against harassment of any sort of coworkers—presumably because this man brings in large amounts of research funding.

The experiences at this job have hastened my arrival at a decision to leave the world of academic research science. I have considered several alternative careers, including industrial research, teaching at a 4-year college, and teaching high school. I have recently embarked on a master's degree program leading to state certification in secondary school mathematics and physics. In another year, I could be teaching high school or, if the right job in industry presents itself, I may try that for some time. Whether the next phase of my career is a crowd-pleaser is no longer a major concern. Instead, I am looking for meaningful work that also allows for a satisfying personal life, and the time to pursue interests outside of work.

Have I become a success or a failure? My family thinks it is ridiculous that someone with so much education and experience should be paid so little (my present salary is $28,100 per year, set by NIH funding requirements), and that I should be going back to school to start a new career. I fear they also think that I have failed. Being a high school teacher is generally not viewed as a special, difficult, and unusual thing—nor does it carry a status comparable to a PhD scientist doing cancer research. My doctoral advisor and committee members would surely see me as a failure. I do not have a long string of publications in highly visible journals, and I am not on my way to a tenured professorship at a good university. Industry might represent second-tier success, but surely high school teaching would be considered a failure. A lot of effort and money has been poured into my education and training; taxpayers who have contributed their dollars to support me through government-funded fellowships sponsored by the National Institutes of Health might think I am wasting their investment. Dr. Hull and Dr. Degani regret what they see as science's loss, and try to convince me to change my mind. I also fear that my friends and supporters in women's studies at Duke might think I have failed, because I am not going to be a powerful woman scientist in the academy who can speak out for the rights of women students and the issues that feminism addresses. I more than likely will disappoint a lot of people in the search for my own happiness and satisfaction.

My reasons for leaving the world of research are actually based on a genuine love for science, rather than a growing distaste. I thoroughly enjoy the theoretical aspects and hands-on work of bench science: designing experiments, collecting and analyzing data, developing an interpretation, and discussing the work with other scientists. From where I stand, this work seems to be done almost exclusively by graduate students, technicians, and postdoctoral researchers. It is ironic that successful scientists are rewarded by being systematically deprived of the opportunity to excel at what they do best. The more "successful" one becomes and the further one climbs up the traditional career ladder, the less time one spends actually doing any laboratory work. The tenure-track professors and heads of research laboratories write grants, administrate, pontificate at meetings, and collect and trade power and influence. Those who manage to keep a foot in the laboratory seem to do so at a great personal and professional cost.

I do not think I am saying anything new in describing this view of academic science. What I am saying is that I am not interested in this type of "success." I know I am capable of writing grants, and administrating; I am capable of supervising students, technicians, and postdocs. I just do not want to do it. I cannot see myself appropriating the major share of credit for work actually done by subordinates to foster my own career and standing in the profession. Furthermore, I am not willing to fight the long and weary battles necessary to attempt structuring a laboratory group in an alternative configuration in a world in which the rewards go predominantly to the standard apprenticeship-based model. I am rejecting the traditional and masculine version of the success story.

There is valuable and rewarding work to do in high school teaching. As a woman with a doctorate and a history in research, I can serve as an early role model to high school girls contemplating scientific careers. My life experiences and association with women's studies have shown me the importance of gender equity in education. These issues are even more critical in science and mathematics education. I had so few women professors and so few fellow women students in my college mathematics and science classes in part because so few girls in high school are encouraged to exercise their mathematics and science abilities.

Other scientists, and particularly women scientists still struggling to succeed in the traditional model, often do not like to hear stories like mine. They want to hear about obstacles overcome and odds defeated. We want all our women to succeed, because their success offers us the encouragement that we can strive for our goals and realize them. More important, we do not want a failure around for men to point at. We do not want to add to the weight of "evidence" that women just drop out of science for mysterious or illogical reasons. There will be people who insist on reading my story in that way. They will locate the illogical reason for my alleged "failure" within me, not in the experiences I have endured. Perhaps I should have ditched my husband sooner, compromised less, fought longer, worked harder. I would suggest to those people that they ask the kinds of questions posed in women's studies. What does this version of success mean? Who is it for? Why do we value it so highly? What are the costs, and are they worth it? Is something different possible? By whose standards should we judge ourselves, and others?

I want professors to start expecting their students to have a life—a real life outside the laboratory. They should expect this of both women and men. Science is not a sacred priesthood to which one must consecrate their life. Professors continue to promulgate propaganda such as "Science doesn't stop at 5 on Fridays"; or "One cannot be a good scientist unless science is ever and always the most important thing in your life"; and "A serious scientist does not let his or her personal life impinge on his or her career." When these beliefs are set forth implicitly or explicitly to people who would be scientists, damage is inflicted. And the damage is asymmetrically gendered, as it was in my marriage with Gordon. The men who are able to fulfill the requirements of these beliefs cut themselves off from important parts of life for the sake of work, and they need women to bear the costs of the success they are purchasing. The women who try to do as the men are doing may find that they are cut off from relationships completely, because rare is the man who would make a good wife. Furthermore, the women who try for the balancing act are punished with the withdrawal of support and mentoring because they are not acting like men.

Professors also indoctrinate their students with the belief that the best career path and the only one worth pursuing is the one that they have chosen: the path leading to the tenured professorship prize. This is not only a rigid and limiting view of the existing possibilities, it is also downright irresponsible in the current job market. Academic research has its rewards, but so do many other choices. I encountered almost no one in science or engineering who seriously questioned this model of success, or who looked on alternative careers as anything but a second-rate choice to be settled for only when the "first prize" could not be attained.

The place where I learned to question this model was in women's studies. Duke's Women's Studies Department helped set up a number of interdisciplinary graduate reading groups, and over a period of 2 years I worked on this questioning with the seven other members of the group to which I belonged. We gave each other support and respect for our research endeavors, and we explored the ramifications of attaining the kinds of successes we thought we ought to strive for. We talked about relationships and their impact on our work. Some of us were married, some were dating or were in long-term heterosexual or lesbian relationships, but all of us felt torn by the need to maintain connections with our loved ones while trying to be serious academics.

No good scientist would ever consider setting out on a course of experimentation with a blind determination to make it to the end no matter what. A good scientist pays attention to the results along the way, with reevaluation and redesign of the experimental protocols and goals as needed. Good scientists have all experienced the excitement of an unexpected result that totally changes the direction of the proposed research. However, we expect our scientists-in-training to approach that training in a totally unscientific manner.

One is not to question the program, the design, or the ultimate goal. One is instead expected to forge ahead unquestioning to a predetermined destination.

Women's studies, on the other hand, teaches its students to critically examine everything. The development of critical analysis that women's studies fostered made me a better scientist, and it gave me the option of thinking about a new design for a more satisfying scientific life than the traditional structure held out to me. I want to emphasize that women's studies was not asking me to reject science or to replace the traditional definition of success with a different and equally rigid one. Women's studies was not asking me to be a failure. Instead it asked something much more difficult of me. It asked me to contemplate the series of questions I listed at the end of the previous section, and to develop my own personal and particular answers to those questions.

Science should do as well by those it recruits.

Wanting "a life" outside of science is a common complaint forwarded by women. In fact, one of the greatest barriers to success identified by women is the commonly held ethic in the academy that science must be a way of life rather than a career. In other words, to be successful, science must become what *you are* as opposed to something that *you do*. This, possibly more than anything, selects against women entering and remaining in scientific fields. It simultaneously creates an environment in which men are far more likely to succeed by virtue of the fact that they can typically assign family obligations to women in their lives, enabling a one-dimensional focus on career development, whereas the careers of women are more likely to derail due to precisely the same set of conditions. For men in science the effect is activating; for women in science it is stifling. This double standard is well known. However, merely stating the double-standard oversimplifies the problem. Fundamentally, it is the ethic itself that women find objectionable, the double standard being important but secondary. A majority of women want multidimensional rather than one-dimensional lives. It is common for women to summarize their reasons for exiting a science career with the phrase "I want a life." The sacrifices are characterized as being just too great. The academy typically responds by stating that people not willing to make the sacrifices do not belong in science in the first place. However, it is important to explore if women are speaking generally or specifically when they state that the sacrifices are too great. It is interesting to note that more often than not, women are eager and willing to endure the sacrifices necessary to learn and master a body of academic material, technical literature, and specific techniques that is required to create a body of research. However, they often draw the line at being one-dimensional—when the expectation is that science must be a way of life rather than a career—the *supreme sacrifice*. For women with a family, the supreme sacrifice is simply not possible. Moreover, for most women, regardless of family status, it is not desirable either.

An issue raised by Suzanne Franks in the previous essay argues that the culture of science points aspiring students in only one direction. Alternative career possibilities are rarely presented. My own experience is a case in point. Graduate training in the Department of Biology at Indiana University prepared us all to strive for the same coveted goal: a tenure-track research position at a major university. Thus, it was assumed that following completion of my doctoral dissertation research, I would conduct postdoctoral research in a "highly visible" laboratory at a premier research institution. Any other choice was viewed as "a step down." The implication was that such a move would not only negatively reflect on my own career, but also on the institution. Thus, to choose something different from the departmentally sanctioned path of success was tantamount to disappointing everyone who participated in my training. The subject of alternative career choices was simply not discussed. As a result, like many before me, I followed the sanctioned path. It was not until I was well into the postdoctoral period that I began to view my scientific training in broader terms.

- I had been trained to solve problems. My abilities extended beyond situations dealing solely with molecules.

- I had been trained in research techniques. My expertise could be applied to problems outside of science.

- I had been trained to think critically, a skill that is valued in many fields.

- I had extensive training in communications: public speaking, preparing copy-ready documents for publication, preparing and delivering audiovisual presentations, and technical writing.

- I had training in proposal writing, a skill valued in many arenas outside of science.

- I had been trained to be a scientific entrepreneur—to pinpoint areas in need of investigation and launch a laboratory venture to address them. If I could write a successful grant proposal, I could write a successful business plan.

The culture in which graduate students and postdoctoral research associates receive their training does not promote such an examination of the breadth and value of their abilities and talents. However, in an environment in which significantly more students are accepted into graduate programs than there are available jobs following completion of their degrees, exploring all possible career opportunities is crucial. It is my opinion that a graduate program does students a great disservice if they cling to the old tradition of exclusively funneling students into the tenure-track research-scientist path.

Arati Prabhakar's story provides a clear example of the rewards that can come from viewing one's scientific training in broader terms than intended by a graduate program. She was the first woman to earn a doctorate in applied physics from the California Institute of Technology. However, it was not an easy road. She struggled with the course work and her department did not offer a friendly environment for women. She seriously considered leaving CalTech without a degree, but her advisor persuaded her that a doctorate would prove beneficial even if she did not pursue a research career. This counsel enabled Prabhakar to begin thinking about her career possibilities in terms broader than conventional standards. Rather than follow a career in research, she took a position as a congressional fellow at the Office of Technology Assessment (OTA). Prabhakar recalled the faculty reaction to her decision: "One faculty member said he didn't understand why we wasted time educating women if they were going to do something like that" (Gibbons, 1993, p. 399). Undaunted, she forged ahead, and the congressional fellowship launched her into a career at the interface of technology and policy, a newly emerging area of international importance. She is a former director of the Microelectronic Technology Office at the Advanced Research Projects Agency (ARPA), a position in which she made significant contributions in shaping U.S. microelectronics research. She is also a former presidential apointee as director of the National Institute of Standards and Technology. Currently she holds the position of chief technology officer and senior vice president at Raychem Corporation in Menlo Park, California. It is not surprising that opinions held about her unorthodox career move are much different now. She was recently invited back to CalTech to speak about her work.

> The moment richest in irony . . . was when CalTech president Thomas Everhart shook [my] hand and said, "CalTech is really proud of you." . . . I didn't know whether to laugh or cry. (Gibbons, 1993, p. 399)

Because of our marginalized status in most scientific disciplines, women are often pushed, or forced, out of those career paths in which either male competition is intense or there is a strong sense of male entitlement. It is ironic that this often places women in a more favorable position for exploring unconventional career prospects. Whereas the career risks associated with an unorthodox career possibility might be judged as exceedingly high for a male scientist, the relative risk perceived by a woman might be lower, particularly if her options are limited. As a result, women are generally much more willing to travel the career path without a map than are their male counterparts. As with Prabhakar, along with these risks can come substantial rewards.

This is not to suggest that the scientific establishment is doing women a favor by creating the harsh environment in which women must exist and are expected to succeed. As I have maintained throughout this volume, this *must* change if the academy is serious about increasing women's participation in science. However, change is typically a slow process, and those women presently aspiring for scientific careers might be well advised to consider following in the footsteps of women like Prabhakar and travel the career path without a map.

6

Dogs Eating Dogs and
Science Devouring Women

There is discrimination in almost all cultures, discrimination that is based on very old customs and traditions, and therefore, very difficult to counteract. And even if the discrimination didn't exist, women themselves have problems they encounter when their scientific careers and the very strong demands that career places on us, conflict in our own minds with responsibilities we have in our homes and to our families. (quoted in Cutler & Canellakis, 1989, p. 1781)

—Dr. Maxine F. Singer, National Institutes of Health and
president of the Carnegie Institution of Washington

Science and engineering fields are highly competitive. Large bodies of technical material must be mastered in a rapidly changing environment. New information is constantly being produced, rendering even the most seasoned scientists with the feeling that they are constantly behind and struggling to catch up. Moreover, the preparation time required to be eligible for many scientific positions is exceedingly long, and getting longer all the time. For example, it is typical for a PhD scientist to have completed more than 10 years of postsecondary education and training[1] prior to landing her first tenure-track position. Finally, large numbers of budding scientists are encouraged to aspire for a scarcity of prestigious leadership positions at the top, creating a social Darwinist environment in which scientists struggle against each other to either find a niche or gain an edge that will ultimately propel them to the next level.

These pressures are part of the "culture" of science and are thus encountered by everyone embarking on a scientific career. However, it is the premise of this volume that several additional gender-related factors combine to make the environment typically more harsh for women scientists than for their male counterparts. In the essay that follows, Nina Wokhlu highlights the apprehension with which many women approach the study of science.

My First Experience as a Woman Scientist

Nina Wokhlu

I entered the accelerated premedical program at the New Jersey Institute of Technology (NJIT) and the University of Medicine and Dentistry of New Jersey. As an undergraduate scientist at NJIT, I dreamed of performing groundbreaking medical research, of achieving the highest academic honors in the challenging engineering curriculum, of stretching my mental horizons beyond their limits by experiencing all the scientific disciplines from geosciences to biological sciences, and of gaining the first inklings of understanding health policy planning.

NJIT is located in Newark, New Jersey, an impoverished urban area. The school makes tuition affordable to attract its 3500 undergraduate students from all ethnic, racial, and social backgrounds. With an extremely high percentage of minorities, including international students and faculty, university-wide women and minority support programs exist to maintain harmony. Women receive benefits from membership in such a diverse population. The faculty were responsive to the undergraduate population and took great strides to welcome women and minorities in a male-dominated science and engineering environment. When I was there, the Big Sister/Little Sister Program was active, as was the NJIT chapter of the Society of Women Engineers. Several of my professors in mathematics, chemistry, biology, and management information systems were women. Although I cannot speak for every woman student at NJIT, in my experience, female and male students were usually treated equally by professors and the administration.

With the propagation of societal myths that girls (and hence women) cannot understand mathematics and science, it is not surprising that female enrollment at many technical schools is low. Despite my university's active recruitment of women, I noticed the dearth of female students about which both women and men complained. Among the entire student population, women represent only about one out of every eight science and engineering undergraduates at NJIT. My first-year Physics III recitation contained a grand total of two women, one of whom was me. There were a whopping three women in my statistics class (one of whom dropped out). This lack of women raised questions in my mind about society's role in discouraging women from exploring science and engineering. I also worried that I would not be able to join all-male study or laboratory groups. However, many of my male colleagues did turn out to be relatively open-minded after realizing that I was fairly intelligent.

Although most of my female friends in science and engineering complain that sexism is inherent in the bureaucracy, my school faces a completely different dilemma. There seems to be a grassroots problem in my and, most likely, other technical schools. Male students sometimes consider women too frequently as potential dates rather than as intelligent coworkers. It is not as if the male students do not have visible examples of intelligent and successful women. For the past 2 years, the undergraduate valedictorians have been women in difficult majors such as actuarial science and computer engineering. The past four presidents of the NJIT student senate have been women. However, the condescending attitude of male students still continues. It seems that the male student population generally views these women as atypical and homogenizes all other women into the single category of *potential date*.

I have not always taken action against inappropriate behavior. One evening, when I was working in a quiet study area, a "seedy" movie was being played in a nearby room. While I felt offended by such an action, I did not object. I rationalized that I was protecting freedom of choice: The viewers had the right to view the movie of their choice just as I had the right to refuse to see such a movie. I later realized that I had allowed my own rights to be violated. What I, and other equally silent women, forgot that night was that it was *our* study area as well. Our freedom to make use of the neighboring room was taken away, as was our ability to engage in quiet uninterrupted study. As Supreme Court Justice Oliver Wendell Holmes, Jr., once said, "The right to swing my fist ends where the other man's nose begins" (Cummings & Wise, 1974, p. 99). Although every person has freedom of choice, that right must not impinge on the freedoms of others. Today, I would handle the situation differently.

Problems such as these are not isolated to female students. Some of my male friends spoke of their female professors as incompetent, confused, or disorganized. When the female professors were considered competent, the students would still cut their classes more frequently than those taught by male professors. However, rather than being overcome with discouragement, these women professors worked even more diligently to successfully create an aura of professionalism and authority. I was encouraged by the persistence of these professors.

In trying to survive my male-dominated classes, I desensitized myself to any unpleasant circumstances. However, I eventually enrolled in a campus women's studies course. This was one of the most positive experiences that I can remember. My original feelings and sensitivities were rekindled. I remembered who I was and what my purpose was. I realized that society may expect me to act in one fashion, but is that behavior really beneficial to me?

Although NJIT is not free of sexism, students are actively trying to end discrimination from the bottom up. Recently, I presented a conference on discrimination. Students were receptive to the conference; they emerged asking questions about themselves. In addition, there was a campus forum on harassment that was also received well. Although each woman does not have to make it her personal crusade to wipe out sexism, she does have a responsibility to herself and other women to speak up when it touches her life and those around her.

I have many aspirations for the future. I hope to practice clinical medicine, perform medical research, become involved in health policy planning, and explore women's health issues. I will attend medical school and will subsequently pursue a master's degree in public policy. I see a potential obstacle in my interest in health policy planning. Major positions in the federal government are generally held by men. Most policy planning positions are appointed by elected officials. How will I as a woman be able to overcome the "old boy network"? I do not know. However, my undergraduate years have proven to me that passivity is not the answer.

It is impossible to definitively forecast the type of environment Nina Wokhlu will encounter on entering medical school. However, a survey conducted on a cross section of 283 female physicians by Leah Dickstein (1990), professor of psychiatry and associate dean for faculty and student advocacy at the University of Louisville School of Medicine in Louisville, suggests that it might be much worse. The women in Dr. Dickstein's survey reported that they often felt lonely in medical school, that they experienced gender discrimination, and that being female affected their career goals. An overwhelming majority (more than 97%) wished that there had been more female medical students, female residents and practitioners, and female faculty members from whom they could have obtained support. Several of the older women physicians in the sample reported having received a lower salary because they were female or having been demoted when they were married. Younger physicians attended school in the company of enough women that they truly expected equality, and they were surprised not to find it.

Because the concentration is typically focused on career derailment, other effects of the harsh environment faced by women in science tend to be overlooked. For example, this environment may significantly influence decisions regarding a specialty area that a woman in science chooses to pursue. Several of the physicians in Dickstein's (1990) sample reported that they chose a particular residency of specialty because it was "open to women" or appropriate for women. As Susan Allen notes in the essay below, women in science often make career choices that are more motivated out of a desire to find a hospitable environment than out of a consuming interest in a particular specialty area.

Cutting Loose

_____ *Susan S. Allen* _____

Growing up in the 1970s, I was transfixed by weekly television episodes of *Marcus Welby, MD* and *Medical Center*, and I decided at an early age that I wanted to be a physician. I wondered what happened behind those massive doors leading to the operating suites where machines bleeped and doctors toiled beneath brightly lit ceilings. How did those practitioners change a patient suffering from a serious malady into a vibrant individual effervescing with gratitude for the handsome healers in long, white coats? It is interesting to note that the women professionals in these televised series fell into two categories: those who implemented the orders of male physicians and delivered hands-on patient care and those who stood silently by the side of the scrub-clad surgeon in the operating room, wiping *his* brow as *he* labored during a delicate procedure. The fact that there were no women doctors deliberating with Dr. Welby or Dr. Gannon about the treatment plan for the patient-of-the-day seemed of minor importance to a 10-year-old. That fact would later change.

Having determined a career path, I undertook the requisite junior high and high school courses in biology, physics, chemistry, and calculus with relative ease. In June of 1977, I became a student at the University of Florida, acquired the dreaded "premed" label, and decided to major in chemistry.

Somehow, it was not surprising that the number of women classmates decreased as I pursued my studies in chemistry. I expected this gender imbalance. However, I was far less prepared for the isolation I experienced near the end of my sophomore year as I started upper-division classes. Taking three to four science courses with their associated laboratory components each quarter meant many evening and weekend hours of tedious work with little time for social events. In addition, although I took great pride in the quality of my accomplishments, these achievements did little to endear me to other classmates. They came to view me as a source of fierce competition rather than as an individual with an intuitive sense for, and understanding of, science. Undaunted, I accepted the fact that such realities were unpleasant but necessary in order to achieve my goals. I went on to graduate from college in June of 1981 with Phi Beta Kappa honors, aware that the path I had chosen would be a lonely one.

Later that summer, I became a member of the class of 1985 at the University of South Florida College of Medicine in Tampa, Florida. Sitting in the school's main auditorium during orientation, I felt an enormous amount of pride at having made it to medical school. There was an accompanying certainty that all of my previous trials and tribulations had been worthwhile because I was entering one of the most respected, challenging, and (I hoped) rewarding fields of science. Having grown accustomed to being one of only a few women in my undergraduate science courses, I was pleased to note that women accounted for approximately one fourth of my medical school class.

However, as one department chairperson after another addressed my class that first day, a feeling of uneasiness swept over me as I realized that few women faculty were welcoming me into my chosen field.

Medical school was not unlike the military. During the first 2 years, I learned that conformity was the key rule to be followed for acceptance. Information was fed to me on an hourly basis in a manner determined by the faculty. My job was to input every piece of medical information I was given into memory without questioning its relevance, then regurgitate it on demand during examination week.

The third and fourth years of medical school were characterized by contrast, providing some of the most rewarding as well as the most painful experiences of my training. For the first time, I was examining, diagnosing, and treating patients. The magnitude of the responsibility I would have as a physician seemed overwhelming. The rewards came through my patients—those women and men who came to me in ill health, told me their stories, and allowed me to examine their bodies, poking, probing, and at times causing discomfort. They were my true instructors—individuals who, as a result of my interactions with them, taught me that I had the knowledge and skills to manage their care, decrease their pain, and sometimes help affect a cure. Their confidence melted away any apprehensions and insecurities that I had.

It was also during these 2 years that the reality of being a woman in a traditionally male-dominated scientific field became painfully apparent. While working on the hospital wards, I was continually subjected to comments and behaviors by attending physicians and other staff that led me to believe that, because of my gender, I would be considered a lesser grade of doctor than would a man. This included sexist remarks made by chief residents on a daily basis; questions selectively directed to my male classmates, preventing me from demonstrating my knowledge; ridicule for exhibiting compassionate behavior deemed appropriate only for nurses; molestation and near rape by a faculty member. These and other events taught me that the medical world portrayed in those televised series I had revered as a child was a myth.

Unconsciously suppressing a growing anger, I down-played the importance of these gender-based challenges and potential boundaries to success, preventing them from interfering with the work I had to accomplish. In June of 1985, I graduated from medical school and received the Outstanding Student in Surgery award from the university. One month later, I began my internship in general surgery at the University of South Florida Affiliated Hospitals in Tampa, Florida, never imagining to what degree that year would change my life and redirect the course of my career.

All medical school graduates experience a stark terror on their first day as bona fide, resident physicians. I was no exception. Four years of intensive study in medical school could not quell the fear in the pit of my stomach when my pager beckoned me at 3:00 in the morning during my first night on call, and I realized that it was now my job to direct the recovery of a patient who had just gone into cardiac arrest. This initial fear faded with time and experience, but was ultimately replaced by a feeling of loneliness. Despite three of ten surgical interns being women, the number of surgery services requiring staff management meant that we rarely worked together on a ward, and were lucky if we saw each other in passing while walking down the hospital corridors. In addition, only two of the surgery faculty members were women—one, a general surgeon with whom I never worked nor even had a opportunity to converse; the other, a neurosurgeon whom I encountered only briefly during a 1-month rotation at Tampa General Hospital. Neither woman was approachable on a professional or personal level, effectively isolating me from the very individuals who could have helped define my identity as a woman doctor and surgeon. This isolation from women colleagues and mentors, coupled with frequent harassment and chronic fatigue from numerous sleepless nights, began to take its toll.

Near the end of the year, an event occurred that dramatically altered my view of medicine and of myself. For several months, I had endured repeated, humiliating comments from one of the chief residents in general surgery. One evening while on hospital rounds, this individual referred to me as an "ignorant bitch who never deserved to be a doctor" in front of several medical students, other resident physicians, and a patient whose care I was managing. I felt as if I had been physically struck, and I was engulfed by an overwhelming rage. My tolerance for such reprehensible behavior vanished. I turned my back to the group huddled around the patient's bed, walked out of the room, and exited the hospital with no intention of ever returning. Medicine—the field of study to which I had dedicated the previous 8 years of my life—had become utterly despicable. Nevertheless, I acquired a sense of my worth as both a woman and a physician when I left the ward that day. As I sat at home later that evening contemplating the events that had occurred, I realized that walking out of that situation was a sign of newfound strength, not of weakness. Although his insulting behavior had ignited my anger, I was fully cognizant that it was fueled by a history of discriminatory and offensive treatment spanning the past 5 years. I had finally reached my limit and could not deny, suppress, nor sublimate these occurrences in lieu of achieving a coveted goal any longer.

Aware of the fact that I had to complete 1 year of postgraduate clinical training in order to be eligible for medical licensure, I knew that I had to return to the ward. Before going to bed that night, I called the hospital and had the offending chief resident paged. When he came on the line, I told him to meet me in his office at 5:00 the next morning, prior to rounds. Standing face to face with him the next day, I calmly but firmly informed him that any future negative comments about the quality of my work were to be made in private and never again in front of my colleagues and patients. The power with which those words left my mouth was intoxicating. From that point on, I refused to accept abuse as a standard component of my medical training. Through gritted teeth, I completed my internship and acquired my medical license. I then promptly placed my white coat and stethoscope in an unlabeled box, sealing the top, and vowed never to practice medicine again.

I moved to California and spent several months debating whether to consider another specialty in medicine or leave the field entirely. After a great deal of thought and some much needed rest, I decided to pursue, and subsequently completed, a residency in preventive medicine and public health. I was conferred with a Master's in Public Health degree in epidemiology from the University of California at Berkeley. The years that I spent in this training program were not only informative, they were restorative. I was surrounded by women scientists—biostatisticians, epidemiologists, clinicians—and was able to redefine myself not only as a physician, but as an assertive, feminist woman. In addition, I made it a point to develop friends and identify colleagues on whom I could rely for social an emotional support.

Despite the intellectual challenge of studies in epidemiology and statistical analysis, I began to miss patient care. After a 2-year hiatus, I resumed the practice of medicine with a positive attitude and a new agenda: helping women to control their fertility and ensure their reproductive health. Over the next 5 years, I provided contraceptive, abortion, and outpatient gynecologic services. I also became a public advocate for women's choice and reproductive rights. As an abortion provider, I had not only returned to medical practice, but was involved in a specialty area steeped in political controversy. I often felt that I had jumped from the proverbial frying pan into the mother of all fires, but the provision of compassionate and safe pregnancy termination services to women in need was worth the heat.

While working as a clinician, I participated as a principal investigator in a research study evaluating the safety and efficacy of a new barrier contraceptive device for women. My background in epidemiology provided good preparation for this effort, and my interest in clinical trial design led me to accept a position as a research coordinator for a government-funded contra-ceptive research and development organization located in Washington, DC.

For the next 2.5 years, my work entailed the design and supervision of clinical studies on new contraceptive methods for use by women and men in developing countries. Despite the woman-focused nature of this work, the individuals directing a majority of these research programs were men. In my naïveté, I assumed that the gender imbalance present in the upper management of these organizations would be easily corrected if more women entered the field of contraceptive research. I viewed my entry into that arena as an important opportunity not only to positively affect the lives of women through the development of scientifically sound and woman-sensitive methodology in medical research, but also to enhance the visibility of women scientists.

Not unexpectedly, the former was more easily accomplished than the latter. The meticulous effort I extended when designing clinical protocols to ensure safety, comfort, and fully informed consent for women study volun-teers was, and still is, a source of great personal pride. Despite knowing that I brought a much needed woman's perspective to this field of research, I quickly found that many of the men with whom I was working were threatened by change and by the prospect of relinquishing control and power to women. As I looked around me at the numerous bright, articulate women scientists employed by many similar organizations, I realized that all of us held titles in our jobs that implied authority but that in reality we were powerless. Although we were led to believe that our voices would be heard and our recommenda-tions heeded, decisions affecting the lives of women both nationally and internationally were made *around* us, not *with* us. As a result, I have watched many talented, young women scientists come to these institutions full of enthusiasm and energy, only to leave a few years later frustrated by an inability to affect even minor changes in systems paralyzed by outmoded, yet tradi-tional, ways of doing business. I too became one of these women who chose to move on and expend my efforts elsewhere.

Since the completion of medical school, I am often asked by young women aspiring to be physicians why careers in medicine (and science in general) are more difficult for women than for men. I can only offer the following opinion based on my past experiences. Those of us indoctrinated into fields of science are taught to closely mimic the behavior of others, to be unemotional in our interactions with colleagues, and to express ourselves verbally in a traditional language established by men. Yet as women, society teaches us that creativity, emotional warmth, and intuition are valuable traits. These characteristics are the opposite of those often viewed as desirable by men in science and medicine. Being a woman scientist becomes a delicate balancing act in which one must exude a male-defined "professional" aura in order to be recognized as a competent scientist, while often suppressing those qualities with which one defines one's self as a woman. This struggle comprises what I believe to be the *extra* effort women must exert on a daily basis simply to be accepted as scientists.

For many of the reasons mentioned, scientific paths are never easy and frequently require sheer determination and a healthy bolus of stubbornness to be traversed. Looking back over my personal experiences in science and medicine, I recognize that three other elements were crucial to overcoming the obstacles that I faced: (a) the creation of a social support system, (b) periodic self-renewal and reevaluation, and (c) perseverance. The significance of perseverance is always reinforced during a visit with one of my closest friends and physician colleagues. Once or twice per year at the conclusion of a medical conference, she and I find ourselves having a familiar conversation over dinner. In our discussion of the tasks we have accomplished and the hardships we have faced since we last saw one another, we routinely come back to the same question, "Why do we, as women, keep fighting the battle to fit into this system that so often seems unaccepting of us?" One of the two of us automatically provides the same response to this question each time that it is posed: "Because we have to!" As women scientists we may often find ourselves bound by traditions that can impede our efforts. When we do, the ties that would restrict the advancement of our careers must be cut, but those that unite us as women must be preserved at all costs.

Joining Susan Allen and Nina Wokhlu, several other contributors to this volume stress that it is the cumulative affect of more subtle factors that cause a woman's career to derail, rather than a single major event. These are referred to as subtle only because they tend not even to be recognized as boundaries to success by the scientific establishment. However, as Dr. Allen emphasizes, their magnitude on the women experiencing them is not subtle at all. For example, imagine how you would react to a member of your family being subjected to the working conditions that Dr. Icy Macy Hoobler, recipient of a PhD in physiological chemistry from Yale and director of the Research Laboratory of the Children's Fund of Michigan for a quarter of a century, describes.

In my first apprentice position in 1920, I was appointed assistant biochemist in a 500-bed hospital. Being the first woman to occupy this post, problems arose in the management of the laboratory and the hospital. Only restrooms for men were provided, and I was assigned to a public restroom in the hospital building a half block or so from the laboratory. My work load was heavy, and so I accustomed myself to infrequent trips to the restroom. I developed acute nephritis that became severe, and after a few months the doctors recommended as treatment a year's leave of absence with complete rest.

My employment as a woman scientist caused other problems for the administration. My predecessors, being men, were accepted in the doctors' dining room for their meals, since the hospital staff doctors were all male. I, being a woman, could not be assigned to the doctors' dining room for my meals, nor could I be assigned in the nurses' dining room for bureaucratic reasons. I was finally assigned to dine with the help and hospital employees. That dining room was open from eleven a.m. to one p.m. Since I was required to take all the blood samples in the hospital daily routine, my schedule was such that I could not eat lunch until after the dining room was closed. . . . Although difficult for me, I worked up courage to take my predicament to the chief of the laboratory, who had employed me. He took my complaint lightly with a smile, saying that conditions would improve and "I would soon get used to them." (quoted in Mason, 1987, p. 283)

One might contend that this account is dated and therefore not applicable in today's contemporary work setting. However, the reverse is true. Although progress has been made in establishing policy prohibiting discrimination based on gender in the workplace, the policy often remains a stagnant, abstract concept rather than one of action. Women in science are still largely expected to *adjust* to the harsh conditions. Despite their careers being separated by nearly 70 years, Minna Mahlab writes in this volume of women's restrooms located several floors below her designated work area.

Workplace discrimination, prohibited under the 1964 Civil Rights Act, involves judging women (and other minorities) as members of a devalued class rather than on their job performance or other suitable criteria. It is manifested by differential hiring, work assignments, salaries, promotions and other conditions of work based on gender, including exclusion from social and peer networks in which business occurs, information is shared, or decisions are made.

Psychologist Naomi Weisstein provides an apt illustration of discriminatory obstacles women face in establishing a scientific career:

My discovery that women were not welcome in psychology started when I got to Harvard, on the first day of class. That day, at a lunch attended by all the first-year graduate students, the chairman of the department leaned back in his chair, lit his pipe, and remarked that women did not belong in graduate school. Then, as if by prearranged signal, the male graduate students all leaned back in their chairs, puffed on their newly bought pipes, and agreed. I was totally unprepared for such a display, and thought it an initiation ceremony, like having to wear a freshman beanie, or getting beer poured on your clothes. Tomorrow, no doubt, we'll be telling the males that they're unfit for graduate study because of their extra layer of fat. (Weisstein, 1976, p. 2226).

However, rather than being told they did not belong in graduate school, the male students in Weisstein's class became valued protégés in the premier research laboratories at Harvard. Meanwhile, things continued to get worse for Weisstein and her female colleagues.

When I wanted to do my dissertation research, I couldn't get access to the equipment necessary for the research. The excuse was that I might break the equipment. This was certainly true. The equipment was eminently breakable and the male graduate students working with it broke it every week. I did not expect to be any different. (Weisstein, 1976, p. 2226)

Undaunted, Weisstein moved to New Haven and collected her data at Yale. She returned to Harvard and was awarded her doctorate in 1964. However, she was unable to secure academic employment.

Here I had graduated *Phi Beta Kappa* from Wellesley, had obtained my Ph.D. in psychology at Harvard in 2.5 years where I ranked first in my graduate class, it was the year jobs were so numerous they were giving them away free at the bottom of cereal boxes, and I couldn't get a job. (Weisstein, 1976, p. 2226)

Awarded a National Science Foundation postdoctoral fellowship in mathematical biology, Weisstein attempted to conduct research at the University of Chicago. Instead, she was quickly funneled into a lecturer position, where university policy prohibited her from applying for research grants and there was no possibility of a faculty appointment. Weisstein eventually landed a junior faculty position at Loyola University in Chicago. However, she faced obstacles to successfully conducting productive research at every turn. Moreover, she was denied access to the informal networks of communication where news, comment, and criticism about the latest data in the field are exchanged.[2] There were other barriers as well. Weisstein noted that women in science are dealt with in ways that men never encounter.

> For example, I sent an article to a journal editor whose interests I knew to be close to what was reported in my paper. My paper described an experiment I had done which constituted a significant step forward in the area. The editor replied that there were some control conditions that should be run, and some methodological loose ends, so they could not publish the paper. Fair enough. He then went on to say that they had much better equipment at his institution and they would like to do the experiment themselves. Would I mind? (Would I mind? Why should I mind? How many really good ideas do you get in your lifetime? One? Two? Why not give them away?) I responded and told them I thought it was a bit unusual, and asked if they were suggesting a collaboration, concluding that I would be most happy to visit with them and collaborate on my experiment.
>
> The editor replied with a testy letter telling me the experiment was trivial, that they only collaborated with distinguished scientists, and that they were too busy to pursue the matter further.
>
> Obviously, what they meant by did I mind, was did I mind if they took my idea and the experiment themselves. Now as we all know, instances of plagiarism are not at all that uncommon in science. But the striking thing about my experience was that the editor was arrogant enough, and assumed that I would be submissive enough, so that he could openly ask me whether I would agree to the suggested arrangement. (Weisstein, 1976, p. 2227)

A crucial point raised by both Susan Allen's essay and Naomi Weisstein's example is that research issues important to women scientists may not be valued (a) because the focus is on women, and (b) because women are conducting the research. The career of Barbara McClintock, recipient of the 1983 Nobel prize in medicine, provides a classic illustration of this phenomenon. McClintock spent her entire scientific career affiliated with Cornell University. She was awarded a baccalaureate in 1923, a doctorate in botany in 1927, and then remained at the university to conduct her groundbreaking research. McClintock was characterized as an eccentric by much of the scientific community. Her theory of "jumping genes"—that certain genetic elements possess the ability to excise themselves and reinsert into a different position of the genome—was considered so radical at the time she proposed it that McClintock was subjected to ridicule, often depicted as hallucinating, and her supporting evidence (albeit strong) discounted. There is little doubt that her "radical" mobile genetic element theory was considered even more outlandish because it was being forwarded by a woman. As a consequence, McClintock spent most of her career in obscurity. It is a testament to her courage and tenacity that McClintock was able to forge a magnificently rich research career despite facing boundaries to success at virtually every turn (Keller, 1983).

Have times changed? The preamble from a 1984 report coming out of the National Institutes of Health, the agency responsible for funding 85% of the biomedical research in the United States, would certainly suggest that they have.

> Women . . . now have improved their chances of obtaining advanced degrees; of the doctoral degrees awarded in the biological and medical sciences in the last ten years,[3] 30% and 35%, respectively, were to women. (quoted in *Report of the Institutional Training Grants Study Group, 1984; also Mason, 1987*)

Given that more than 10 years have past since these encouraging data were presented, one might expect that women have achieved even higher percentages of representation in biomedical science, particularly at the senior levels of responsibility. However, nothing could be further from the truth. For example, a 1993 report by the Task Force on Intramural Women Scientists at the National Institutes of Health found significant gender differences in salary, tenure, promotions, and recognition of achievements (*Report of the Task Force on the Status of NIH Intramural Women Scientists,* 1993). A 1994 study on resources available to scientists in one division of the National Cancer Institute of the NIH also revealed significant gender differences. Women scientists, on average, were found to have 63% of the personnel and less than two thirds the budgets appropriated to male scientists at the same rank of seniority (Seachrist, 1994). The situation is not any better in academia. Phyllis Carr and her colleagues performed a controlled study of faculty in 107 major teaching hospitals throughout the United States and found that women in academic medicine have lower rank and are paid less than their male counterparts, despite shouldering comparable responsibility and achieving similar levels of academic productivity (Carr, Friedman, Moskowitz, & Kazis, 1993). As Pat Eng reports in the essay that follows, the climate for women in engineering is just as depressing, if not worse.

Putting It on the Table

_____ *Patricia L. Eng* _____

I was raised in an ethnically diverse neighborhood in Chicago, Illinois. Many of my schoolmates were first-generation Americans with parents from Europe or the Middle East. We all accepted each other at face value. I cannot remember any incident in which racial prejudice was an issue. As a child, I did not have any particular interest in science. I was much more interested in dance and gymnastics. As a fairly introverted Asian female, I found that using space and choreographing my movements to music was a most enjoyable and splendid activity. When I saw my first ballet, I was convinced that dancing in a chiffon skirt was the most wonderful profession imaginable.

Despite my quiet nature, I was somewhat of a precocious child, and one day, I decided to see if I could ask my teacher a question that she would be unable to answer. So, out of the blue, I asked her why a ball bounced. Rather than answer my question directly, she instead encouraged me to study physics when I got to high school. She told me that the secret to why everything was the way it was, and acted the way it did, could be found in physics. At the time, I did not know what physics was, but I remembered what she said.

My family moved to an all-White, suburban, affluent neighborhood my first year of high school. I found that a majority of the students had attended the same grammar and middle school together. Therefore, the cliques were well established. It was at this point that I learned that I was Asian and very *different* from everyone else. I was not included or welcomed at many of the school social activities. Therefore, I found solace in my studies and in gymnastics. My high school counselor noted that I had an aptitude for mathematics from my high school placement exams and designed my curriculum to be heavy in mathematics and science. That was fine with me. I enjoyed the classes. The material was logical, and the girls who had snubbed me were not in those classes.

Remembering the advice of my third-grade science teacher, I signed up for physics in my junior year. To my surprise, it was not as hard as I expected. Physics also provided the added benefit of helping me to understand the mechanics of gymnastics. Vectors explained why I had to lean backward during the approach to the vaulting horse in order to achieve enough height to do a handspring vault. I started to do better in gymnastic competitions and to improve my form. I also noticed one day that I was the only girl in my physics class. It did not bother me. The only thing that mattered was learning the material.

In my senior year of high school, I scored well on advanced placement tests in both mathematics and physics. This situated me in sophomore-level mathematics and physics classes on entering the University of Illinois. My first 3 years were a real struggle. By my junior year, there were only 3 female physics majors out of a total of about 300, and we wound up forming a study group. Physics and mathematics were somehow harder to understand at this level and I found myself pulling C's. My male peers told me that a physics major had to have a doctoral degree in order to find a decent job. This concerned me because I believed that my mere average grades would not get me into a decent graduate school. Furthermore, I was beginning to tire of going to school. I wanted to obtain a job and earn a living. I began to wonder if I would ever succeed.

I participated in an open house hosted by the College of Engineering during my junior year. During breaks from staffing my exhibit, I toured the others in the hall and discovered that the University of Illinois has a Nuclear Engineering Department. I stopped to discuss what Nuclear Engineering is and learned that it is very closely aligned with physics. I was intrigued and, after some investigation, transferred from physics into nuclear engineering. Although I had many classes to catch up on, I managed to graduate with a degree in nuclear engineering within 15 months.

Two weeks prior to graduation, the chair of the Nuclear Engineering Department requested that I report to the TRIGA reactor on campus to have my picture taken for the university newspaper. They wanted to do a feature article on the first person to obtain a bachelor's degree in Nuclear Engineering from the University of Illinois. It seemed that no one had actually pursued the undergraduate degree before! So my picture was published in the school newspaper and a press release was issued to a number of newspapers across the country. As a result, I began to receive letters from companies who were interested in hiring me. Recruiters began to call me and my parents. This was a little overwhelming. After all, I had been *only* a C student.

I carefully considered all of the offers and subsequently took a job as an intern working at the Hanford Reservation in Washington State. As an intern, I spent several 4- to 6-month rotations at different jobs throughout the company. This valuable learning experience enabled me to sample a number of jobs before settling into a permanent position. It also afforded Westinghouse Management the opportunity to assess my skills and potential during this internship period.

Within 4 weeks of my arrival in Washington State, a woman came to see me. She introduced herself as the president of the Eastern Washington Section of the Society of Women Engineers (SWE) and invited me to attend the local meetings. I was 2500 miles away from home, in a strange place, with no friends. I took her up on it and went to the meeting. I met about 20 women who worked all over the Hanford Reservation and who were willing to chat with me about anything. I felt welcomed and respected. Here were women that could be my confidants and big sisters. Friendships were quickly made, some of which continue to this day.

I became very involved in SWE, organizing and chairing two career development conferences. I made many contacts in the community through these efforts and developed my project management and coordination skills. Westinghouse Management was supportive of my involvement and encouraged me to pursue a leadership role within SWE. Eventually, I became president of the local section. This made me stand out among my peers. I was different. I was involved in activities in which most engineers do not engage, let alone in their spare time. My efforts were reported in the company newspaper and my peers complimented me on my community involvement.

My career also seemed to be progressing nicely. I chose a permanent position and my work assignments increased in scope and responsibility. But all good things come to an end, and as a result of cuts in the federal research budget, I found my projects being terminated. I left Westinghouse and over the next few years, found myself moving through a series of jobs that took me back and forth across the country. Each time that I changed jobs, I joined an organization that worked hard at getting the job done. No one seemed to notice or care that I was an Asian female. They were more concerned with my technical skills and abilities. In retrospect, I cannot remember the topics of discrimination and sexual harassment being discussed in the workplace during those years. The atmosphere was one of learning and doing the best job one could. I also remained a member of SWE and became involved in local activities whenever I moved to a new location.

In 1983, I joined the federal workforce as a reactor inspector for the Nuclear Regulatory Commission (NRC). Two things distinguished me. Not only was I the first female reactor inspector, I was also the youngest in the

Midwest Field Office. As a consequence, I was once again very different from my peers. I later became one of the NRC's Resident Inspectors—this is an inspector who is permanently assigned to a power plant and inspects plant operations on a daily basis. I was one of four such women in the country at the time.

I continued my involvement with SWE and was now an officer in the Chicago section. Shortly after becoming a resident inspector, I received a call from the national president of SWE. She asked me to conduct a survey of the members of SWE in order to better understand what women engineers were like. I pointed out that my training as a nuclear engineer did not include much in the way of statistics, demographics, or social science. I stated that I had done everything I could to avoid those subjects. But she would not give up and, in the end, I accepted.

Despite my involvement with the members of SWE, I had no information on where I fit as a woman engineer. As I looked at the available data, I found that there were lots of things that I wanted to know. How much alike, and how different, was I from my female colleagues? How did they feel about their relationship with management, their careers, and their families? What were their perspectives on career obstacles and their general treatment in the workplace? Was my experience prior to joining the NRC typical? Armed with these and other questions, I set about to design a survey.

I would never have had the opportunity to conduct a social research project such as this through my everyday work as an engineer. SWE, or any professional society, is a wonderful environment in which to learn and become involved in projects outside of the workplace. Through conducting the survey, I developed project management skills that have transferred directly into the workplace. Over a 2-year period, I solicited and acquired assistance in the form of analytical expertise for the survey from the Engineering Work Force Commission and was successful in convincing Proctor and Gamble to underwrite the initial pilot study.

Based on the results of the pilot study, I was successful at obtaining funding for a national survey, which was administered and coordinated by the Engineering Work Force Commission. During the following 4 years, SWE conducted a national study of the engineers from 22 engineering societies. The results were published by the Society of Women Engineers in 1993. Topics included basic demographic data such as marital status, children, number of employers, and salary, as well as data on answers to attitudinal questions regarding satisfaction with various aspects of career, management, and equality of treatment.

Some of the more interesting findings of the survey pertain to salary and satisfaction. As long suspected, and now proven, women begin their engineering careers with salaries that are slightly higher than men. At about age 31, this situation changes; men begin to earn more and continue to do so throughout the remainder of their careers.

After publication of the survey report, I evaluated the responses to the open-ended question, "What is the biggest obstacle in your career?" The interesting thing about the responses is that men consistently blamed external forces, specifically the economy, for their woes. Conversely, women in their 20s blamed themselves in the guise of insufficient knowledge or training, whereas those in their 30s reported difficulties balancing work and home. Women in their 40s tended to cite discrimination and the economy as obstacles. Finally, discrimination based on age or gender was the major complaint of women in their 50s. Several more mature respondents expressed great dissatisfaction with their careers, citing difficulties in interactions with management and their male peers, and indicated that they were considering leaving the profession altogether. At the time I conducted the analysis, I could not imagine why one would leave the profession, especially when these women had indicated that they found engineering to be a rewarding career.

About a year after the survey was published, I was promoted to a senior position within the NRC and found myself working for an older White male engineer. During my first month on the job, I asked him to tell me what he expected of me as a senior member of his staff. He replied that he did not really expect much from me, because I had been placed in his group by senior management as part of the Equal Employment Opportunity program. He subsequently informed me that I was neither his first nor even his second choice for the position; however, because we were "stuck" with each other, we would have to work it out.

I was stunned and confused. I could not believe that my gender and ethnicity made that much of a difference. After all, discrimination only happened to others—not to me. I knew that in the past, I had simply worked hard and my work had spoken for me. So I resolved to work very hard in order to change my supervisor's mind. However, this was not to be the case.

My supervisor began a sustained psychological assault that was so subtle that I did not recognize it at first. I had never experienced anything like it before. He constantly found fault with my work assignments. He often questioned the rationale behind my conclusions. The technical content was usually acceptable, but every report was returned with several comments on the correct usage of grammar and punctuation. After I incorporated his comments, I would resubmit the report to him, only to have it returned to me with more grammatical errors. In several instances, he found fault with corrections that he had required on a previous revision.[4]

These "improvements" often delayed issuance of my reports by as much as 6 weeks. I was frequently told that I did not understand the work of the group because I lacked the proper background and my field experience was dated. This explanation was again invoked when I asked what criteria I had to meet to be awarded an outstanding performance appraisal. I was informed that receiving that level of recognition would be impossible. Slowly, my work assignments dwindled until I was left with only two, requiring about 1 hour to complete, whereas others in my group were assigned in excess of seven major tasks.[5] I was also encouraged to arrange for Chinese New Year celebrations and to provide information on Chinese cooking to my peers. My supervisor developed a nickname for me that he thought sounded "Chinese" and used it in work gatherings before my coworkers. My female colleagues noticed that this supervisor was treating me poorly before I did and recommended that I seek employment elsewhere. As I approached the age of 40, I found myself thinking that I was stymied and worthless as an engineer, and began to entertain thoughts of changing my vocation. I then realized that I was more like the women responding to the survey than I had previously believed. Many of the women in the 30- to 40-year range expressed feelings of frustration in the workplace, noting that they were not taken as serious candidates for promotions and that choice work assignments regularly went to younger, usually male, colleagues. Some stated that they were considering leaving the profession to do other things.

The situation finally became intolerable when this supervisor told me, in front of my associates in the hallway, "Why don't you just sit in your office? You don't know what you're doing anyway—you should mind your own business."

I was speechless. I could not believe that he would publicly humiliate me in front of my peers. He subsequently called me into a closed-door, one-on-one, counseling session where he informed me that as my supervisor, he could order me to do anything, including answering telephones and cleaning his office. I was nothing more than one of his employees, and I should be grateful to even have a job.

One does not hear the message until one is ready. Up to that point, I thought of discrimination and harassment as something that happened to others. My competency and worth had *never* been questioned. I suddenly found that I was experiencing the instillation of insecurity and demeaning treatment that so many other women had talked about. The good news was that having previously talked to many others, I did not get depressed—I got quietly angry. I realized that I was being subjected to a type of psychological torture that was eating away at my self-esteem and confidence. Through his comments and treatment, my supervisor was instilling insecurity into my life.

Instilling insecurity is the process by which people, including men, teachers, and parents, convince women and girls that they are not capable. It is a very subtle, yet pervasive, phenomenon. The effects of this are discussed in detail in the American Association of University Women's report *How Schools Shortchange Girls* (AAUW, 1992). Even Congress acknowledged that gender-biased treatment of students has a negative effect on girls when they passed the Gender Equity in Education Act in 1994. The act provides funding to sensitize teachers to the effects of gender-biased language and treatment on students in the classroom.

The day after my "counseling session," I approached my supervisor's boss, explained what had happened, how I felt about the situation, and asked for a transfer. After a few months of negotiation, I was transferred to another senior position in a different organization where I am very happy and challenged.

This incident has shaped the message that I give to young women that I mentor. I stress four main points. First, seek out and interact with successful women of a like situation. I find the Society of Women Engineers and similar organizations to be great resources. Someone may have been where you are going and might be able to provide some helpful insight about how to handle specific situations. Contrary to some beliefs, women should and can be their own best resources. I will start worrying about the competition of other women when 50% of my peers and management are female. In the meantime, we all need to pull together to make it better for all of us.

Second, I emphasize that when something does not sound or feel right, do not wonder or stew over it—put it on the table. That is, get it out in the open. In retrospect, when my supervisor told me that he never wanted me in his work group, I should have asked for a meeting with his boss to discuss it openly. It is better to be transferred than to work for someone who dislikes you and makes it known during your first few days on the job. This same advice also applies for questionable remarks. Today, when confronted with a veiled or snide comment about my gender or race, I reply, "Excuse me? What exactly are you trying to say?"

Third, I stress to women how important it is to safeguard their self-esteem. Women pursuing a scientific education today face just as much sexism as those in previous generations, as the contributions to this volume demonstrate. The difference, as I see it, is that women in previous generations *expected* to face sexism and discrimination. They were therefore better prepared to deal with it and still manage to forge a career. Conversely, women today enter science and engineering fields expecting fair and equal treatment. When they do not find it, they are stymied and feel betrayed by a society that told them that they could "be anything they want to be."

Although some claim that the climate for women in the technical workforce is progressively getting better, I do not necessarily agree. In my opinion, the major change is that the method of instilling insecurity in women is more subtle and therefore harder to identify, creating the false illusion that things are better. This can cause women to believe, as I did, that they are responsible for any difficulties experienced. In my case, I erroneously concluded that if I just tried harder, I could *prove* to my supervisor that he was wrong. However, this was an impossible task because of his sexism and racial prejudices. Like countless other women in similar situations, I eventually fell into the pattern of believing him. As a result, I nearly lost my career.

Fourth, once one graduates from school, the need for support remains. Seek support from women in the workplace. Find outside sources of encouragement such as technical and educational societies. This point cannot be overemphasized because one never knows when one will face harassment, sexism, or discrimination. A case in point is that my first personal encounter with overt discrimination took place when I was in my late 30s, *after* establishing my career!

Throughout my career, I have found that the synergism, camaraderie, and friendship of women in organizations such as the Society of Women Engineers, the Association of Women in Science, and the American Association of University Women provide a safe forum for open discussion about the workplace and for putting things on the table. Remember, too, that we have to help those who come after us. Providing support and serving as a sounding board for each other is vital. Who knows? You might mentor a future Nobel laureate.

Similar to Pat Eng, Princeton University molecular biologist Shirley Tilghman reports that she did not confront gender discrimination until later in her highly successful career as a senior scientist.

> My conviction is that the unconscious biases against women are the last frontier that we face. But these are so subtle, so unintentional, and culturally bound that we must be ever-vigilant. Here is a serious example: In 1988, I ran a Gordon Conference on molecular genetics which was funded by the N.I.H. About 33% of the speakers and 45% of the attendees were women. Two years later, another conference on the same topic was arranged by some of my male colleagues. And only two of the speakers were women. I don't think you can attribute this to anything but an unconscious bias. In the biological sciences, there's been a tendency to think that we are doing so well that the problem is over. And most women would like to believe this. I believed it. But that is nonsense. (Morell, 1992)

As a group, women scientists may show concern for, and value, women's health research more than men, but it is less probable that they will occupy positions to influence research priorities. Perhaps the most graphic contemporary example of women's devaluation in the research arena is that, until only recently, research on breast cancer in men, comparatively rare in occurrence, far outpaced breast cancer research focusing on women. Furthermore, issues important to women may be valued when the research is conducted by men but not by women. Consider the case of Margaret Jensvold. During medical school and a psychiatric residency, Dr. Jensvold had initiated research on the treatment of menstrual-cycle-related depressive symptoms by modifying the dosage of antidepressant medication over the menstrual cycle period. She accepted a psychiatric research fellow position at the National Institute of Mental Health (NIMH) in the Menstrually Related Mood Disorder Program fully expecting to continue this important work. To her surprise, Dr. Jensvold was informed that the NIMH would not allow controlled investigations of antidepressant therapy for menstrual-cycle-related depressive symptoms to be conducted. She later learned that this was untrue and that the project had been delegated to a male colleague. Meanwhile, Dr. Jensvold was assigned to study the abuse histories of patients with premenstrual syndrome (PMS). Her survey uncovered widespread abuse in the backgrounds of PMS patients, contrasting that reported in some community-based studies (Jensvold, Muller, Putnam, & Rubinow, 1989). The results were apparently incongruent with the expectations of her male colleagues at the NIMH. As a consequence, she was denounced as having psychological difficulties, her scientific competence was called into question, and her fellowship was prematurely terminated. Dr. Jensvold filed formal allegations of discrimination with the NIMH. In response, her supervisor refused to allow blood samples she had collected from another study to be analyzed, and NIMH attorneys warned her not to publish any findings derived from data that she collected during her psychiatric research fellowship.

> Two years later, when an EEOC investigation into her complaint had not been opened, she filed a lawsuit alleging sex discrimination and retaliation. Nearly five years after her departure from NIMH, Dr. Jensvold's case went to trial. In April 1994, a jury of eight Maryland citizens found unanimously that Dr. Jensvold's NIMH supervisor had discriminated against her and that his refusal to assay her samples after she filed a complaint constituted illegal retaliation. In addition, they found that her supervisor's treatment of her constituted "discriminatory mentoring." The lawsuit was precedent setting, establishing mentoring as protected activity under the Title VII discrimination law. (Jensvold, Hamilton, & Mackey, 1994, p. 111)

Despite the termination of her fellowship, Dr. Jensvold managed to independently continue her research program. Her 1992 published study on variable antidepressant dosing as a treatment for menstrual-cycle-related depressive symptoms (Jensvold, Reed, Jarrett, & Hamilton, 1992) was highlighted by the General Accounting Office (U.S. GAO, 1992) as an illustration of the type of significant contributions that will be lost if the scientific research community does not acknowledge the distinctive needs and perspectives of women (Jensvold et al., 1994).

As Margaret Jensvold's case illustrates, when a woman scientist refuses to "adjust" to the harsh conditions and becomes a whistle-blower, she is branded a turncoat, an instigator of dissent, characterized as on an antiscience campaign, and is abandoned—even by some women colleagues (Glazer, 1983). The institution usually counters her complaint by initiating "damage control" measures including, (a) disputing that any discrimination or harassment occurred, (b) denying that it was deliberate, (c) asserting that the woman instigated it all, or (d) arguing that the positive virtues of the alleged perpetrator(s) outweigh the negative consequences of their actions, and, therefore, disciplinary measures should be waived. Colleagues routinely decline to provide substantiating information previously given in private. In addition, retaliation against the woman for exposing discriminatory practices is apt to occur, accompanied by underrating her contributions and maligning her character. Important work is often redistributed to others. As a consequence, the work environment becomes increasingly unbearable. Too often family and friends routinely blame the victim by disbelieving her allegations or suggesting that she may be exaggerating and fail to support her efforts to fight against discrimination (Schrier, 1990). Women such as Margaret Jensvold are often victimized twice: first by the discriminatory practice, and then again when they report it. Rather than accept a second round of victimization, which can often be far more vicious than the first, many women choose to remain silent and are left to languish in work environments infested with discrimination.

It is also unfortunately a common experience of women in science to have credit for contributions made to a research program either discounted or misappropriated. Being in an environment in which there are few women contemporaries and women mentors with whom to seek out perspective and support may contribute to the feelings of helplessness created by unfair treatment such as this, which often evolves to the apathy directly preceding career derailment. I faced such a situation in graduate school. I spent months working out the conditions for a technique that eventually proved to be highly useful both for the laboratory and ultimately for my dissertation research. However, a male graduate student in the laboratory, with seniority over me in that he was nearing the completion of his doctoral studies, coopted my work, seeing it as an opportunity to add another chapter to his dissertation. I protested, but to no avail. My specific contribution was trivialized to the level of "a general biological reagent," and my angry reaction was characterized as "irrational." My objection was to his coopting the work as if it was his own, not to him using the technique to advance his research. This individual's dissertation contained no acknowledgment of my contribution to the success of his research, despite the fact that even the most incidental contributions made by male colleagues were mentioned.

Katherine Sanford, an internationally distinguished researcher at the National Cancer Institute since 1947, very painfully learned that seniority and level of scientific accomplishment do not guarantee protection against discrimination or harassment. Dr. Sanford was the first person to clone a mammalian cell, which proved to be a crucial breakthrough for such areas as the ongoing development of vaccines and molecular genetics. She recently developed and patented a test that identifies a type of DNA repair problem present in the cells of individuals with several cancer-prone genetic diseases (Sanford et al., 1990). Given the significance of her research and her record of major accomplishments, one might expect that Dr. Sanford's research would have been enthusiastically supported at the NIH. However, while Dr. Sanford was developing this test, her institutional support was drastically decreased and her staff pared from a total of 12 to a single laboratory technician and a glass-washer. Her primary collaborator was transferred to an administrative position in an alleged retaliation for his support of her. The official explanation for this extreme set of actions was that a panel of outside scientists reviewed her research program and found it to be "below par." Dr. Sanford examined the credentials of the reviewers and concluded that they lacked sufficient expertise to perform an adequate evaluation. However, her objections were ignored. Other detrimental actions followed. For example, she was prevented from presenting her work at conferences and her name was removed from the NIH telephone directory. An EEOC review found probable cause of discrimination, but the NIH disregarded the findings. Finally, after the filing of two complaints with the NIH, a negotiated settlement was reached. However, Dr. Sanford was left to conduct her research under limited support and staff (Jensvold et al., 1994).

Women scientists are public entities who draw attention with anything that they do. They have a pioneer status, functioning as stand-ins for all women. They are symbols of how women can achieve in this society. Perhaps their most challenging obstacle is to find a way to conform to a male-dominated work environment without simultaneously becoming self-alienated (Kanter, 1977).

> There is an element of derailment built into the system for women—the pressure created by having to be a role model and a "first" along with personal competency. Men don't have to deal with this added pressure. (Morrison, White, & Van Velsor, 1992, p. 16)

Women professionals perform in a glass house and dread even the thought of failing on the job, because it would not only affect their own advancement but also restrict the opportunities afforded to the women who come after them.

> "I feel that if I fail, it will be a long time before they hire another woman for the job," one executive confided. Carrying that burden can lead women to play it safe, to be ultraconservative, to opt out if a situation looks chancy. (Morrison et al., 1986, p. 146)

The burden is in being a minority, marginalized by gender before anything is said or done, and in assuming the onus of exemplifying women as a group because there is no one, or few others, to share that responsibility.

Women are a minority in this business. A woman coming into a high-level meeting will see few other women. They have difficulty finding a supportive ear or shoulder. So they feel distinctly different. (Morrison et al., 1992, p. 16)

As Denise Gürer notes, being a woman where few, if any, women have been before is a liability that creates stress.

Journey to a Career in Science

Denise Gürer

Like many women scientists, I found initial encouragement to pursue a scientific career from my parents. They instilled in me the belief that I could do whatever I chose in life. In addition, they served as my first role models, because both of them have scientific careers: My mother is a nurse practitioner and my father is a physicist. Their strong encouragement, coupled with my interest and fascination with mathematics, led me to apply to Indiana University of Pennsylvania (IUP) as a physics major, where my father was a professor in the Physics Department.

IUP is a medium-sized university in the college town of Indiana, Pennsylvania. Even though IUP enrolls a large number of students, approximately 13,000 a year, my graduating class in physics had only nine students, two of whom were women, counting myself. When I attended IUP (1980–1985) the physics faculty numbered 14, and there were no women.

In my first physics class of about 100 students, the professor announced that it was his opinion (and he made it quite clear that his opinion was of the utmost importance) that women should *not* pursue physics careers. It was his belief that women better served our society by staying at home, and that working professional women were ruining the economy and the standard of living for single-income households.

Needless to say, these "welcoming" remarks from an amateur economist left me in a slight state of shock. However, rather than taking his statements to heart, I ignored what he had to say and retaliated by dropping off Equal Rights Amendment statements in his mailbox on a regular basis.

After graduating from IUP with honors, I entered the doctoral program in the Physics Department at Lehigh University. Lehigh is a small private university with 4,500 undergraduates and 2,000 graduate students located in Pennsylvania. There were approximately 20 faculty members—all male—and about 40 graduate students. Of these, 4 were women.

The environment was much harsher and more constrained in graduate school. For the first time I experienced sexual harassment from my peers. Comments were always made about how I looked; mostly negative comments about my weight, makeup, clothing, and hair. I became so self-conscious about my looks that I started wearing baggy shirts and jeans to school. I wanted to look as unfeminine as possible and blend into the woodwork.

The comments about my appearance sent overt messages that I was different and not welcome. This greatly affected my self-esteem and my ability to interact with colleagues and professors.

Another problem was getting respect for my opinions from peers, even though my class work was above average. I remember a case in which I pointed out a mistake in a fellow classmate's calculations and explained in detail why they were incorrect. He refused to believe me and as a result got that part of the homework wrong. However, this incident did not cause him to think more highly of my comments. He still insisted on ignoring or dismissing my input.

When graduate students enter the physics program, they spend a majority of their first 2 years working at the Physics Building, and in most cases, socializing is done solely with their classmates. It is a very cloistered and intensive atmosphere in which one does not see many other graduate students until qualifying exams are passed. In order to survive the first 2 years, one has to rely on, and work with, one's peers—such as taking part in study groups and discussions. However, this support structure is not always open to women students. We are outsiders—excluded from much of the networking and socializing—and are not taken seriously. This proves to be quite harmful, because there are typically not enough women classmates to form a comparable support structure.

My interactions with the professors seemed pleasant on the surface. Because I was different, I was given more attention. However, I never had the feeling that my scholastic achievements were valued. A professor even told a visitor to the department, "It's nice to have Denise around. It's good to have a pretty face here." I'm sure that the professor meant it kindly and as a compliment. However, it made me feel insignificant; as if my only value was cosmetic.

This treatment took quite a toll on my self-confidence. I found that I started blaming myself for any problems I had with fellow classmates and professors. I dreaded coming in to my office every morning. I started to believe that I was neither sufficiently smart nor capable to succeed in physics, and this understandably affected my schoolwork. As a consequence, I began to put off doing my work because I was afraid I would not be able to successfully complete it. The fun and excitement of physics was slowly being beaten out of me. Eventually, things deteriorated to the point at which I obtained an MS in physics and transferred to the doctoral program in computer science.

There was a much higher percentage of women in Lehigh's graduate program in electrical engineering and computer science–approximately 15% of the 200 students. This certainly did not represent parity, but I immediately felt the impact of having more women in the EECS Department. This is often referred to as a *critical mass.* I define it as enough women to take some pressure off of simply being a woman. No longer one of four females spread out in the entire physics department, I felt that I was not the sole representation of womankind. To illustrate, I often felt as if mistakes that I made reflected on all women studying physics and professors would add that event as evidence to their assumption that women do not belong in science. Conversely, when a woman made a mistake in the EECS Department, it was because she did something wrong, not because she was a woman. I attribute this difference to the critical mass in EECS. It was also good to see other women working at tough problems and subsequently being taken seriously by their peers. I no longer felt like an outsider and was more comfortable. Another positive aspect was that there were more role models. If I saw a woman colleague taking a difficult class, I thought, "Hey, I can do that too!"

Despite a critical mass of graduate student women, there were a paucity of women faculty. As a consequence, there were not many female role models for women beyond graduate student status, and the male faculty were not accustomed to working with women on equal footing. Although most faculty did not seem to mind having women graduate students, there were some notable exceptions. For example, I once overheard a conversation between professors in which one complained, "Lehigh went downhill when they admitted women!"

A paucity of women faculty also affected how the undergraduate males perceived women in higher positions in the academic environment. My advisor, who was the sole female faculty member in the College of Engineering for many years, related horror stories about her teaching experiences with the undergraduate male students. Her office door was consistently vandalized with graffiti and she was constantly dealing with insolence and hostility.

Role models are an important variable in retaining women in science during their undergraduate and graduate years. Women need to see and speak with other women who are successful in science-related professions. Interactions with women professionals need not be constant. I remember two encounters in my 6 years at Lehigh that were critical in fostering the encouragement and motivation to finish the PhD program. Both were invited speakers in our department's seminar series. Graduate students who were working in areas of similar interest to those of the speakers were provided an opportunity to meet with them for a short time and were also invited to join a group of faculty and students for dinner following their presentation. I arranged to meet briefly with one of the speakers, who was very well known and respected in the area of cognitive science. I expected her to be in a hurry and unwilling to take the time to talk to a student, but I was wrong. Despite having only a short time to converse, she managed to have a profound impact on me. It felt good to have someone take an interest in my work. She impressed me with her approachability, as well as her willingness to consider my ideas and provide input. Our interaction also encouraged me in that I could look into the future and see myself in her shoes. Thus, a seemingly incidental encounter provided me with a role model and a source of motivation in my dissertation research.

A second woman speaker also had a large influence on me. The department allowed graduate students to invite some speakers of their choice with the condition that they organize the visit and stay within a budget. I promptly took advantage of the opportunity and invited a woman I had met at a conference the year before. When she visited Lehigh, she and I talked at length about my dissertation work, which was in the proposal stage at the time. One of her comments I remember well. She said, "This is certainly cutting-edge work." I was unsure about what I was proposing and her comment really gave me the boost that I needed. Once again, I had a role model, an example of someone like myself that reached a high level of status in the research field.

In addition to role models, mentors are equally important but are much more difficult to find. Mentors are around for a longer period of time than guest speakers and help protégés learn the system and good scientific practices. In many cases, one needs more than one mentor for different areas. During my time in the EECS Department, I received much of my mentoring from two people: my husband and my graduate advisor. My advisor is a tenured faculty member and is also a woman. My husband, a physicist, gave me constant support when I felt discouraged. His belief in me helped to sustain me through difficult times. He also taught me about research, including networking, reading and writing research papers, and attitude. There are many skills to learn as a budding researcher, but attitude is crucial and the most difficult. My husband taught me to trust my instincts, and that if I strongly believed in something to stand up to criticism and forge ahead. In addition, he taught me good scientific conduct, such as being critical of one's own work in order to produce the best possible model system and experiments designed to test it. There were times when I felt like giving up and quitting graduate school, but his constant encouragement kept me going, and his advice helped me to become a better scientist.

My graduate advisor also served as a mentor, but in a different way. She taught me good writing skills and most important gave me a push when I needed it. I remember one time when I was reading papers and trying to get an understanding of the state of research in intelligent tutoring systems. At one of our weekly meetings she said that she thought I was ready to submit my dissertation proposal, which includes a written and oral presentation. My first reaction was to panic and I protested. I felt that I needed at least another month to adequately prepare! However, she stood by her decision and stated her conviction that I was ready. Reassured by her confidence in me, I started to put something together and wrote up a proposal. All went well and in hindsight, I recognize that I really needed to be prodded and encouraged. I would have continued reading for months before considering myself ready.

Not only did my advisor aid me in earning my PhD, but she also encouraged me to become involved in women's groups centered around the university. I became a member of the Presidential Advisory Committee for Women. One of our projects was to submit suggestions for improvements in making the campus a better place for women to the president of the university. Two tangible results from that committee were the development of a women's center and a child care center for university employees and students.

I originated the idea for the women's center and enthusiastically pursued its establishment, while simultaneously working on my PhD. I wanted to provide a place where women felt safe; where women could talk about their problems and not be ridiculed or dismissed. I also wanted the women's center to be instrumental in sponsoring gatherings and discussions, such as brown bag lunches and presentations by off-campus speakers on women's issues. I teamed with the woman who started the child care center and, with support from the upper administration, we managed to obtain three rooms in a building near the center of campus.

My involvement on the advisory committee and the initiation of the women's center helped to convert my negative experiences at the Physics Department into something useful, not only for myself but for other women at Lehigh. My activities gave me back the self-esteem I had lost and connected me to other professional women at Lehigh, thus providing a strong support network. I felt I was making a difference, securing the best from my educational experience. Most important, I was not a victim of the academic process.

Many programs have been developed in the past few years with the goal of attracting and retaining more women in scientific professions. Many of these programs are good and have achieved varying levels of success. However, as this volume suggests, they do not always get to the heart of the problem—which is that women face more and more hostility and discrimination as they progress up the academic career ladder.

It is my opinion that one of the leading contributors to the inability of some departments to retain women is their harsh environment. This is particularly difficult to eradicate, because many attitudes and sexist traditions are embedded in the system and perpetuated by faculty. Because individual departments have unique qualities, a one-size-fits-all solution is not practical. Instead, each department must perform an inward examination, identifying and addressing specific areas of concern. It is crucial that the administration fully support activities centered around creating an academic environment that is less hostile toward women.

7

Female Impersonators
and Honorary Males

[Women] leave [science] because while it's fun to do the work, it's not fun to be in that environment. What we can do is help make them aware of the underlying sexism so they will know how and when to choose their battles. Help them let the distasteful stuff flow on by them and know what they have to do. Help them find mentors. (quoted in Geppert, 1995, p. 42)

—Jan Brown, an independent consultant in technology management, transfer, and commercialization based in Austin, Texas

Women in science owe a debt to feminism. It has been through feminist analysis and critique that many of the barriers to success outlined in this volume were first exposed. In *Female-Friendly Science,* Dr. Sue Rosser identified the feminist study of language and classroom behaviors as two important areas of contribution.

A large body of feminist research has documented how language, both written and spoken, transmits bias regarding roles and stereotypes relating to gender. Textbooks and classroom discussions frequently communicate this bias by using male pronouns and other masculine terminology when in fact the reference is inclusive of all genders. It is argued that this convention allows the important points to shine through without being smothered in additional levels of complexity created by the tedious practice of using inclusive terminology, such as "her or his experiment"; "she or he calibrates the equipment"; and "professors expect women and men to work hard." Furthermore, it has been historically assumed that a majority of society understands that masculine terminology has both exclusive and inclusive usages, and that the difference is readily apparent through context. If true, a clear prediction from this assumption is that when masculine terminology is used in its inclusive context, listeners should generate images of women and men about equally. However, in a classic study, Wendy Martyna (1980) demonstrated that people rarely visualize women when masculine terms such as *he* or *man* are used in a generic context. Thus, in addition to low visibility contributing to an environment in which women in science feel alienated, everyday language usage constantly reinforces an image of what a scientist is—and it is almost always male.

Gender referencing is another form of language usage that transmits bias. It occurs when statements are made that, either explicitly or implicitly, present one gender as the norm and the other as atypical. Examples include "The scientist conducted the experiment while *his* technician recorded the data in *her* notebook"; "The doctor examines *his* patient"; and "The nurse makes *her* patient's bed." Statements such as "men and ladies," or "The engineer and his doctor wife attended the reception" represent other ways in which language supports stereotypical roles (Rosser, 1990).

It is often the case that science faculty are unaware that their language reflects stereotypical and sexist biases. Furthermore, even when they are made aware, it is difficult to alter lifelong language patterns. People usually make a feeble attempt, only to fall back into old and familiar patterns of language usage. A common excuse for not following through and implementing change is to render insignificant the effect of language on overall career development. However, just as with other double standards exposed in this volume, language patterns are *only* deemed insignificant if the negative consequences do not directly impact on the careers of men. The effects on girls and women are far from insignificant. Gender-biased language affects how we think about ourselves, stifles creativity, and constrains potential. Furthermore, if gender-biased language patterns are truly insignificant as alleged, one has to wonder why change is so difficult. Why is implementing policy to eliminate gender bias so thoroughly resisted within academia and industry?

Of course, in the short term, it is always easier to do nothing when confronted with a prospect for change. However, in the long term, doing nothing can have extremely negative consequences. Among these is that it systematically steers potentially productive women away from science. I believe that eliminating gender bias in everyday language usage will be a long process. However, there is no better time to start than now, and no better way to begin than by examining our own use of language. The Association of American Colleges (1986) has recommended the following two general guidelines for recognizing gender-biased statements in your language: (a) Would you say the same thing about a person of the opposite sex?; (b) Would you like it said about you?

As previously mentioned in chapter 4 of this volume, the manner in which scientific accomplishments are recognized tends to render women invisible. A case in point is the discovery of the homeobox, a conserved DNA-binding sequence common to a class of developmental regulatory genetic loci known as homeotic genes. The discovery is generally credited to Swiss researcher Walter Gehring and American researcher Matthew Scott, independently studying homeotic genes in the common fruit fly, *Drosophila melanogaster.* News that developmentally important DNA sequences are conserved among species (including humans) created quite a flurry when it was announced. The discovery was reported in the popular press in such prestigious daily news-papers as the *New York Times.* Nevertheless, lost in the step-by-step media accounts of the homeobox discovery was that Amy Weiner, a graduate student conducting doctoral dissertation research in the laboratory of Thomas Kauf-man at Indiana University, performed much of the bench work experiments and was the primary author on the scientific publication coming out of the United States. The other author, Matthew Scott—to whom the discovery is credited—was a postdoctoral research associate in Kaufman's laboratory at the time, but waited to publish the findings until he had moved to a faculty position at the University of Colorado at Boulder. Whereas the names Walter Gehring and Matthew Scott became synonymous with the homeobox, the only place where Amy Weiner is given true recognition for her part in the homeobox discovery is at Indiana University, on the fifth floor of Jordan Hall, in Thomas Kaufman's laboratory.

Sue Rosser (1990) noted that the convention of referring to scientists making important discoveries by their last names (e.g., the discovery of nuclear fission by Meitner), is parallel treatment but disproportionately fails to acknowledge contributions made by women. The image present for most people is that of a male scientist, because the major proportion of scientists are men. While conducting postdoctoral research at NIH in Bethesda, Mary-land, I inquired among several of my colleagues if they knew the institutional affiliation of Meitner at the time the nuclear fission discovery was made. My question contained no gender reference—only a last name. However the response nearly always referred to Meitner as male ("Wasn't he at . . . ," or "I'm not sure, but I think he did his work at . . ."). In fact, Lise Meitner was a talented woman scientist—one who out of conscience refused to extend her work to developing weaponry of human destruction (Vare & Ptacek, 1987). These represent a few among many ways that women's scientific achievement is rendered invisible by conventional practices. It would seem to me that if the scientific academy is serious about increasing women's participation in science, a good place to start would be by recognizing the past and present accomplishments of women scientists.

A second area in which feminist research has contributed significantly is in the area of classroom dynamics. For example, studies of groups containing both women and men have demonstrated that men generally talk and control the topic of discussion more than women (Kramarae, 1980). Don Zimmerman and Candace West (1975) similarly found that men interrupt women more frequently than the reverse, and their interruptions typically interject trivial remarks that either end or change the focus of women's discussion.

Sue Rosser (1990) has elaborated.

> Forms of verbal interaction, such as knowing and addressing the male students more frequently by name and interrupting female students more frequently than males, may be unconscious behaviors on the part of faculty that discourage female participation. Humorous or teasing reference to physical or sexual characteristics (more frequently applied to females) or humorous treatment of serious topics such as rape, lesbianism, or depression are likely to be offensive to women and make them feel uncomfortable in the classroom interaction. (pp. 13–14).

Rosser (1990) went on to note that differential encouragement to males at the expense of females can also occur nonverbally. For example, faculty have been observed to preferentially make eye contact with men. Myra Sadker and David Sadker (1979) also have found that faculty more often nod or present other gestures of encouragement in response to men's questions, and tend to allow men more time to answer a question before moving on to another student. Finally, Bernice Sandler and Roberta Hall (1986) reported that women are more often asked lower-order questions, such as those requiring memorization of facts, whereas men are characteristically asked higher-order questions, such as those requiring analytical reasoning and synthesis. They also found that women tend to be squeezed into the back rows during laboratory demonstrations, often leaving them walled out by taller males occupying the prime viewing positions. These factors collectively operate to place women pursuing science careers at a distinct disadvantage.

A third area in which feminist analysis has contributed substantially is by critically examining researcher bias in designing and interpreting experiments. This work exploded the myth that scientists are dispassionate observers dedicated to pure ideals and the noble goal of unlocking the mysteries of nature and the universe. This was the image presented to me as a young girl. Like priests, scientists were presumed to be above the temptations of the flesh plaguing the remainder of society. It never occurred to me in my youth that motivations other than a noble quest for the truth, such as the Three Big Ps (**Power**, **Profit**, and **Politics**), were possible for scientists.

Feminism questioned the assumption that scientists are dispassionate observers immune to outside influence. Science is not conducted in a vacuum. It is an integral part of culture rather than a "holy" entity hovering benevolently above it. Scientific research is located within a particular time, historical context, and political framework. For example, it should come as no surprise that tremendous advances in surgical techniques, the development of antibiotics for treating infection, aeronautical design, and communications occurred during the First and Second World Wars.

Researchers also come from varied backgrounds and life experiences, factors that can unconsciously seep their way into research design and interpretation. For example, the scientific establishment has only recently begun to address the underrepresentation of women and ethnic minorities in clinical trials (e.g., Brooks, Smith, & Anderson, 1991; Schmuker, & Vessell, 1993; Wermeling & Selvitz, 1993). Moreover, Jerry Weaver and Sharron Garrett (1978) reported that even when included in clinical research protocols, women and ethnic minorities often receive inferior and insensitive treatment.

Economics and politics also influence the direction of research. Private industry funds a minority, but significant, proportion of scientific research and it is curious that conclusions drawn from the data collected in these studies tend to favor the industry funding source. The tobacco and pesticide industries are two among several examples. One could hardly characterize the so-called genetic and biological "experiments" conducted on human prisoners during the Nazi era as a noble quest for the truth conducted by scientists with pure ideals. The research was the cancerous outgrowth of a political agenda. Finally, the U.S. government actively promotes research in certain areas while banning entirely funding for research in others, such as directly studying sexuality and sexual behavior in persons under the age of 18 years.

Given that the motives behind scientific research are not always as pure as alleged, feminists asked when scientists are engaged in a noble quest for the truth, what truth are they searching for? Who decides what phenomena need explanation and what is problematic about them (Harding, 1986)? There are many possible directions that scientific research could take, but some paths are very well trodden, others infrequently, and many others not at all. Two external forces constraining the direction of scientific research are resource availability and technological limitations. For example, it would be unfair to compare the abundance of genetic information known about fruit flies to the dearth available on extraterrestrial life, when to date no verifiable sample of the latter has been discovered. Nevertheless, technological capabilities aside, the determination of what is scientifically interesting, and hence where resources will be allocated, is largely made by senior scientists. Therefore, the decisions have historically and predominantly been made by men. Even when they do participate in proposal review, women's perspectives on problematics can easily be swamped by the male majority and effectively silenced. Taken together, feminist analysis has exposed that science is not necessarily engaged in a search for the *whole truth* but a selective version of the truth based on what those in power define as problematic.

Feminist criticisms of science are often discounted as self-evident and pointless by the scientific establishment. In addition, scientists appeal to the notion that because they occupy the highest ranks of the intelligentsia, and a significant degree of expertise is required to perform scientific analysis, no one but a fellow scientist can fully understand what they are trying to accomplish. Thus, science has traditionally placed itself above criticism.[1]

During the transition from a group connected primarily through public activism to women's studies as an academic discipline, feminism also placed itself above criticism (Patai & Koertge, 1994). It is alleged that women's status as an oppressed group renders it impossible for men and nonenlightened women to objectively review feminist projects. Thus, only a feminist can fully understand what feminist research is trying to accomplish. Similar to science, a few hot topics are deemed problematic and heavily pursued.

Daphne Patai and Noretta Koertge pointed out in their book *Professing Feminism: Cautionary Tales From the Strange World of Women's Studies* (1994) that the transition to the classroom has given feminism a legitimacy that it lacked in the past. Furthermore, university affiliations have afforded professors with opportunities to obtain outside funding for feminist projects and the ability to publish in well-circulated periodicals and journals. An infrastructure grew out of feminism's move into academia that included the creation of associations and organizations, the development of specific rules for properly conducting feminist research, and the establishment of feminist journals in which to publish and gain credibility within the feminist and academic communities. Finally, the transition of feminism to the classroom provided easy access to a large pool of young women that in prior decades were largely unreachable. Course work could be designed and reading materials chosen that guided impressionable women to focus on any or all of the hot topics deemed problematic by the academy.

It is interesting to note that science has its own associations and organizations, rules for properly conducting scientific research, and specific journals in which scientists can publish and gain credibility within the scientific and academic communities. Therefore, it would seem that science and feminism are more alike than either discipline would like to believe. In fact, the structural commonalities abound. However, because both disciplines have placed themselves above criticism, neither is willing to objectively listen to outside opinions. Dissent from within and critical views coming from the outside are typically seen as an attack that could potentially jeopardize the entire discipline. Massive defense efforts are consequently mounted to counteract them. Hence, the battle lines are drawn—feminists on one side and scientists on the other—a majority of women opposing a majority of men. However, where does a woman in science fit into the picture? As Angela Rella points out in the following essay, right in the middle.

Who's Afraid of Virginia Woolf Now?

———— *Angela Rella* ————

So this is how it is: I am working at a bookstore for $5 an hour. After spending 5 years of my life (and 5 years of my parent's money), I still do not know where I am going, or to be more precise, what I am going to be doing next year. One of my coworkers said to me the other day, "So you just graduated and you have no idea what you want to do? Wow, just like in the movies!" My life has never resembled this brand of chaos before, and it is not very comforting to realize that one is classic "Generation X," so I am at a loss. I look toward two things to clear my mind: numbers and Virginia Woolf. Fresh out of college, the only numerical connection my numbed and weary brain can find is the prevalence of the number 5 in my life ($5 dollars an hour, 5 years gone, $500 dollars in the bank, five friends left, five letters in my last name, 5 years until I am twenty-seven . . .). Unconsoled, I turn to Virginia Woolf's *A Room of One's Own* to reaffirm my thoughts and existence, as her more than 60-year-old writing reaffirms the necessity and hardships of women in male-dominated fields in a logical, irrefutable, indisputable way.

I graduated from high school in 1989 and headed for the University of Rochester. On my parent's advice, I decided to take up study in one of the last bastions of male domination: electrical engineering. I had always been a strong math student, and this fact combined with an interest in the subject propelled me rather unthinkingly toward a career in the sciences. After 2 years of this curriculum, during which time I longed for rare liberal arts courses to balance my brain, I transferred to the State University of New York at Binghamton, located in upstate New York, where low tuition would allow me an extra year to major both in electrical engineering and English literature.

I went to SUNY Binghamton hoping to bridge two gaps: the gap between those who study science and those who study words, and also the gap between women and men. When I met with my advisor during orientation, I was heartily discouraged from keeping the former plan. He told me that I could always read in my spare time or return to school for my English degree later. Most of the engineering professors treated me as if I were less serious about my studies than the other students. This may have been because they did not know *how* to deal with me, but, nevertheless, if one of the goals of education is to provide an environment in which people are allowed, encouraged, and aided in achieving their dreams, I must say that in no way did my engineering education meet this goal.

The gap between liberal arts and engineering that I had been hoping to bridge was certainly not any less wide than the second gap I wished to transcend: the one between women and men. In fact, this second divide was a much more frustrating one because it was always visible, being brought to my attention constantly. Lured to the school by a videotape showing a female electrical engineering professor, I soon realized that she and another woman were the only female professors in the department, and they were untenured assistant professors. This disparity was amplified in the classroom. My first-year engineering class of more than 50 students included 2 other women and myself.

Such low representation gave each one of us the feeling of isolation, as well as a lot of attention. I am not speaking of polite attention; I am speaking of the attention that makes itself evident in not-so-subtle ways. It is a little unnerving to sit through class knowing you are being watched; it is more than a little unnerving to have your headband and hair pulled during the class, and it is downright distracting to have unsolicited spitballs and crumpled-up notes hurled at you in the middle of a course on beginning circuit analysis. This behavior made me feel that I was not there to learn but to be a plaything or a distraction so that the other students could remain amused. One day, I had brought something to read during the breaks. With the attention focused on me as usual, the book was grabbed out of my hands, discovered to be a report on women in science and technology, and sexual innuendoes were hurled about me and the professor who had given it to me. These innuendoes, while offered in jest, nevertheless caused me to be more careful in my relations with male professors and thus distance myself from a valuable resource of learning.

This singular attention was not limited to students. One of the professors—noted more for his presence at the campus pub, drinking with the guys, than his teaching skills—refused to learn my name. He repeatedly mixed me up with the only other woman in the class, leaving me with the impression that he failed to recognize the differences between us and only saw us in terms of our gender. In another incident, a guest lecturer from IBM was outlining a potential situation that an engineer might face in the workplace. After using the male pronoun, he turned to me to use as the engineer in his example. Instead of adding the phrase "or she" to his story, he realized that he could not fit me into the mock situation as he had constructed it. Thus, he turned to the man next to me, who could be included into the language he had chosen, and used him in place of me. These slights by professors or authority figures were much more damaging than the ones by my peers. I could get angry at the students, I could yell at them as I sometimes did, and I could even ignore them. Professors cannot really be ignored, however, and their attitudes gave me a feeling of futility. Attitudes in people so much older and more powerful are not easily changed, and therefore I could not see any hope for equal treatment. The student behavior did not offer any consolation either; a long pedigree line of transference of sexist attitudes was evident and absent of any change for the better. I had no motivation to excel in my schoolwork. My experiences left me to conclude that I would always be on the outside regardless of any positive efforts to improve things on my part.

Even my graduation ceremony was not free of little reminders that I did not quite belong. One of the speakers was fondly relating a story about the aforementioned professor who enjoyed fraternizing with male students at the campus tavern. He asked who could forget the times during lab when this professor had called out to them, "OK guys, let's hurry up and finish so we can go get a few drinks." I surely could forget because the statement was never directed toward me. However, I was *not* going to forget that on my last day in the school, the student speaker had decided to use an anecdote that excluded me because of my gender.

These exclusions might appear to some as too subtle to amount to much, but I did not encounter them at all in my English classes and it made a huge difference. Whether it was the large number of female students in the classes or the large number of female faculty members in the department, I do not know, but the attention of the students and professors was not constantly focused on me or other female students. This was an environment in which I was not afraid to draw some attention to myself by raising my hand or answering a question.

Although I did not encounter condescension from students and professors in my liberal arts classes because of my gender, at times there was an attitude of discomfort because of the fact that I was an engineering major. The students were particularly uncomfortable around me, even the ones who considered themselves feminists. For example, the most prominent factor in introductions was my status as an engineering student—as if to tell everyone that I was different. Some of the students thought that it was admirable that I was working so hard, especially in a male-dominated field, but a majority cloaked their disdain in superficial compliments. After talking to several women, each stating, "I could never be an engineer!" in tones of awe, these compliments came to signify that participating in such a hostile, patriarchal environment would be in direct contradiction to their feminist politics. The implication was that my interest in engineering meant that I could *not* be a feminist. It was their view that trying to change the male domination of the sciences by working within the structure was tantamount to joining in and becoming one of "them."[2] Thus, the sanctioned feminist position was a polarization of liberal arts and "hard" science majors.

These attitudes resulted in more isolation. I was made to feel as if I was betraying all women because of my chosen field of study. If I were a "true" feminist, I would be devoting my energies to women's studies instead of engineering. As a consequence, I did not get support from a majority of my colleagues in engineering or liberal arts. Instead I was an outcast in both of these highly polarized groups because of my gender—in engineering because the stereotype is that women *cannot* be successful engineers, and in liberal arts because the prevailing belief is that women *should not* be successful engineers.

So where does Virginia Woolf fit into all this? Her lectures to women students in 1929 have always been a little problematic for me. Much of *A Room of One's Own,* which deals with the absence of women as writers, can be applied to today's absence of women as scientists. But until this point in my life, I have never agreed with her assertion that in order for a work to be genius or whole, the creator's mind must have "consumed all impediments and become incandescent" (Woolf, 1929, p. 57). Much to my irritation, Woolf condemns the feminist movement that brought women the vote because it had made men and women both conscious of their genders and unable to devote themselves entirely to their creative work. This point escaped me until only recently, when I read Woolf's assertion that a woman artist's "mind must have been strained and her vitality lowered by the need of opposing this, of disproving that" (Woolf, 1929, pp. 53–54). Woolf wrote that most of the books authored by women in the past are flawed because, in each, the author was conscious of the criticism.

> She was admitting that she was "only a woman" or protesting that she was "as good as a man." She met that criticism as her temperament dictated, with docility and diffidence, or with anger and emphasis. It does not matter which it was; she was thinking of something other than the thing itself. (Woolf, 1929, p. 71)

I, who was overly conscious of the criticisms, was definitely thinking of something other than electrical engineering. I was thinking of the high-school-ish arrangement of the classes. I was thinking of the guys, who after informing me that they were majoring in psychology, a subject supposedly "too technical for me to understand," got a scared look in their eyes when they learned of my majors. I did not want any part of it; that is how I met the criticisms. I had to do it differently—dress differently, act differently, have different friends, date different guys. And who knows to what extent I did it differently not because I really wanted to, but because I was scared that I could not do it the same as others and as well? That last question is the one that undermines the feminist scientist, the one that causes her to doubt herself, to wonder whose fault it is that there are not more women scientists. And even now I cannot separate myself from that question, from these doubts. I am sitting here wondering if that question is a form of blaming the victim or if this whole essay has been an exercise in whining, a catalog of petty injustices, a clearing of my conscience for not trying my hardest. In my sanest hours I believe that there is a fault in the collegiate science environment; I was forced to meet the criticisms and avoid the comparisons. I did this by doing it differently, by concentrating on the fault in the system rather than the science itself, and now I have been thinking of anything but electrical engineering for so long that I am not sure if I even like the subject—if I even wish to continue with it. Someday in the future maybe women will not become distracted so easily. Woolf described a woman who "had certain advantages which women of far greater gift lacked even half a century ago. Men were no longer 'the opposing faction'; she need not waste her time railing against them; . . . she wrote as a woman, but as a woman who has forgotten that she is a woman" (Woolf, 1929, p. 88). Someday I hope this will be the case for every woman, and those instances of excess attention and minor exclusions that I listed, which may not seem that daunting in themselves, will not cause women to become distracted from electrical engineering, or science, or anything at all.

Given that science is characterized by feminists as the last bastion of the patriarchy, one might predict that feminist support of women scientists would be strong. After all, it is reasonable to expect that feminists would lend their greatest support to women existing under the most oppressive patriarchal conditions. Using this criterion, women in science would certainly qualify. As Angela Rella points out, however, feminist support has been conspicuously absent. Instead, women in science are demonized. The extreme severity of the feminist critique of science has resulted in a mind-set in which women pursuing scientific careers are viewed as betraying their gender: In effect, they are cast as *female impersonators.*

My dual major in biology and secondary education caused the university feminist community to view my involvement in their projects with some reservation. Nevertheless, I participated to the degree that a student with a full course load was able. Articles criticizing science as a discipline as well as a mode of inquiry were routinely given to me—I suppose with the hope that I would eventually "see the light." Confronted with the knowledge that science is unequivocally patriarchal and antiwoman—a theme common to all of the articles—the sole solution open to me as a responsible member of the feminist community would be to change my major. Given this underlying expectation, my announcement to pursue a graduate degree in genetics was met first with a reaction of shock, followed by strong disapproval. The criticisms of science voiced in my assigned reading material were suddenly levied vehemently against me. I *became* science. As a consequence, I weathered a host of derogatory statements. Among them was that I was leaving the feminist community to become an *honorary male*—PhD standing for **P**hallus **H**onorary **D**ecree. However, I never expressed a desire to leave the feminist community. Instead, I was ostracized because my career choice was deemed incompatible with a feminist agenda. It is interesting to note that the label *honorary male* was not applied to feminist professors at the university, most of whom held doctoral degrees. They too could have been characterized as self-serving coveters of the **P**hallus **H**onorary **D**ecree. However, none were. Most were highly respected and held up as role models to emulate within the university feminist community. The *female impersonator/honorary male* label was selectively applied to me and other women similarly aspiring for scientific careers. Analogous to how marriage and pregnancy are often viewed as the death of a woman's career within scientific circles, the university feminist community viewed my choice of a career in science as my death as a feminist.

Thus, women in science are isolated at many levels. We cannot just *be* scientists, nor can we just *be* women within, as well as outside, the scientific establishment. In the following essay, Donna Riley touches on the skeptical mistrust of technology by feminists as another factor contributing to women in science feeling alienated in feminist circles.

Feminist/Scientist:

Ambiguities and Contradictions

_____ *Donna Riley* _____

I attended an all-girls high school in Pasadena, California, where I learned that women can do and be anything in the world. My interests in environmental issues, mathematics, and science led me to consider a career in environmental science; with my father's example and encouragement, I ultimately chose chemical engineering. Although I was aware of the women's movement in high school, I thought of it as ancient history; in my mind, sexism had come and gone, even for women in science.

I majored in chemical engineering at Princeton University, a private school in suburban New Jersey. The enrollment was approximately 4500 undergraduate and 2500 graduate students, with a 60 to 40 male to female ratio overall, and an 80 to 20 ratio in engineering. The engineering school (excluding computer science) had 1 female faculty member out of 100, and she was not tenured.

My high school education had prepared me well academically, but I was completely unprepared for the hostile environment and blatant sexism I encountered at Princeton; it felt like running into an ivy-covered brick wall. In December of my first year, international headlines documented new evidence of hostility toward women in science; Marc Lepine gunned down 14 female engineers at the University of Montreal simply because they were women and engineers (AP, 1989). A man in my first-year chemistry class, on discovering that I was pursuing a degree in chemical engineering, remarked, "Oh, you're an engineer? Where's my gun?" Everyone laughed except me.

Although a large number of my male peers seemed convinced of female inferiority, or were at least too competitive to relinquish their male privilege, many professors expressed concern about the lack of female engineers and offered female students a great deal of respect and encouragement. Sadly, even these supportive professors were silent when a mechanical engineering professor defended the "right" of his male graduate student to post centerfold pinups in a shared laboratory space. Pornography contributed to a hostile aesthetic environment.

More amusing is "Upstart 2," the statue that looms outside the entrance to the School of Engineering—undeniably resembling a 21-foot phallus. Although this work of art may mean different things in other contexts, its strategic location made it a tongue-in-cheek symbol of my experience—a not-so-subtle reminder of my struggles to prove myself as an equal mind, to avoid becoming a sex object in the eyes of professors and peers, and to affirm my identity as a woman through it all.

I became involved in the campus women's center, a student group committed to feminist advocacy and education. I also served 3 years on the University President's Standing Committee on the Status of Women, where I acquired the tools I needed to understand and analyze my situation and the strength and opportunity to work for change.

When the *f*-word is mentioned to most female engineers, they typically insist, "I believe in equal rights for women, but I'm not a feminist." Nevertheless, creating a space for women in fields that have been traditionally dominated by men is precisely what feminism has meant to generations of women. Despite their fear of feminism, nearly all of the women pursuing careers in engineering at Princeton were active in the Society of Women Engineers (SWE), a group promoting professional development and networking among female engineers. To my utter horror, SWE hosted a fashion show, modeling career clothes and teaching women to "dress for success"; I wondered how male engineers could ever take women seriously if our career development activities were limited to hosting seminars on how much makeup is too much at the office.

When I arrived as a graduate student in the Department of Engineering and Public Policy at Carnegie Mellon University in Pittsburgh, Pennsylvania, I expected to establish an immediate connection with the only other woman in our class of ten new graduate students. The two of us attended a meeting for a group of graduate women in science, the purpose of which is to allow graduate women from different departments to meet each other and to discuss issues of mutual concern such as dual-career couples, child care, and sexual harassment. My classmate interrupted the meeting, demanding to know, "What's the point?" She questioned the validity of these issues, asking "Do you think that [sexual harassment] really happens? I always thought women made those things up." By invalidating my own experiences of sexual harassment by male peers, this comment sealed my isolation. Some nonfeminist women in science think that denying the oppression of other women makes them stronger. Having completely bought the male science system of competition and elimination, they do not understand that playing "Uncle Tom" in gender politics hurts all women in the field.

My exploration of feminist issues at Princeton led me to take a women's studies class on the history of gender and science, where I discovered a different kind of isolation. In a class of anthropologists, sociologists, and historians, I was the sole engineer. They questioned me intently: "So how does it feel to be an engineer?" I entered the class believing the authority of experience would make me an expert, but instead I became an object of study to academics who did not necessarily understand my experiences. As a result, I was always seen as a female engineer in that class, and never as a women's studies student.

Once again, I found myself having to prove my abilities—this time not as a woman in a hostile field but as an engineer in foreign territory. As in engineering, I was proving my abilities to myself as much as to my peers and professors. I had awkward interactions with some students who assumed I had no background in basic feminist theory. They seemed to think that if my perspective differed from the readings, it was because I did not understand it, or because I had "sold out" to the male engineering patriarchy. If, on the other hand, my women's studies classmates disagreed with the readings, their comments were taken as informed criticisms. In that respect, I felt excluded from the lively classroom debates.

This type of isolation crystallized in my interactions with some feminists on campus who viewed science as inherently and irreparably oppressive to women. Let me say outright that the feminist and women's studies communities at Princeton are not monoliths; they include people of many differing views on all topics, including this one. Most of the women in the women's center and other groups were extremely supportive of women in science. However, the views of a few antiscience feminists were enough to make me feel ill at ease in the feminist community, just as the views of a few sexist engineering professors made me feel ill at ease in my academic community. These technophobic feminists could not fathom my desire to stay in a field so hostile to women.

This view is evident even in feminist academia. In her book *Gyn/Ecology: The Metaethics of Radical Feminism,* Mary Daly observed that there are female gynecologists who may seek to offer women true healing. However, she noted that these women go through the same education and training and contribute to the same literature and professional conferences as male gynecologists. She concluded, quoting Gena Corea, "Female doctors who are 'honorary white males' don't defend female patients against harmful obstetrical practices, unnecessary surgery, unsafe contraceptives, and forced sterilizations." According to Mary Daly, all female gynecologists who have been educated in mainstream American medical schools are "token torturers" of women, liaisons to the patriarchy. There is no room in Daly's view for female gynecologists to use the powerful knowledge men have monopolized, subverting it to help other women (Daly, 1978).

As a feminist scientist, I welcome critiques of my field, especially those that may result in positive changes in science. However, the technophobic feminists' belief that "the master's tools will never dismantle the master's house" does not permit them to see how feminist scientists can use the master's tools in new ways—ways the master never intended, nor even imagined (Lorde, 1984).

The sexual stereotypes that go with engineering culture only made things worse. I began to see the damned-if-you-do, damned-if-you-don't plight of female engineers; women who best adapted to this masculine environment were often accused of acting too much like men, whereas women who maintained their "femininity" were not taken seriously. I was more concerned with being seen as a serious student, and I bought into the myth that this could only happen at the cost of my attractiveness to others. Still dependent at that point on male approval for self-worth, this severely shook my self-confidence.

Male engineers are often characterized as repressed and sex starved, placing more strain on the already uncomfortable relationships between women and men in engineering. The "Engineer's Cheer"—a staple of engineering culture at Princeton—states

> Label the axes y and x,
> To hell with football, we want sex.

My male engineer friends complained ad nauseam, "This school is totally devoid of women." When I reminded them that 20% of engineers (including me!) were female, they would qualify, "Well, there are no good-looking women," or, "Well, you don't count." These remarks are not only without tact, they also demonstrate the invisibility that women in engineering face.

The notion that women must be asexual to enter a male world is not a novel idea. In early Christianity, virgins were given leadership roles; women's vows of chastity offered them personal autonomy and freedom from traditional gender roles (Pagels, 1988). Abstention from sex was seen as the way for women to approach the male-identified spiritual world. The Gospel of Thomas, a Gnostic text from the second century, quotes Jesus, "For every woman who will make herself male will enter the Kingdom of Heaven." Elaine Pagels interpreted this to mean that "the men form the legitimate body of the community, while women are allowed to participate only when they assimilate themselves to men" (Pagels, 1989, p. 49). Now, as then, women's lives are fragmented; we are presented with false choices between the autonomy of our careers, and the personal fulfillment of sexuality, family, and other pursuits.

My first 2 years as an undergraduate at Princeton shattered my academic confidence; the process of regaining my self-assurance began with an independent research project at Princeton's Center for Energy and Environmental Studies (CEES) during my junior year. I took on the project (despite resistance from the Chemical Engineering Department) because it offered me four opportunities I had sought: (a) to conduct actual research, (b) to get outside my department, which was impersonal and intimidating, (c) to explore environmental issues, and (d) to work with a female scientist. The positive research experiences I had at CEES were the single most important factor in transcending my self-doubt, allowing me to discover my abilities as a scientist, and ultimately motivating me to continue study in graduate school.

Valerie Thomas, my advisor at CEES, taught me to use my chemical engineering tools on projects that had an environmental component. My work with her grew into my senior thesis. Its interdisciplinary nature allowed me to consider the policy implications of the scientific research that I was conducting. Furthermore, I enjoyed the subjective judgments involved with my research as much as the "objective" scientific analysis. Finally, I had found a mentor in the field I wished to pursue, and she made all the difference.

An additional confidence builder was my activism, which enabled me to deal positively with many of the problems I faced. I worked with the Committee on the Status of Women to implement university policies designed to improve the recruitment and retention of women in science. Concrete steps were taken to make the climate less hostile for women; the administration implemented an explicit policy against the public display of degrading sexual images of women in campus work spaces. In addition, taking self-defense classes, organizing marches against sexual violence, and planning other feminist activities with the women's center enabled me to find my own voice and effectively confront sexism on campus.

When it came time to apply to graduate school, I intentionally sought a department with female faculty in my research area and a support network for female graduate students. I chose the Department of Engineering and Public Policy (EPP) at Carnegie Mellon (where my mentor from Princeton had done her postdoctoral work). EPP has an uncommonly positive and welcoming environment for women; although it still has no tenured female faculty, the department's cochair, Indira Nair, is an expert on women in science. Her sense of integrity and genuine concern for students makes Dr. Nair an excellent advocate and counselor. Of course, the department is not perfect; the fraction of female professors affiliated with EPP has historically approached 10%, but it is somewhat lower now. The usual stories about inappropriate comments and bad attitudes among certain male faculty still circulate, but it eases my mind to know I have a strong advocate and support system.

EPP is interdisciplinary, and although this causes a degree of fragmentation, it is the very thing that attracts me to the field. Breaking through the rigidity of disciplinary boundaries helps shatter the usual scientific hierarchies and methodologies, opening research problems to new questions and novel approaches. Because the technical and policy issues are often intertwined, the ideal of "objectivity" no longer reigns supreme. EPP provides space for scientists concerned with the social ramifications of their work, and this contributes to making the environment more comfortable for women.

The Department of Engineering and Public Policy is located at Carnegie Mellon University, which is decades behind even Princeton in responding to the needs of female students. It is a private school of a similar size to Princeton, but more intensely bifurcated into science/technology and fine arts. The male to female ratio here is 70 to 30 overall (80 to 20 in my department), and the hostility of the male engineering culture permeates the campus. CMU's administration is smaller and less politically sophisticated than Princeton's; most administrators appear to be indifferent at best, although there are a few outstanding exceptions.

Now, more than ever, I feel tension between my activism and my work. Many women in science complain that too much of the burden is placed on them to organize events and develop policies that will help women. We feel we cannot just be students because we are female engineers; we work double time as students and activists (triple time if we have families). At the same time, my activism has taught me the importance of organizing and implementing one's own empowerment; my activism (whether it is about women in science, queer rights, or reproductive freedom) gives me the strength to continue conducting my research in a hostile environment. I am continually seeking to strike a balance—I want to do enough activism to inspire my determination, to boost my confidence, and still have enough time left to focus on my work.

Forces from all sides set up obstacles; sexist men say that women cannot do science; technophobic feminists demand women abandon science in order to withdraw energy from the patriarchy; antifeminist women in science attack feminist scientists as weak whiny victims; rigid holders to traditional disciplines frown on my female-friendly, interdisciplinary field as "too subjective"; time constraints make me choose between fighting oppression and doing good academic work; my own self-doubt creeps around telling me I cannot, I am not good enough. All I can do is rise up defiantly, and say, "I'm going to do it anyway."

It would be inaccurate and unfair to universally portray feminism as hostile toward women in science. As Donna Riley notes above, feminists are often cast as a homogenized group of women with a single purpose and agenda, when in reality *feminist* is a blanket term denoting a diversity of women with a spectrum of views and opinions. However, acknowledging this diversity does *not* diminish the isolating effect that the antiscience stance held by some vocal and influential feminists can have on individual women in science. My previously shared undergraduate experience is a case in point. Despite the fact that the Northeastern Illinois University feminist community did not actually represent all feminists, the nature and intensity of the collegiate environment effectively meant that at the time they *did* represent all feminists to me. As a consequence, I viewed ostracism by this select group of feminists as a banishment from the *entire* feminist community. My graduate years at Indiana University, Bloomington, as well as my postdoctoral years in the Washington, DC, area, were therefore largely spent isolated from the feminist community. Nevertheless, contrasting the accounts presented thus far in this chapter, several other contributors to this volume report positive experiences with women's studies. In particular, Sue Franks notes that her affiliation with women's studies provided a framework for understanding the culture of science that ultimately enabled her to complete a graduate degree. In addition, many of the programs designed to capture interest and increase women's participation in science currently in place were developed by people acutely attuned to issues raised by feminism. Furthermore, Sue Rosser (1990) has suggested that feminist pedagogical methodology can be applied to create a science classroom in which all students are encouraged and supported.

> During the past two decades, the feminist community has sharpened its critique within the academy, extending women's studies to the scientific disciplines. . . . Pedagogical methods developed by teachers in women's studies and ethnic studies may help create a [science] classroom climate which is more conducive to learning for women and people of color. . . . Although most teachers in institutions of higher education strive to create an environment conducive to learning, their efforts may be undercut if they fail to be sensitive to factors such as sexism and racism, which are an obstacle to learning. (pp. 10–11).

As I stated at the beginning of this chapter, women in science clearly owe a debt to feminism. However, in their zeal to transform science into a discipline in which women can feel empowered, feminists have contributed to the harsh environment faced by those women choosing to work within the present scientific system. This is inappropriate and it must stop. Women face enough alienation and isolation within the culture of science. The last thing that we need is to be blind sided by an attack portraying them as female impersonators when they seek refuge in feminist circles or women's studies programs. Feminists should recognize that the transformation of science to a discipline in which women are empowered will remain an abstraction unless enough people currently in the system make it a priority and reach levels in which their voices are heard. Thus, rather than separate itself from women in science, feminism must take a more active role in supporting them.

The final essay of this chapter examines how the enthusiasm on the part of feminists to transform science has erected an enormous barrier to women's achievement in science. The author calls for a feminism that empowers women within the current culture of science as opposed to requiring that women boycott science until the desired transformation is effected.

Feminism:

A Mixed Blessing to Women in Science

_____ Noretta Koertge _____

Why are there still so few women in the natural sciences? Thanks to the women's movement and other social changes, women are now entering the legal and medical professions in record numbers, and the percentage of female graduate students and professors in most disciplines is climbing steadily. Yet at my university (all too typical of research institutions), only 7% of tenure-track positions in the natural and mathematical sciences are occupied by women. There are no female faculty members of any rank in computer science, only one each in chemistry and geology, and a total of two each in our large physics and mathematics departments.

Why? Are the hard sciences really the last bastions of male chauvinism, or is something more complex going on? Could certain feminist stances even be part of the problem? Before the era of women's suffrage, the reasons for the absence of women would have been obvious—there were legal barriers thwarting them at every turn. In 1900 when Emmy Noether passed her university entrance exams, women could only audit classes with the professors' permission, although the Prussian Ministry of Education did have a policy stating that access "must not be determined by the degree of the individual lecturer's distaste for co-education" (Dick, 1981).[3] Noether was able to audit classes with Hermann Minkowski, Felix Klein, and David Hilbert, all now famous for their contributions to the foundations of physics, and when the law changed in 1904 she quickly received formal credit for her work.

However, it was still illegal for her to teach in Germany. Hilbert protested the regulation, saying that he could not see why the gender of the person should be relevant to her admission as a lecturer; after all, this was a university, not a bathing establishment! When his arguments were unsuccessful, Hilbert nevertheless listed Noether's name on his own seminars and she became a de facto lecturer and thesis supervisor. It was during this period that she conducted the groundbreaking work on differential invariants that was of fundamental importance for Einstein's general theory of relativity. In 1919, the year when women gained the vote in Germany, more lecturers were needed to teach the returning World War I veterans, and the law was finally changed. Noether then taught at Göttingen until 1933 when she, as a Jew, was suspended by the Hitler regime. Hermann Weyl, who was then at Princeton, arranged a job for her at Bryn Mawr, but she died almost exactly 2 years later at the age of 52 from complications following an operation to remove a tumor.

I can well imagine that by her Bryn Mawr period, Noether would have been quite optimistic about the future prospects for women in math and science. There had been amazing legal breakthroughs in her time and she had benefited from male mentors throughout her life, beginning with her father, who was also an excellent mathematician. Her work was appreciated not only in Germany and America, but also in Italy and the Soviet Union, and praised by both mathematicians and physicists. Although she was not known as a brilliant lecturer, her graduate students admired her greatly—she continued to meet with them at her apartment after the Hitler edict and several made important contributions to mathematics. Her first official PhD student was a woman, as was the Bryn Mawr student who turned out to be her last. Surely, there would be many more women who would be captivated by the beauty of mathematics. As Einstein wrote in describing Noether's work in her *New York*

Times obituary, "Pure mathematics is, in its way, the poetry of logical ideas" (quoted in Dick, 1981, p. 93).

The optimistic mood of American women in the middle of this century can be symbolized by the World War II poster of "Rosie the Riveter." Young patriotic women were rolling up their sleeves and demanding access to traditionally male jobs. How silly to think that women were too delicate to be welders and handle explosives, or that they did not have the kind of mind needed to understand radar and computers. This conviction that women could succeed at science and technology was an important strand during the beginning years of what is now called Second Wave Feminism. In the early 1970s, feminists organized workshops in auto mechanics, because most women had been shunted off into home economics classes and had not been privy to the little lessons in how to change oil or check the lawn mower's spark plugs that many boys get along the way. Those lesbians who had long found many aspects of the traditional girl gender role limiting were often leaders in the grassroots movement to support women who wished to enter the trades and become electricians, or plumbers, or foresters.

At the same time, women were also systematically protesting unequal opportunities to pursue a career in science. The California Institute of Technology finally opened its doors to women students in 1969.[4] Women still encountered formidable obstacles; MIT students complained about getting physically shoved away from scarce computer terminals and not being allowed to work with heavy equipment such as tanks of compressed nitrogen.[5] But the dominant feminist response was a confident conviction that women's aspirations would eventually prevail. As one popular t-shirt of the time put it, "In order to succeed, women have to be better than men—luckily, that isn't difficult!"

According to this optimistic feminist analysis, there were two sorts of factors deterring women from the study of science: the external legal or institutional barriers, such as those faced by Noether or the women who could not get into CalTech, and then the more subtle internalized impediments caused by socialization into gender stereotypes. The women's movement at that time hoped to solve the problem through a two-pronged campaign. The external obstacles would be removed through political action, whereas feminist education and consciousness-raising would provide women with the experience and confidence they needed to enter technical fields. It was in this spirit that people designed curricular remedies for math anxiety, set up classes to introduce women to computers, wrote triumphal histories about the scientific accomplishments of forgotten foremothers, and encouraged those women already in science to serve as mentors and networking nodes.

Some of these feminist initiatives to encourage women to pursue scientific careers are still going on today, but they have certainly been supplemented by and, I would argue, seriously compromised by a quite different feminist response to the question of women's "proper role" in science. According to this radical feminist analysis, both the content and methods of traditional science are patriarchal and oppressive. Feminist polemical writings describe the essence of science as "necrophilia" (Daly, 1978), the fruits of science as "weapons of the phallocracy" (Daly, 1987), and the much-vaunted scientific quest for objectivity as "politics by other means" (Harding, 1991). More influential, perhaps, are the works written in a more scholarly style that argue that women have special "ways of knowing" that are both superior to, and incompatible with, the emphasis on analysis, quantitative measurement, and controlled experiment that are so central to and so highly regarded within scientific reasoning (e.g., Belenky, Clinchy, Goldberger, & Tarule, 1986). These radical feminist critics believe that science will have to be revolutionized before it can be an acceptable calling for women. Any feminist who decides to become a scientist will therefore have to think of herself as a missionary and exercise vigilance to keep from going native! By implication, the feminist credentials of any woman who does manage to succeed in science today are called into question.

The full story of how so many intellectuals at the end of the century have come to repudiate science—and rationality as well—has not yet been written (although see Gross & Levitt's *Higher Superstition,* 1994, for many useful insights). Feminists have both been influenced by and contributed to the Left's drift away from material and institutional explanatory factors and its current fascination with ideology. But much of their alienation from science came directly out of the feminist emphasis on women's traditional culture.

Women have historically been denied access to theological training and leadership roles in religious institutions, but they have often found opportunities to express themselves in mystical writings and marginal religious activities. Second-wave feminists set out to reclaim and expand upon women's contributions to the traditions of witchcraft, fortune-telling, chiromancy, and other forms of divination. It is no accident that many of the leaders of "New Age Spirituality" are feminists. By the same token, women who have historically been excluded from the study of the scientific medicine of their day have often become specialists in folk medicine and alternative approaches to healing. Feminists have continued this long tradition of automatic suspicion of the medical establishment and have encouraged women not just to question conventional medical wisdom (a quite sensible attitude), but also to rely on herbal remedies, acupuncture, and massage, as well as various magical practices involving crystals, auras, and talismans. Especially popular are attempts to improve one's physical health through visualization techniques or an analysis of how the site of the current physical pain symbolically encodes old psychological traumas.

Women have historically been viewed by psychologists and physicians as emotionally fragile and prone to hysteria, depression, and other forms of mental illness. Feminists reinforced other critics of traditional psychotherapy, but instead of calling for a more careful, scientific approach to the alleviation of psychological distress, they borrowed methods indiscriminately, not just from respectable self-help groups such as Alcoholics Anonymous, but also from the most bizarre proponents of reincarnation, regression to past lives, and reconstruction of fetal memories. Feminists have played a central role in therapies that purport to retrieve repressed memories of sexual abuse and satanic rituals or spaceship abductions (Pendergrast, 1995). In extreme cases, women were told that their very sanity was contingent on their ability to reject not just science, but in addition the evidential norms of common sense.

It thus came to pass that feminist bookstores, feminist festivals, and even feminist academic conferences, such as meetings of the National Women's Studies Association, became permeated with the books, artifacts, and practices of spiritualism, soothsaying, and all varieties of pseudoscience.[6] This general nonscientific milieu was then punctuated with numerous writings, some scholarly, some not, that presented an amazing variety of explicit critiques of science. It is impossible to survey this vast literature—a bibliography compiled in 1989 lists more than 1000 items—but suffice it to say that as the term *critique* suggests, none of them presented science as a female-friendly enterprise (Wylie, Okruhlik, Morton, & Thielen-Wilson, 1989).

Much was made of the sexist content or metaphors of old scientific speculations and theories, such as Aristotle's theory of reproduction according to which males contributed the active form while females furnish only passive nutrients, or Victorian medical theories about the debilitating effects of the monthly loss of blood on women's bodies and minds. Too frequently these old ideas were not placed in historical context: For example, the same nineteenth-century physicians who worried about menstruation were also very concerned about the effects of the discharge of semen on men and even had a name for this condition, *spermatorrhea.* Neither were these anecdotes supplemented with old scientific speculations that downplayed the role of males in reproduction, such as the seventeenth-century preformationist doctrine of *emboitement* that posited little homunculae nested like Russian dolls, which had all come from Eve's ovum!

And most important, no emphasis was placed on the fact that however sexist, racist, or oppressive these old ideas might be, it was the normal critical methods of science itself, not the political process, that had shown them to be erroneous. All too many feminists were quick to conclude that not only did scientific results lack credibility but that scientists were actively conspiring to repress knowledge that would be useful to women, such as methods of parthenogenesis or the facts that women were the "first sex" (the Y chromosome has been said to be a late mutation derived from an amputated X chromosome) and that prehistoric societies were peaceful, ecologically enlightened, vegetarian matriarchies. There were, of course, many feminist biologists, archaeologists, and anthropologists, as well as educated lay people, who were in a position to criticize these fantastical accounts, but many feminists were not really interested in exploring the distinctions between myth and history, or logical possibility and physical reality.

The most potentially devastating attack on science was the attempt to establish what feminist bibliographers cited above all: "the radical feminist conclusion that science is by nature deeply and unavoidably androcentric" (Wylie et al., 1989, p. 2). If this claim were accepted, it would explain why women have not hitherto entered science in great numbers. Who wants to participate in a deeply androcentric activity? And it would also suggest that women who do not wish to sustain the patriarchy should participate in science only in order to transform it into something quite different.

Now what sort of arguments could possibly be advanced in favor of the proposition that science is unavoidably androcentric by nature? There are at least three distinguishable lines of attack. First, there is the charge of necrophilia. Romantics such as the German *Naturphilosophen* have long argued that science can only study nature by tearing it into bits. They see early modern science as dominated by a mechanical philosophy, which viewed the physical world as a giant clockwork. (One recalls the parallels Cartesians drew between the yelps of a dog in pain and squeaky door hinges.) The aim of science was to learn to manipulate those mechanisms and then have power over nature. What feminists have added to the Romantic critique is the claim that the project of dominating nature was an intensely sexual one, and they take very seriously Bacon's descriptions of "putting Nature on the rack" and "penetrating her innermost secrets."[7] As Mother Earth was transformed from a source of awe into a rape victim, so were ordinary women turned into sex objects.

There are also allegations that scientific creativity is a manifestation of womb envy (e.g., talk about "fathering" the atom bomb), and much is made of the close connections between science and warfare—both are then seen as intrinsically violent, life-destroying pursuits (e.g., Caputi, 1983, chapter titled "Unthinkable Fathering").

A second line of attack alleges that the much-praised methods of science, which are supposed to guarantee universal objective truths, are in fact gendered. Although the arguments are not always presented so tidily, the basic strategy here seems to be to draw parallels between stereotypical male cognitive attributes and the preferred modes of scientific reasoning. It is then claimed that female cognitive styles are denigrated as being unscientific and are thus excluded from the scientists' repertoire, just as women are excluded from organized science. The proposed dualities will be familiar: quantitative versus qualitative, logical versus intuitive, abstract versus concrete (e.g., Musil, 1992). But it is at first very surprising to hear this sort of argument coming from people who claim to be feminists. One can only imagine how perplexed Emmy Noether would be to hear that her approach to mathematics, which tended to be more abstract and closer to pure logic than those of her contemporaries, was uncongenial to women's ways of knowing! (On the other hand, maybe she would have agreed—after all, she never married and her colleagues referred to her as "der Noether.") But not only do these dualities play on misleading gender stereotypes, they also caricature scientific reasoning. No one, not even the positivists, denies the importance of intuition in scientific discovery. There is even a technical term for it, *Fingerspitzengefühl*. Barbara McClintock's "feeling for the organism" is a widely shared experience of working scientists. What scientific method does require is that both our intuitively plausible theories and abstract mathematical models be critically evaluated on the basis of concrete, tangible, well-constructed experimental or carefully analyzed experiences and observations. In fact it is the dialectic between the dualities feminists claim to be gendered that keeps science going. This is not to deny, of course, that there are frequent controversies over scientific styles, between atomists and continuity theorists, reductionists and emergentists, "lumpers" and "splitters," those who would stress nature and those would stress nurture, gradualists and catastrophists, algebraists and geometers. But it is just silly to try to label one side as more feminist, or more progressive, or whatever, merely on the basis of their methods and approaches. There are differences, at least in priorities, between the cognitive values of scientists and those of mystics, artists, and stockbrokers, but trying to map these differences onto gender stereotypes impedes efforts to understand and evaluate them.

A third line of attack marches under the slogan that science is just politics by other means.[8] This critique relies on and endorses recent attempts by sociologists of knowledge to argue that scientific results are ideologically constrained social constructions formed through negotiations among science entrepreneurs who are trying to maximize their own professional interests. On this view, although there is a lot of rhetoric about science being driven by criticism, objectivity, independent testing, empirical adequacy, and error elimination, this is just talk that distracts us from the most important factors: the scientists' own interests. If you want to understand which theories are hot and which are not, it is no use going to the work of trying to compare the evidential basis for or heuristic promise of the two competitors. Instead, just ask, "*Cui bono?*"

Feminists go on to add that the hegemonic ideological agenda has historically always been oppressive to women, minorities, and so forth, and it has thus far been in the professional interests of those few women who have gone into science to participate in that patriarchal agenda. (If they do not do the kind of science that "boys" like, then they really are marginalized.) On this view, if women are to change science, they must enter subfields in large numbers and set up their own societies and journals. They must then evaluate all research in that area according to how well it furthers the feminist agenda. Such a science will be politicized, but this time consciously so and with the *right politics!* There will still be debates in science but now the most important issue will be made explicit: "Which theory is best for women?"[9]

Such criticism of the traditional values of science seems so extreme that one might imagine—or hope—that it would have little effect outside the hothouse environment of feminist theorizing. Unfortunately, though, it is gaining credibility. In researching our book *Professing Feminism: Cautionary Tales From the Strange World of Women's Studies* (1994), Daphne Patai, professor of women's studies at the University of Massachusetts at Amherst, and I learned how strong the antiscience element in feminism had become and the impact it was having on young women scientists. A research biologist told us she hesitated to tell feminist acquaintances what she did because of their antipathy to science. The chilly climate within feminism deterred her from serving as a role model for prospective science majors. A senior sociologist, highly regarded as a scholar and a founding member of the National Organization for Women, described to us the hostility of feminist graduate students toward courses on statistics and quantitative methods. She also noted their resistance to any sort of critical scrutiny of the numbers they eagerly quoted about rape, harassment, and other mistreatment of women. She was dismayed further by feminist colleagues' out-of-hand dismissal of any research that included biological perspectives on social issues (Patai & Koertge, 1994).

We concluded that the ethos of contemporary women's studies might very well discourage young women from seeking a career in science and even make them feel morally and politically enlightened in remaining ignorant about it. Comparatively few undergraduates enroll in women's studies courses, but feminist theorizing about the alleged incompatibility between the ways women think and the standard accounts of scientific reasoning is also having an impact in schools of education and secondary school science curricula. Some of the pedagogical suggestions are sensible: Don't have so many story problems about football and the trajectory of artillery shells and increase the amount of practical, hands-on experience with the material being studied. Other recommendations are extremely controversial, such as making the study of science as nontheoretical and nonmathematical as possible. But what is most tendentious are the reasons given for these pedagogical proposals. It is claimed that girls find it less congenial to think abstractly than do little boys and that asking them to deal with logic or mathematics is putting arbitrary and unfair obstacles in their path. Here is an unusually explicit formulation of such a position that appears in a volume on mathematics education, no less:

> In the context provided by Irigaray we can see an opposition between the linear time of mathematics problems of related rates, distance formulas, and linear acceleration versus the dominant experiential cyclical time of the menstrual body. Is it obvious to the female mind–body that intervals have endpoints, that parabolas neatly divide the plane, and, indeed, that the linear mathematics of schooling describes the world of experience in intuitively obvious ways? (quoted in Damarin, 1995)

It is hard to believe that such a position is considered to be feminist. To me it is much more reminiscent of Victorian misogynist speculation and perhaps even harder to imagine that this conclusion is considered to be based on the kind of research that should inform the design of science curricula. Yet when we remember the feminist critiques of scientific method and the advocacy of incorporating politics into research, we should not be surprised if feminist research submits itself only to feminist standards of appraisal, the most important of which are, "Does the result resonate with women's intuitive experience, and can the result be used politically to advance women?"

I do not doubt that many women are put off by quantitative and theoretical reasoning. After all, "Barbie hates math," or said she did until feminists, presumably those who had not read Irigaray, protested. And it might be possible to entice more little girls, as well as all of those little boys who hate math, into better tolerating elementary science classes if we dropped from the curriculum items such as Boyle's law (inverse proportions are confusing) or the concept of density (everyone starts out intuitively convinced that a pound of iron is heavier than a pound of feathers). But such a watered-down approach to science would neither prepare students to become scientists nor give them the basic scientific literacy needed to read the newspaper and live in a technological society. If little girls as a group are in fact biologically disinclined toward math, then they should have more of it in school, not less, just as little boys may need extra lessons in expressing themselves verbally. Of course, science pedagogy should make science as accessible to as many people as possible, but not by a low-math, low-theory surrogate in the pretense that this will somehow help women and minorities.

By this time the reader may be growing impatient with my critiques of feminist critiques of science. After all, the fact still remains that there are pitifully few women scientists and even if radical feminism is now exacerbating the problem or proposing cures worse than the disease, they certainly did not create the problem. Why are there so few women in science? And what can be done to change the situation?

The purpose of this volume is to raise the level of discussion of just these issues, and I am delighted to participate in what I hope will be a more open and less ideologically driven investigation. Let me begin by saying that although there is much more to learn about the factors that influence a person's interest in and aptitude for science, we already know that in the case of women as a group there must be a myriad of small inhibitors. Although there is a lot of talk about "glass ceilings" or "critical turning points," sociological studies show that at every level women—who by all indicators appear to be as well qualified as men—are in fact on the average less apt to succeed at the next level. Girls who do well in beginning math courses are less apt to take another one; well-qualified females are more likely to quit graduate school than their male peers; women with PhDs from good schools are less apt to publish. Now it is easy to say that this simply demonstrates the pervasiveness of sexism— and that may be true for all I know—but such a monosyllabic answer gives us very little insight into how to change the situation. Just calling for a revolution in the *Zeitgeist* or a mathematics based on menstrual cycles does not promote effective change in the here and now.

When researchers and analysts have looked in detail at the various choice points along the trajectory leading to a scientific career, they find a wide variety of factors that impede women's success rate. Some are large, but many are small. Furthermore, many of the deterrents lie within the sphere of women's own agency and could conceivably be changed by women working together, even if there were no changes at all in traditional male attitudes. So, for example, when Dorothy Holland and Margaret Eisenhart (1990) did a longitudinal study of female undergraduate science majors, they found that many of the dropouts fit the following pattern: The girls had been straight-A students in high school and that fact was an important component of their self-esteem. When they entered college, not surprisingly they would get the occasional A- or B+ in their technical subjects. Even though they still liked science a lot, they now felt inadequate and either switched to an easier major (i.e., one with a higher curve) or drastically lowered their educational goals and became heavily involved with dating and partying. To the researchers' surprise, it was not their boyfriends who lured them away from science. Rather, they first lost their confidence and then started looking for romance.

Of course one can read such a study as a story about unfair societal demands on girls to be good little obedient students who will eventually become good little obedient wives. But be that as it may, the research also suggests that all beginning science students—and perhaps women especially—need to be fully informed about grade inflation in the humanities and given an explicit interpretation of what that A- or B+ really means. Letter grades could at least be indexed (sometimes that disappointing A- was the highest grade in the class), and academic advisors should continually comment on what the student's record implies as far as prospects for graduate school or a good job as a technician is concerned.

I am firmly convinced that the best strategy for change is to attend in a practical fashion to the tremendously varied small inhibiting factors that can add up to just enough to deflect women away from what might have otherwise been an ideal career choice. The current ethos of academic feminism also directs our attention to a myriad of small negative factors, but too often the analysis turns into a search for petty injustices that are then magnified through mutual commiseration and used to fuel angry confrontations that all too often result in formal, bureaucratic gains for women but a loss in collegiality and trust.

This volume provides a detailed, personalized picture of the problems faced by young women in science and of their varying experiences with the different currents of feminism. Both anecdotal evidence and more systematic surveys indicate that today there is an extraordinary range of attitudes toward women in science. Some laboratories are inclusive and supportive; others foster an atmosphere of cutthroat competition and distrust. So local conditions will dictate what responses are appropriate. However, I would like to offer, for what it is worth, some general advice to women in science, based on my early experience as a laboratory technician and a college chemistry teacher, my extended studies of the history and philosophy of science, my participation in feminist activities, and my more recent research on women's studies programs.

First of all, although scientists as individuals are as fraught with human frailties as anyone else, I believe that the knowledge produced by science is by and large the best available and that professional scientists by and large try very hard to be fair in their attributions of credit to colleagues. Just as it is reasonable to tentatively accept the results published in a good journal unless one has specific grounds for doubt, so I believe it is reasonable for women entering science to adopt an attitude of provisional trust toward their teachers and peers unless there is substantial evidence to the contrary. Here I disagree with those feminists who believe that sexism and racism is so institutionalized that the default setting should be one of suspicion.

Second, it is important to recognize that science today is one of the most demanding of professions, arguably more time- and energy-consuming than medicine and with less secure job prospects. This means that everyone concerned tends to be on task and disinclined to deal with matters they consider to be peripheral. It is easy for female graduate students to take this personally or to attribute such an atmosphere to male insensitivity. However, it is worth remembering that female ballet dancers, figure skaters, and gymnasts also tend to be consumed with a quest for excellence. As long as there are a shortage of good jobs and limited research funds, there will be pressure to be productive. For this reason, it is especially important for women in the sciences that there be good day care facilities and formal guarantees of family leave opportunities. It would be wise for women's organizations wishing to reform science to ignore superficial manifestations of sexism, such as infelicitous pronouns or male-bonding beer parties and to concentrate instead on winning crucial improvements, such as family leave policies. It is my repeated observation that "chilly climate" investigations or allegations of sexual harassment in the new, extended sense of the term are counterproductive for women in both the short and long run. The accusatory process takes activist women away from doing science and it alienates all women from male colleagues. Women scientists always need to keep their priorities clearly in mind: Are they really trying to improve scientific institutions or are they more interested in wide-scale social engineering? If the latter, perhaps there are better sites for their political efforts.

I also think young women scientists are ill-advised to go out of their way to seek out women research directors or to spend most of their time at national meetings networking or caucusing with other women. We all need supportive friends and people to commiserate with. But anyone who is in danger of being marginalized or seen as a strange, unknown quantity for any reason needs to take extra care to be seen as approachable and interested in participating. This holds for Americans at a conference in Germany, Protestants at an Irish wake, or vegetarians in a steak house. It may be more comfortable for members of a minority group to cluster together in a corner, but it is not a good way to become part of the larger enterprise.

An especially dubious form of academic separatism is the common feminist practice of starting alternative journals in order to promote feminist scholarship and to provide women with a congenial place to publish. This tactic can undoubtedly lead to short-term success in fields that encourage the proliferation of novel interpretative frameworks and in which there is relatively little consensus on either methods or results. But it seems self-defeating to import this practice into the sciences. Consider, for example, the so-called feminist approach to economics, which opposes the rational economic man model. Let us assume for the sake of this argument that the proposed alternative has no historical antecedents and was developed de novo by women inspired by second-wave political feminism.[10] If the new approach solves lots of standard problems in economics, then it will be taken up by all sorts of economists, even sexist ones. There is no reason to keep it separate from mainstream journals. However, if the new account turns out to be of little value in describing or explaining economic phenomena, then it will quickly turn into a marginal subject, not a good place for aspiring young women economists to put their research efforts. No matter how politically attractive an approach may seem to its proponents, that aspect counts for very little when it is appraised in the scientific arena.

More than 50 years ago, on the eve of World War II, Robert Merton wrote a series of important essays in which he described the normative structure of science and showed how it was being subverted in Nazi Germany. The most important canon was the one Merton called *universalism* (as opposed to *particularism*): "The acceptance or rejection of claims entering the lists of science is not to depend on the personal or social attributes of their protagonist; his race, nationality, religion, class, and personal qualities are as such irrelevant" (Merton, 1973, p. 270). In his essay, Merton described many deviations from that norm—the Nazis' repudiation of Jewish physics, the Marxist-Leninist call for a class-based science, as well as French critiques of so-called German science after World War I. Merton did not explicitly list gender among the illegitimate factors that might enter into the unfair appraisal of a researcher's contribution, and feminists needed to correct that omission. The important thing for women to notice now, however, is how very congenial the traditional norms of science are to their full participation. Unlike many organized religions or folk cultures, science is not intrinsically sexist. There are no misogynist creation myths or rules about who can be ordained as priests. Quite the contrary. According to the basic ideals of science, scientific claims are to be evaluated solely on logical and empirical grounds; scientific knowledge is to be made freely available to everyone; scientific credit is to be awarded strictly on merit. In their struggle to participate fully in science today, women's best strategy is to call on scientists and scientific institutions to honor their own most fundamental values. Any feminist theory that repudiates those values is a dubious ally.

8

Abolishing Gender Apartheid

Sex differences in rank and tenure status continue to exist in a major way, and the recent data do not show a significant improvement. . . . You would think there was something mystical about the figure for the proportion of women at full professor, because it just doesn't change. It just sits there stagnating—almost independent of the changing pool of female Ph.D.-level scientists. . . . The basic obstacle is simply the old boy network, which is still very much in place. . . . There are lots of hard-charging women out there, so the only reason I can see why women aren't making it to the top is that men feel comfortable working with men. (quoted in Gibbons, 1992a, p. 1368)

—Margrete S. Klein, former director of women's programs at the National Science Foundation

Taken together, the major components of the extra stuff, outlined in the preceding chapters, work to isolate women. The effects are often crippling. A number of detrimental consequences are connected with isolation, including stigma, impairment of self-confidence, and exclusion from access to informal networks of professional communication. Informal associations are essential for professional growth, career enhancement, and the scientific process. Affiliation with helpful colleagues enhances the conditions for scientific accomplishment; a poverty of supportive interaction inhibits it. Isolated women are not only deprived of social psychological support, but also the social resources underlying achievement (Etzkowitz et al., 1994).

The following two essays speak for themselves. Molly Gleiser's personal story and research call attention to the crippling effect that isolation can have

on women in science. Wendy Katkin follows with a description of Project
WISE, an innovative program to combat isolation and support women's
success in scientific endeavors.

The Glass Wall

____ Molly Gleiser ____

I was an ambitious and watchful child. Even before I attended school I
painfully observed that boys were more privileged than girls, a message fully
apparent in my family where, in the tradition of Orthodox Jews, my parents
thought their son more important than their daughters. Intelligence was one
of the great values of our family. Almost before we went to primary school,
my siblings and I knew we would go to college. But there was a difference.
For a girl, a degree was an *insurance policy*. She might be widowed, or not
get married. For boys, their profession would be the focal point of their lives,
its use not contingent on other eventualities.

Our house, piled high with books, fostered intellectual exploration. And
my father favored most those books connected with science. When I was about
8, he roped me into his garage workshop to help him. I learned such skills as
how to countersink screws and how to cut wood on a treadle fret saw, a
machine similar to an early sewing machine in which the saw is moved up and
down by a foot treadle.

His teaching at its best was much deeper than mere details. Rather, it
promoted critical thinking and a passion for investigation. For example, he
became very angry one day on seeing me at the kitchen table trying to force
apart a broken wristwatch in an attempt to get at the flywheels.

"Never try to force anything. That's the lazy way around," he admonished.
"Try to figure out how it works."

I decided to become a chemist when I was 11, soon after I successfully
performed my first experiment: the precipitation of copper sulfate from an
aqueous solution. I watched with great excitement as the brilliant blue crystals
precipitated out of solution, while my mind inquisitively wandered on. Just
how large would the crystals grow? For what could they be used? Did other

chemicals produce equally beautiful crystals? I did not encounter any road-blocks until 2 years later.

That year, our third in high school, when we were 13, a change was made. Rather than judged according to ability and promise, students were divided into two groups based solely on their gender. Girls, from this time on, were to study biology, in its early stages merely a descriptive science. Boys were challenged with the more rigorous study of advanced chemistry and physics. I wanted to be a chemist. I had encountered my first glass wall. How could I become a chemist if I were not allowed to take the course work necessary to achieve my goal? And why were *all* girls channeled out of these disciplines, when some of us were clearly capable of doing the work, and *all* boys channeled into them? But nowhere, except in my mind, did I hear a word of protest. I sat in the classroom glowering all term. The glass wall was steadfast, and I remained outside. But powerful forces acted in my favor. World War II broke out. My family left London and eventually settled in Nottingham, where I attended a girls' school. There, freed from the problem of what constitutes the right footing with boys, I became an outstanding student in both chemistry and math.

I later attended the University of Nottingham. After 2 years the war ended. My attachment to the school was weak. Social difficulties bothered me. I thought then that they arose from the fact that I had moved so many times. Then again, I was not physically attractive. My weight never rose above 83 pounds until I was 25. It suddenly occurred to me one day that I did not have to remain at Nottingham. I had heard of crack places where one could study science, places like the Imperial College of Science and Technology in London. Following the suggestion of my academic advisor that I "give it a try," I went to London to take the entry exam.

About a week after returning home, a small white envelope bearing the Imperial College insignia fluttered through our mail slot. My heart thumped as I picked it up. Would I return to the provincial backwater of Nottingham? Or would I be admitted to one of the most prestigious schools in Europe? I ripped open the envelope, fingers trembling. My eyes flashed on the contents. Clutched in my hand, I held my passport out of the periphery of science into the heart of its territory. I had evaded the glass wall, and my life as a scientist had officially begun.

By the time I had completed my baccalaureate, it was quite clear to me that I would become a physical chemist, probably a thermodynamicist. An oddity in the field of chemistry, thermodynamics is the least compartmentalized discipline, and is also taught in physics and engineering. Thermodynamics quite took me by the throat, so powerful was its appeal that lay far beyond that of any of the other narrower specialties we studied. I later chose it for my doctoral dissertation research.

Three possibilities then opened up for me after earning my PhD. I could take an industrial job. On the other hand, the British Iron and Steel Research Association, who had given me a bursary to cover my doctoral studies, now offered me a third year as a postdoctoral researcher. Or I could accept my sister Shummy's invitation to stay with her in Buenos Aires, Argentina, where she had married and was expecting her first child.

My graduate advisor then proposed a fourth option: a slot at the National Physical Laboratory. "You could stay there until you retire," he encouraged.

But I shuddered. If I accepted his proposal I would take the well-trodden path from the tube station to Teddington just outside London each morning and receive regular pay raises. The National Physical Laboratory was known as a secure place. Still, security is just another name for *prison,* in my mind. Thousands of miles away lay pampas, gauchos, South American dictators, and revolutions. In contrast, at Teddington I would be climbing on and off laboratory stools endlessly putting iron samples in furnaces, and I would end up knowing more about putting iron samples in furnaces than anyone else. A wave of nausea swept over me.

"I have decided to go to South America," I said.

A month later with all of the *joie de vivre* of a released prisoner I found myself standing under the blinding blue of the jacaranda trees in Buenos Aires. When I left a year later, the old Molly was gone. A new Molly, 20 pounds heavier, smiling, presentable, and much more confident than before, had taken her place. I was in love with Argentina, but it was no use staying. There just were not enough chemical jobs available. So I wrote to Professor Briscoe, the chair of the Chemistry Department at Imperial, and asked him to help me to find work in the United States. Meanwhile, I returned to London and after 4 months of searching, about four times as long as it took a majority of the men, I found work.

The handsome exterior of my office mate at Glacier Metal Company in London was complemented by a coarse interior that created an instant disagreeable impression on me.

"What's that?" He pointed to my bench where I tinkered with some brightly colored spheres joined together by metal sticks.

"They're molecular models," I replied with the hope of engaging in an intellectual conversation with him.

"This is a research division, not a kindergarten," he said sarcastically, and donning his motorcycle helmet, slammed out of the office.

By the end of the year my weight had fallen to its college level, and I felt too demoralized to go on. But at my lowest point, deliverance came in the form of a letter arriving from the Ohio State University in Columbus, Ohio. Professor Briscoe had found me a job in the United States.

A little flurry greeted my arrival at Ohio State where I promptly fell in love with one of the graduate students on my project. As the girlfriend of *one of the boys,* I was included in everything. When they went to the Red Cross to donate blood, I was triumphant among those that did not faint. When they threw their quarterly party, I was among the jovial crowd, and when they went to the "library," a euphemism for a Friday afternoon movie, I went along too. But when the relationship ended, I found myself an outcast, included in nothing.

There were signals all along that I did not share their mentality. The boys' girl-watching at the lab's window was a prime example.

"Gee, there's a girl almost as well-stacked as one of your pin-ups," a newcomer to the laboratory noted as he watched students emerge from their 5 o'clock classes. He began to sing softly:

> Let the sun shine in.
> Face it with a grin.
> Open up your pants
> And let the germs fly in.

A fellow lab member emitted a wolf whistle and nodded his approval. "Boy, what a big, dumb, nice, average girl," he remarked in admiration. The unspoken message came through all too clearly: I was among supermen for whom the archetypal women were the only suitable mates. And how could I, insignificant, undersized, flesh-and-blood me, who had committed the crime of being intelligent, hope to gain their respect as a person and a colleague?

Once I complained to my supervisor about how isolated I felt.

"You shouldn't complain," he sneered. "We didn't ask you for a photograph before you came here."

In a separate encounter, the group leader on the project suggested that I should get out and make friends "on my own level." However, in that great university of 20,000 students only one other woman research associate existed. Of course, he must have known that. Moreover, it was not clear if he was suggesting that I seek out the company of other women, seek out people who were less intellectually inclined, or if he considered the two one and the same.

The other graduate students, who were all male, seemed like stick figures to me. A glass wall separated us that had only superficial similarity with today's glass ceiling that inhibits women's promotion, and instead has everything to do with women's failure. It was a wall that allowed me to see the privileges and advantages accrued to those on the other side, but at the same time effectively inhibited even the most common interactions. Simple greetings such as, "Good morning," or "Nice day, isn't it?" were present on the other side of the glass wall, but absent from my reality. In this ambience, I became increasingly withdrawn; but I had not been demoralized completely into submission.

Only with great reluctance did the group leader finally agree to a meeting to discuss our project. Even then he failed to give me any specific direction until one day he found me fiddling with the x-ray machine and asked what I was doing.

"I'm taking x-ray diffraction patterns of the molybdates at different temperatures," I replied.

"I don't want you to do that," he said. "Take the molybdenum oxide John obtained in his experiments and get its composition."

At last an instruction! We could publish the results. And by summer I would surely have a new job.

"Okay," I answered enthusiastically and disappeared into the chemistry library for the usual literature search not to return to the laboratory until the following Monday.

"Where have you been all week?" The group leader interrogated me.

"In the chemistry library," I informed him, "Researching molybdenum oxides."

"I didn't tell you to do that," he barked. "I told you to analyze the oxide we have at hand."

"I was only looking up papers to determine which technique would be the best to use," I explained.

"When I want you to do research in the library, I'll let you know. Just stay in the lab and do what I tell you," he ordered.

"You've given me no directions for a year," I charged, shaking with rage. "Now you're giving me one that's irrational. Obviously I have to know what others have done before I start experimental work. I'm willing to follow your instruction, but I'm not going to do anything that makes no scientific sense."

"Just do what I'm telling you," he roared.

At that moment I felt something give way in the glass wall, something that released the tightness within my chest. "And I'm telling you this," I counterblasted, "When you use your position to make a fool of me, which you have done repeatedly, and when you use your power to make a mockery of my work, you're a son-of-a-bitch!"

"You're fired," he screamed. "You're incompetent!" He stepped over to the telephone and dialed the Research Foundation. "Pay Dr. Gleiser 2 week's wages," he instructed. "She's fired." He turned angrily to me. "I don't care what you do with your time or your money!"

Contrary to the state of panic and depression that should have accompanied such a circumstance, being fired from that job as a chemist has always been the happiest day of my life. I stopped shaking. A warmth spread through me. Never again would I wear out my feet on the stone floor. Never again would I sit in research seminars, a sea of empty seats around me. Perhaps without references I was through with chemistry forever. However, it did not seem to matter. Unexplored vistas opened up before me.

People were staring; no one dared utter a sound. Restraining the smile that bubbled up in me and threatened to break into a laugh, I collected my belongings and headed down the corridor to the exit. The group leader followed behind, taunting me like a spoiled brat.

"You're uncreative! You're unimaginative! You're incompetent! I've always known you were incompetent. You've been incompetent since the first day you came here."

At the end of the corridor, I turned calmly and inquired, "Then why have you paid me more money each year to persuade me to stay here?"

"Because . . . " he paused, searching for something to say, "because I felt sorry for you."

And as I opened the door to make my exit, even he laughed at the absurdity of his claim.

I found the discrimination at my next job at the Massachusetts Institute of Technology to be even worse. Part of it was institutional. For example, although MIT had accepted women students almost since its inception in the nineteenth century, somewhere along the way a rule was instituted that all undergraduate women must be housed in dormitories. Because places in them were limited to 12 women, the policy effectively imposed a cap on the number of women who could be enrolled at any given time. It remained so during my stay there from 1957 to 1962.

The numbers of women, individuals from other countries, and Jews who had graduated and wanted to work at MIT were controlled by placing them in the Department of Sponsored Research (DSR). As a member of all three of the above categories, I was brought in under the DSR program. None of us knew on being hired that our days were numbered. In fact, the policy for faculty was the exact opposite of the policy for DSR staff. Faculty were considered for tenure after about 5 years' service, whereas DSR staff were automatically terminated after 5 years.

With rules like these it is not surprising that I met only one other woman scientist in my early years at MIT. And she left shortly when her husband, a lawyer, took a job in Washington, D.C. Later, Asha and her husband Ram, both chemists from India, joined us. We became firm friends, and I felt less lonely. But this occurred only after a long time during which I experienced what I disliked the most: isolation. For at least in the United States, it is not active virulence that constituted the worst characteristic of the glass wall, but isolation. It was partly the constant isolation that engendered in me a growing dislike for science. MIT was the kind of place where one professor thought nothing of saying to another publicly: "Why do you bother with women? They're almost as bad as foreigners."

One did not often hear blatant misogynous remarks like that. There were too few professional women for us to constitute a threat. But like several other women at MIT, as a middle-age Jewish woman, I was triply discriminated against. The effect of each incident of discrimination and verbal abuse for the victim is the same and cumulative: a loss of self-confidence and a decrease in trust. I was no exception.

To a certain extent I enjoyed MIT: its high prestige, its libraries open every day from 8:00 in the morning to midnight, and its respect for good work. I did well there, coauthoring two books and four research articles, while I worked for one of the six leading metallurgists in the country, an honor in itself. Unfortunately, around this time with the opening of the Eichmann trial in 1961, anti-Semitism on the campus increased dramatically. Graffiti began to appear in the basement by the food vending machines: "Dirty Jews!" "Jews and pigs!" "Hang the Jews!"

Anti-Semitic episodes, more than anything else, drove me to Israel when my 5 years at MIT were up. I worked for a year as a researcher at the National Physical Laboratory of Jerusalem. I spent the following year as a technical editor for the Program for Scientific Translations, also in Jerusalem. In January 1966, my temporary resident's visa expired, and I left Israel for what I considered to be my true home, the United States.

I found Boston unchanged. Thus, when a letter arrived offering me a job at the Lawrence Berkeley Laboratory at the University of California, Berkeley, I jumped at the opportunity. But the glass wall there was even higher and more rigid than it had been elsewhere.

On my arrival, I confronted, pinned to a notice board outside my supervisor's office, a list of elements, followed by a second list of binary mixtures of elements. My job, along with the rest of the members of the research group, was to choose one of these *systems,* as we called them, place our initials beside it to indicate that we were working on it, calculate its thermodynamic data such as specific heats, ready the data for publication, and submit it to the supervisor for his final approval. To this day, the bellows of this supervisor ring in my ears.

"Dots, I tell you! I want dots, do you hear? Not crosses. I've told you before! . . . Mark the experimental points with dots!" Although the data were sound and I had done the work expertly, he would slam down in front of me the graph I had drawn the day before solely because the presentation failed to meet his petty idiosyncratic standards.

I realized early on that taking the position at Berkeley had been an unfortunate mistake and therefore put forth great effort to find a new position. However, for all that I searched, not a single job offer did I get. My work became something to endure and the only redeeming feature of my life was attending a biweekly writing class that I had initiated as a hobby. By 1970, I had already sold a couple of articles. But in the laboratory I was at my final gasp. I could not have lasted as long as I did had my supervisor not decided to attend a convention in (then) Soviet Russia. His departure placed me in a quandary. Either I could write the systems my way, which he would not accept, or I could write them his way, which meant introducing at least six grammatical errors on each page. By now he had accumulated so many systems on his desk submitted by those in his laboratory that, like the Leaning Tower of Pisa, they threatened to fall on the floor. His idiosyncratic perfectionist tendencies made it impossible for him to review them or to delegate the task to anyone else. It had become customary in the laboratory to expect a verbal bludgeoning with the inevitable rejection of a system. I finally resolved to do no more systems until he reviewed the work I already had given him.

With our supervisor absent, the morale in the laboratory—which one newcomer, holding his hand 2 feet off the floor to indicate a comparatively high degree—rose. People bounded rather than dragged into work. But it could not last.

One morning I heard a long absent but familiar sound on the stairs. Clump! Clump! Clump! My door flew open. My boss stood there, livid. I had given him no new systems, but he had found a stack of my old unreviewed ones. He flung them in front of me.

"You can't write English either!" He snorted and slammed out the door. Undaunted, this time I ran after him.

"You have repeatedly humiliated, insulted, and denigrated me," I charged. "This cannot go on. Unless we can resolve matters, I shall go to the Lawrence Berkeley Laboratory personnel office to find out what my rights are."

"You've got rights?" he mocked. "This is the first I've heard of it. You're only temporary here, and you're employed by *me,* not the Lawrence Berkeley Laboratory.

"So I've been *temporary* for 4 years? I scoffed. "And if you think to muffle me with misstatements, you won't succeed."

I thought it would be nice if I could simply obtain a transfer to another slot, so I headed to the division head's office. But he informed me with indifference: "There are no transfers." He wound up by warning me to include the latest references in my write-ups of the systems, and I left to ascertain my rights at the personnel office.

The wispy woman with long everted nostrils who listened to my complaints said, "Everyone understands that individual." I smiled with relief. Others had been there before me. She looked up my file. I was permanent, not temporary.

Because my position was, in any case, about to be phased out, I had priority of rehire over all applying from outside the campus for any position for which I had the qualifications. Further, university policy stated that the personnel office and my supervisor *must* assist me in obtaining the new position. "There's only one other woman chemist here among 2000 employees, and she's about to be phased out, too," the secretary added.

I gasped. The laboratory was about to be purged of woman chemists!

"You're incompetent!" my supervisor barked when I confronted him with the facts. Incompetent! I did not budge a millimeter. But the label *incompetent* was one that had been ascribed before. Although it had no basis in fact, this label made a wound in me that suppurated for years. My supervisor emerged from his office a few minutes later and threw on my desk an official letter of dismissal, effective in 6 months.

I turned to the California State Employees Association, and their lawyer cut him to pieces.

"What kind of supervisor are you? Your discharge of her is illegal. It has to go through personnel." The lawyer's light freckled nose jutted forward until it almost touched that of my supervisor. The sight was reminiscent of a baseball team manager vehemently arguing with an umpire, in a full ritualistic display of posturing, over a perceived bad call. "If this comes to court I'll bury you. The judge requires more than your say-so about her performance.

I turned to the other employees for support. One woman laughed wryly. "Oh, Molly!" she sighed, surprised that I had not yet accepted the tenor of the system. "They don't like women. They don't like middle-aged women. They don't like Jewish women. But most of all, they don't like middle-aged Jewish women who make complaints to trade unions." And with one accord all the employees turned down my requests for support. In all fairness, they probably feared for their own jobs. Even my supervisor's secretary refused my request for support.

"Priority of rehire means nothing," she said. "A final evaluation is made behind our backs, completely ignoring our input, and a box is usually marked: 'Not recommended for rehire.' Your boss gives rotten references. He wrote about one fellow who was looking for a job: 'As for his innate abilities I would say he's average or below average.' I typed the letter myself."

I gasped in shock. By writing bad references, my supervisor had held the scientists in his group as peons for years. The business manager of my division confirmed it.

"Your boss has the right to select whom he wants regardless of seniority," he informed me. "Permanent or temporary, and all that baloney, it doesn't matter what your position is called, it's only as permanent as anything else in life."

As I listened my head spun. Permanent meant temporary. Experienced meant inexperienced. Competent meant incompetent.

"Molly," an inner voice whispered to me: "Isn't this fascism?" And even as my face registered shock, I answered, "Yes!"

My one hope lay in my lawyer.

"I've dropped your case," he stated matter-of-factly when I ran across him a few days later.

"What?" I said, aghast. "Why?"

He didn't look at me. "You know why."

"But how will I ever get another job without references? I'll fall on welfare," I cried.

"That's right." My lawyer's gray-suited figure toting a black briefcase flew by without another word.

Never had I felt so tiny as I climbed the stairs of Hearst Mining, the building where I worked. Inside, the hall seemed to engulf me. I shivered. Upstairs a strange silence surrounded me. The glass wall between myself and the scientific establishment had thickened to a wall of ice. I tried to get on with my work. But I felt dazed. Several times I called my lawyer and asked him to explain why he had dropped my case.

"You know why," he continually responded, and I could get no other answer.

I sat staring at the black-and-white linoleum in my kitchen for hours that evening. What had happened? I drew a blank.

Slowly I sat down at my typewriter to enter my other world that had so often blotted out the indignities of the day. However, my feelings were too overwhelming to be sublimated. My fingers faltered. A scene from the previous day took prominence. My supervisor, foot tapping, face clouded, had met me in the doorway of the department.

"Where've you been?" he demanded.

"The library," I replied, and perhaps some note of pride lingered in my voice. "I left a message to that effect with the secretary," I added.

"You're not allowed to go to the library," he scolded.

The phrase struck a warning note. Exactly so, 15 years before, my supervisor at Ohio State had delivered the same outrageous admonishment. Perhaps something about women in libraries threatened these men: the freedom of information, other people's autonomy, or the extreme quiet where position and bullying voices no longer prevailed.

"The division head wants the latest references," I informed him, attempting to detour from a potentially explosive confrontation. "They're not in your information office."

"You're not allowed to go to the library," he sternly repeated. A great gust of rage surged in me. Had anyone ever heard of a chemist who was not allowed to go to the library? And how would I, friendless as I was, meet the division head's criticisms that my work was out of date? Between the two of them they would have me in jail or institutionalized in a mental hospital. I could not go on.

I knew that my supervisor's log currently indicated that I had produced more, and faster, than anyone else. If I left now, his allegations of incompetence would be unsubstantiated and slanderous. Conversely, if I stayed he could badger and harass me until my productivity fell off and his allegations would have substance. I must quit now. I would not bend to tradition and tender my resignation according to policy, thereby preserving a false positive image at my division and the university. I could no longer continue to work for them. I owed them nothing.

I arose from my seat at the kitchen table and against a backdrop of a blood-red sky, I walked back across campus and unlocked the heavy door of Hearst Mining. On my desk upstairs lay completed my last piece of work. Finished, our book would appear in every metallurgy laboratory in the world. My name would be among the authors.

I squared up the sheets and left them there. My body relaxed in a double sigh. From the desk's drawers I withdrew my belongings: a pen, two books, and three air letters. I descended the broad stairway for the last time. The massive door slammed behind me. As I trod the asphalt path, an inner voice said, "You've lost your livelihood. University of California faculty members are on the board of every company around. Who will employ a 45-year-old woman without references anyway? No one."

But my spirits rather than sinking lifted at each step. I would never have to work as a chemist again. I had lost my profession but had been given myself. Perhaps I could piece a living together. I had been given little. I would need little. I could work at my crafts in the morning. Jewelry sold best. I wished I had purchased that blowtorch and silver soldering machine earlier. In the afternoons I would let my imagination rip. I would write the wildest things. And in a vision I saw myself. Autonomous? Yes. Alone? No. Ahead stood a line of authors: some rich, some ragged, some well-known, others unrecognized. To all, an inner dignity clung. These people had testified; I would be among them. No glass wall stood between us. I'd join them quicker if I left the formal path. I felt something inside me coming together. And in a voice cracked from long disuse, I began to sing to the familiar tune of *Happy Birthday*:

> Happy phased out to me.
> Happy phased out to me.
> Happy phased out, dear Molly,
> Happy phased out to me.

> I have testified.

Since leaving the Lawrence Berkeley Laboratory, I have worked as a freelance writer and editor. Writing in the last years, unlike trying to work within the scientific establishment as chemist, has filled me with joy. The project that gave me the most fulfillment is one focusing on the causes of suicide among chemists. I developed a compelling interest in the subject after reading a National Cancer Institute study reporting that the suicide rate among female chemists was five times the national average for white women (Walrath, Li, Hoar, Mead, & Fraumeni, 1985), and along with colleague Richard Seiden, decided to investigate the matter further. The results of our study reveal just how dangerous isolation can be (Seiden & Gleiser, 1990).

The goal of the project was to gather information about the suicides of chemists, identify the causes, and separate them into work-related and non–work-related factors. This last step was critical, as we wanted to ascertain the degree to which work-related factors contributed to triggering suicides and to identify any gender differences in the causes of suicide among chemists. Our sampling strategy yielded the names of 28 female and 63 male suicides. Information about them came primarily from coauthors whose names appear in *Chemical Abstracts.*

Separation of the precipitating events into work-related and non–work-related factors revealed that an overwhelming majority of the suicides were work related; only 4% of the suicides for women were attributable to non–work-related causes compared to 19% among men. Work-related isolation was the most prominent factor associated with suicide for both women and men. However, for women it is almost universal at 96%.[1]

Apart from self-explanatory examples of isolation such as minority group membership, being single, and geographical isolation, we judged women to be isolated when they constituted a numerical minority at work and thus had few others to share common interests and experiences. This essentially meant that all women faced isolation to some degree, with the possible exception of those working in women's colleges. An interesting factor was the high percentage of women who were marginalized in their families of origin because of work-related conflicts with their parents. Mothers were bewildered by their daughters' choice of career and were unable to understand why they could not be satisfied in less demanding, traditionally feminine positions; fathers vilified the drive and enthusiasm of their daughters, thus effectively undermining the self-confidence necessary to survive a stressful career and work situation.

We also found that women endured a wider diversity of isolating experiences; 96% of the women studied faced two or more types of isolating experiences compared to a rate of 36% among men, and one third of the men experienced no isolating experiences under our criteria. This suggests that even if women achieve numerical parity with men, they will still comparatively experience more isolation.

A major feature of work-related causes among women was sex discrimination. It figured in such problems as outsider work slots, parental conflict, slow/no promotion, and supervisor problems. These were not minor issues. One supervisor flatly stated, "Women should not be in biochemistry, the work is too hard." Another male supervisor continually belittled a woman colleague who had achieved professorial rank. He claimed she had insufficient intelligence.

A final factor to be discussed is personality. Suicide is caused neither by personality nor circumstances, but by a combination of the two. A certain type of personality, under a given set of circumstances, will commit suicide. Severe mental illness was the most common personality cause among women chemists, being almost twice as high (44%) as it was among male chemists (24%). Women were also more withdrawn than men and twice as likely to suffer from low self-esteem, coupled with high achievement orientation, than men.

Our data suggest that women chemists have a higher rate of suicide than men. Our work corroborates an older finding of F. D. Li (1969). While examining the death certificates of women chemists, Li found every eleventh certificate to be a suicide. Although his method cannot be used to calculate the suicide rate among women chemists, it does indicate an abnormally high rate.

A majority of women chemists do not commit suicide, of course. However, the same cannot be said about experiencing work-related isolation. Consistent with the theme of this volume, I predict that efforts to increase the number of women scientists without also addressing other aspects of work-related isolation will ultimately result in greater numbers of women feeling the crushing effects of isolation.

As for myself, I never worked as a chemist again. A vision floats in my mind of me at 18, sitting at our dining-room table, my textbooks around me. My mother's voice chatting with a friend drifts through from the living room. "I've had four children at university," she explains, "But none ever sat down to work with such joy as Molly."

My mother's words were true. Tears fill my eyes, but they do not fall. The picture today is quite different. Although I loved chemistry, if anyone had approached me after leaving Lawrence Berkeley Laboratory and threatened me with bodily harm if I did not return to the laboratory, I would have refused and accepted the consequences. My treatment as a scientific researcher was so oppressive that I would have opted for anything else.

It would be nice to record that after I left the Lawrence Berkeley Laboratory my writing flourished and I enjoyed a spectacular success. However, it is not so. I sold a few articles at first, and my income supplemented by savings, craft work, and odd jobs, such as substitute school crossing guard, remained minimal for years. By 1972, I was desperate. In an attempt to survive I applied for numerous jobs in research. Everywhere the door slammed in my face. Repeated protests to the directors and Nobel Prize winners at the Lawrence Berkeley Laboratory about unfair, slanderous references led nowhere. The label of *incompetence* had made the rounds and it had stuck.

True, I have not been one of the architects of the field, only one of thousands of bricklayer-chemists without whom the foundations of modern chemistry could not have been laid. But my coauthorship of four books, nine research articles, and one patent should speak for itself.

In 1975, I applied for several jobs as technical editor at the Lawrence Berkeley Laboratory, and when tipped off by a friend that men less qualified or unqualified had been appointed, I filed a formal complaint with the Equal Employment Opportunity Commission (EEOC). The EEOC found in my favor, but the Lawrence Berkeley Laboratory refused to conciliate. Thus, the case went to trial in civil court. Denied a jury, I lost. But I had the high honor of being the first woman to take the goliath Lawrence Berkeley Laboratory to court on a sex discrimination charge. Other women followed me and won. It is my sincere hope that these victories will decrease discrimination against women.

Today I live and work under the eaves of a little white Victorian house in downtown Berkeley, California, where I am frequently visited by the many friends who have encouraged my contribution to this volume. I have published almost 100 short stories and articles in local and national outlets, ranging from *The Berkeley Barb* to *Harper's* magazine. My specialty is biography. I supplement my writing with editing assignments.

My anger has not disappeared. With no fear of losing my job, I express my outrage at injustice and oppression more readily than before. But because I no longer have to restrain my feelings, I reach out to others more easily too. With men, women, children, friends, or strangers, the bonds of love form more quickly now.

Perhaps this is the most important lesson that I have learned from my experiences as a scientist: the animate is worth more than the inanimate. Of all things animate, the most worthy is love.

Project WISE:

A Community of Wise Women

_____ *Wendy Katkin* _____

Women in Science and Engineering (Project WISE), is an innovative experimental project, initiated at the State University of New York at Stony Brook
(hereinafter Stony Brook or USB) in 1993.[2] It was established to motivate high
school and college women who show academic promise in mathematics or
science to develop their talent, with the long-range goal of pursuing careers
that require advanced scientific, engineering, and mathematical (SEM) training. Project WISE was conceived by women scientists at Stony Brook and
developed collaboratively with colleagues at Brookhaven National Laboratory (BNL), with significant input from high school teachers, administrators,
and students; members of the local branch of the American Association of
University Women (AAUW); and Cold Spring Harbor Laboratory (CSHL)
scientists. Most of its activities are carried out by women scientists. Thus from
its conception through its implementation, Project WISE has been a commu-
nal effort, created by a working group of women professionals, all of whom
are committed to engaging younger women in science, mathematics, or
engineering and to assist them to develop the skills and the confidence to
support their continued pursuit of these subjects; their approach reflects their
underlying goal to establish a community of women scientists that includes
members at every stage in the pipeline.

Yet Project WISE is not a solely female event. From the outset, the project
has enjoyed considerable support from the (all-male)[3] higher administration
at Stony Brook, as well as the participating research laboratories and high
schools, and it has benefited from significant contributions from other colleagues, who have key roles as instructors and research supervisors of participating students. The involvement of male faculty, researchers, and high school
teachers has been steadily increasing as the project has begun to have impact
at the university and participating high schools and as male faculty and
administrators have become sensitive to the issues that divert young women.

A male colleague in physics is now a member of the working group, another serves as the initial academic advisor for incoming college students, and a third hopes to teach the initial Project WISE college course (discussed later) next year. The widespread support the project is gaining and is critical to its becoming institutionalized at Stony Brook and the participating high schools and to its continuing once the funding from the National Science Foundation ceases.

Project Description

Project WISE has two distinct components: a high school component, which, within 3 years, will involve 120 girls per year in Grades 9 through 12; and a college component, which in 3 years will have 140 undergraduate women participating. Although the college component covers all four undergraduate years, its primary focus is on the first two years. We have chosen to emphasize the 5-year period between 10th grade and the second year of college because these years come at a critical time when young women form attitudes and develop skills that shape their subsequent educational and professional lives. This is also the period of major leakage and therefore highest risk in the female SEM (i.e., science, engineering, and mathematics) pipeline, when most academically talented young women take their last math or science course (Hewitt & Seymour, 1991; Madison & Hart, 1990).

Project WISE takes a systemic approach to attracting women to SEM; thus in both the high school and college components, each year's activities build on and expand the previous year's. Although the two components are not formally linked, their participants interact at occasional events and thus gain a perspective of the entire pipeline. Furthermore, both components offer a similar combination of programs that integrate four facets: (a) exposure to the range of opportunities available to individuals with advanced SEM training; (b) gender-focussed considerations that might influence the young women's educational and professional plans; (c) study strategies to facilitate the development of both skills and an enhanced sense of confidence; and (d) substantial research experience, mostly within a group context. Project programs include enrichment activities; hands-on research experiences; informal programs that emphasize applications and careers; social events; individual academic advising; a strong mentoring system; and involvement of teachers, administrators, parents, and friends, all of whom critically influence the values young women develop, as well as their educational course. We have endeavored to incorporate these elements because they have all been identified by the American Association for the Advancement of Science as "key" to successful intervention programs (Matyas & Malcom, 1991);[4] they are also necessary to effect permanent change in the SEM environment for women.

In establishing Project WISE, we have also sought to create models that can be readily integrated into regular high school and college curricula; this is essential if Project WISE is to be maintained and mainstreamed at Stony Brook and the participating high schools and if it is to be expanded to other universities and high schools. This approach will allow the project to reach significantly more women than those participating. We also envision segments of the project being adapted for other targeted populations, such as minority and disabled students.

High School Component

The high school component involves 30 ninth graders per year, all from the same school and selected primarily for their expressed interest in participating, with only minimal consideration given to academic ability. The idea at this early stage is to reach a range of girls with different abilities. In contrast, the 10th-grade program, and every subsequent level program within Project WISE, is targeted at "high-ability" girls. We have chosen to focus on this group in particular because of its potential to become engaged and succeed, and the likelihood that it will not do so without intervention (National Research Council, 1989; Tobias, 1992).

Project WISE accepts six 10th graders and one science or math teacher annually from each of five local high schools with diverse ethnic and socio-economic student populations; the students and teachers remain in the project through 12th grade. We "sell" the students on the project by emphasizing the opportunity to engage in cutting-edge research with active scientists at Stony Brook, Brookhaven, and Cold Spring Harbor Laboratories, all very prestigious institutions on Long Island. We enlist the support of parents by stressing the honor of their daughters' being selected for participation, the unique experience Project WISE will provide, and the potential value of the project on college applications. Although we do not focus explicitly on gender factors, in describing the project at meetings with the parents, we discuss the factors that discourage girls from pursuing SEM and suggest ways in which they can provide support and encouragement. The high school teachers are drawn to the project because of the opportunity to conduct research and update their knowledge, and also because of the project's training sessions, which are designed, again, to sensitize them to issues that deter girls from study of SEM and to educate them about pedagogical strategies and instructional methods that have proved effective with girls.

Because many high school girls may be intrigued by, but not committed to, science, we have designed Project WISE so that it involves them *slowly and gradually* and engages them socially, as well academically. In order to effect this gradual involvement, we have planned the high school component so that the 9th-grade program consists of only five integrated activities, spread throughout the year; the 10th-grade program consists of nine sessions, one per month, and a 2-week residential science adventure during the summer; and the 11th grade has ten regularly scheduled sessions, plus extra research activities and meetings with research advisors. In the 12th grade, the students work out their own individual schedules. In addition, in an effort to attract students who have competing interests and who might not otherwise participate, we have arranged the schedules each year so that activities take place on rotating days (i.e., on Mondays in September, on Tuesdays in October, etc.). To facilitate communication among the students, and to enable them to contact participating teachers and researchers as well, we have placed a dedicated computer and modem in each participating school and assigned an electronic-mail account for each girl and teacher. Once Project WISE is firmly established, we plan to produce a newsletter, to be distributed through electronic mail, which will put current participants in touch with others who have successfully passed through the program to learn about their college experiences.

Table 8.1 provides a by-grade outline of the high school component's main activities. As may be noted, the activities taking place during each year are designed to accomplish specific goals.

9th Grade

This segment, offered in cooperation with the Northern Suffolk County branch of the AAUW and modeled on the national AAUW "shadowing" program, has two objectives: To provide early insight into a broad range of careers and professional opportunities that require mathematical, scientific or technological skills; and to arouse the girls' interest and curiosity sufficiently to stimulate continued study of these subjects. The message is presented in a low-key manner. The girls participate in a series of activities, spread out from

Table 8.1   Activities in the High School Component

Grade	Participants	Activities
9	• 30 students • 2 guidance counselors	• AAUW shadowing program • Counselor training • Career counseling • Shadowing • GEMS
10 (academic year)	• 30 students • 5 teachers	• Introduction to email • Group research projects as USB, BNL, and CSHL • Teacher training • Parent workshop
10 (summer)	• 30 students • 5 teachers	• Science Adventure consisting of field research projects (2 weeks)
11	• 30 students • 5 teachers	• Group research project (USB, BNL)— one per semester
12	• 30 students • 5 teachers	• Individual or group research at USB, BNL, or CSHL • College advisement and assistance • Social Activities with USB undergraduates

October through May, in which they learn about and do research on nontraditional career options, with special emphasis on those requiring quantitative or technical skills. One activity is an all-day Workshop on Gender Equity in Math and Science (GEMS), in which the students have the opportunity to (a) hear talks by women professionals in SEM fields on such topics as the use of mathematics and science in their work or managing a family and a career; (b) role play in skits about gender-equity issues; and (c) engage in hands-on activities that require group cooperation and collaboration and stress team rather than individual effort. The principal event for the 9th graders is a 1-day experience, organized by the local AAUW, during which each girl "shadows" a woman professional in a nontraditional career in order to learn about her work and work environment and gain insight into the education and skills it requires. The girls maintain a log of their day and discuss their observations with one another at a follow-up session. The final activity is their attendance at a symposium at which the 10th- through 12th-grade Project WISE students give presentations relating to their research; our objectives in inviting the 9th graders to the symposium are to enable them to see and hear what colleagues only a year or two ahead of them in school have accomplished and to catch some of the enthusiasm and excitement these "older" students feel as they present their work.

At the end of the academic year, we host a ceremony at which the girls are given certificates signifying their participation in the 9th-grade Project WISE program. The girls are encouraged to invite a female friend, as well as parents, siblings, and teachers, to attend. By sharing their experiences with others at the ceremony, they extend and validate them. The goal here, as it is for many other high school and college segments within Project WISE, is to involve more young women than those participating directly. Finally, a critical element of the 9th-grade program is a training program for the school guidance counselors to make them aware of issues that divert girls from SEM and to help them to develop strategies to address these issues.

10th Through 12th Grade

This segment aims to give the girls positive and inviting experiences in a variety of SEM research settings and to begin to instill in them levels of confidence and commitment that will encourage them to continue. The pedagogical strategy throughout emphasizes teamwork and cooperation and a bottom-up approach that moves from practical to theoretical considerations; this kind of strategy has proved to be more effective with girls than traditional methods (Keith & Keith, 1989; Matyas & Malcom, 1991).

In the 10th grade, the girls are divided into groups of six, each led by a female mathematics or science teacher. The individual groups engage in a series of 3-day experiments, one each in a physical science, a life science, and engineering, developed for Project WISE by active researchers at Stony Brook, Brookhaven National Laboratory, and Cold Spring Harbor Laboratory and carried out at each of these sites. Working collaboratively, the members of each group then follow up the experiments with supplemental research, and they prepare presentations, which are given to their peers. Following experimentation on DNA fingerprinting at the Cold Spring Harbor DNA Learning Laboratory, for example, individual groups conducted research and gave presentations on health, agricultural, forensic, and ethical issues related to DNA. Based on its own experience in doing DNA fingerprinting, the fifth group reported on the importance of accuracy in scientific experimentation.

During the summer, the 10th-grade-level girls take part in a 2-week residential "Summer Science Adventure," organized around the theme "Why is the world the way it is?" Led by researchers, and assisted by the high school teachers and three female graduate students, they engage in a variety of field research projects at such sites as the New York Botanical Gardens, the Brookhaven Science Museum, and the National Wildlife Refuge site, Seatuck, as well on the Stony Brook Marine Sciences Research vessel, the *On-Rust*. They also have instructional sessions involving the computer. Equally important to their research experience, the girls have the opportunity to live on a university campus, participate in many of its activities, and socialize and "bond" with one another in a way that is impossible during the academic year. Such bonding is particularly important for those who lack strong support at home or among their peers in their own communities. The residential experience will also allow them to link their academic and social activities as, for example, when they "drop" into the laboratory in the evening to see how a test they did during the day is working out or when they visit their counselor in her laboratory where, as a graduate student, she is doing her own research.

The 11th-grade program has two thrusts: research and socialization into the SEM environment. Although the aim of the 10th-grade segment is to expose the students broadly to different kinds of scientific research, the 11th-grade segment seeks to give them more in-depth experiences so that they will begin to think of themselves as scientists—which is the first important step in their decision to take their science and mathematics studies seriously. During this year, the girls will participate in two group research experiences, one per semester, at either Stony Brook or Brookhaven National Laboratory. They will be supervised by a researcher and the high school teacher assigned to the group. Although at the time of this writing we have not yet offered the 11th-grade segment, we envision all the research projects as being small and "doable" within the semester so that the girls can achieve a sense of accomplishment. In 1995–96, for example, one group will study the behavioral patterns of different species of fish; another will test the use of different materials and methods to simulate diamonds and then actually create them; a third group will be involved in an ongoing project to develop materials to impede the spread of asbestos in razing a dilapidated bridge. Each group will report on its experiment at an event, modeled on a professional symposium, that will take place at the end of the semester, and be attended by parents, female friends, teachers and researchers, as well as by the Project WISE 9th- and 10th-grade participants.

Their socialization into the SEM environment will be accomplished through regularly scheduled evening sessions attended by women researchers from Stony Brook, Brookhaven, and Cold Spring Harbor Laboratories, high school teachers, and undergraduates and graduate students associated with the college component. On occasion, researchers or undergraduate or graduate students will give presentations relating to their research; on other occasions, visiting women scientists from industry will be invited to speak. Although the formal subject of the talks will be their ongoing work, the speakers will also raise personal matters relating to their professional development and careers. At every session, there will be time set aside for informal discussion so that the girls can begin to see the researchers as "real people" and form relationships with them. Some sessions will be exclusively for the 11th and 12th graders and will focus on college-orientated issues, such as reading a college catalog or questions to ask at a college interview.

In the summer between 11th and 12th grades, the girls will have a more extended research experience. They will have the option to join a summer residential research program at Stony Brook or Brookhaven National Laboratory and spend 6 to 8 weeks as research apprentices, or they may become associated with an individual researcher. Either way, we will endeavor to identify research settings that have at least one female researcher (a faculty member or advanced graduate student) to serve as a role model. Because Project WISE is only just completing its first year (though we offered a pilot version to 15 first-year college women in 1993–94), we have not yet worked out the details for this summer program, but we hope to arrange for the teachers to participate as well. We envision the small groups of girls meeting weekly throughout their apprenticeship with one of the high school teachers. Through these weekly meetings, they will be able to report on their own work and become reacquainted with the projects of the other girls. As they do throughout the high school component, the teachers will be the liaisons between the high school and Project WISE experience, ensuring that the research experience is defined at an appropriate level for the girls and in a supportive setting. During this summer, the teachers will spend half their time also involved in research. In addition to gaining new knowledge and skills, they will become reacquainted with the research milieu and gain firsthand knowledge of factors in the environment that encourage and discourage women. This experience should enhance their own teaching and research supervision and motivate them to incorporate group research projects and new methods in their classrooms.

In the 12th grade, as part of their academic schedule, the girls will be encouraged to take an advanced placement (AP) calculus or science course at their high school or, preferably, an introductory calculus or science course at Stony Brook, where they will be placed in the same sections as first-year Project WISE college students. They will also participate in weekly after-school group study sessions led by advanced undergraduate women majoring in a mathematics or science. Their extracurricular activities will be organized around individual or group research experiences that they will carry out during the entire academic year. The research will culminate in the preparation of a written report and poster for submission to science contests or journals. The students will also have regularly scheduled evening sessions. In the fall semester, at least two sessions will be set aside for them to "practice" their presentations and respond to questions. Other sessions will deal with the "nuts and bolts" of choosing and applying to colleges, and include writing and critiquing college application essays and mock interviews with faculty, some of whom routinely interview students for their own alma maters. The spring sessions will include discussions of college-oriented issues, such as coping with large lectures or dealing with sexism in SEM classes. On occasion, the 12th graders will attend special evening programs offered in conjunction with the college component.

College Component

The college component is directed at women entering Stony Brook who have a demonstrated aptitude for SEM, as measured by a combination of factors: 4 years of high school math or science, a high school GPA of at least 90, a score of 600 or higher on either the SAT quantitative exam or a mathematics or science achievement test, strong letters of recommendation, and an interest in science or mathematics, as demonstrated through research experiences or extracurricular activities. As suggested, we have chosen to focus on this group because of the high dropout rate among women, even those with high ability and a genuine interest in science (Keith & Keith, 1989; Matyas & Malcom, 1991; National Research Council, 1989; Tobias, 1992), during "the troublesome transitions from high school to college" (Madison & Hart, 1990). Furthermore, it has been found that if students bypass science or mathematics courses in this transitional period, they virtually never switch back into them (Green, 1989; Hewitt & Seymour, 1991). Thus large numbers of talented women cut themselves off from an array of potentially exciting and important career opportunities before they even know what they are. Studies cite numerous factors leading to their withdrawal, specifically insecurity and self-doubt about their ability to perform well, the highly competitive nature of their SEM classes, lack of encouragement, and the perception of scientists as unattractive people (Keith & Keith, 1989; Wellesley College Center for Research on Women, 1992).

The college component has been planned therefore to counter these factors by (a) facilitating the transition from high school to college through the second year; (b) engaging the women in SEM *early* in their college careers, *before* they make academic decisions that will shape their subsequent education; and (c) providing experiences, information and support that will motivate them to continue study in SEM fields. We seek to accomplish these objectives through special research-oriented courses and research experiences, informal programs, individual academic advising by faculty to ensure appropriate placement in SEM classes, strong mentoring, and, especially, creating a supportive social environment. By the end of their sophomore year, the women should have sufficient knowledge and self-confidence to pursue a range of options and make informed decisions about their future plans. Although Project WISE does not have any formal program requirements beyond the first 2 years, during their junior and senior years, the women are encouraged to maintain contact with the project through attendance at the monthly evening sessions and through get-togethers once each semester at which they will bring one another up to date on what they are doing. The women will also be advised, and urged, to continue to do research in their major and to take nonquantitative electives, such as literature, or gender and science, which reinforce the themes of Project WISE. Junior- and senior-year participants will be invited to become junior mentors to subsequent Project WISE cohorts.

Table 8.2 provides an outline of each year's activities within the college component. It should be noted that, in addition to the target population, the college component also benefits other groups, specifically advanced women undergraduates who serve as junior mentors, female graduates students who direct research projects, and male and female faculty, who also direct research projects. By involving diverse constituents, sensitizing them to what may be sexist patterns in the classroom and providing training in ways to remedy them, Project WISE seeks to stimulate real and pervasive changes at Stony Brook in the SEM environment for women.

First Academic Year

The college component formally begins during the summer, prior to the incoming women's matriculation at Stony Brook, when they attend orienta-

Table 8.2   Activities in the College Component

Year	Participants	Activities
1	• 35 undergraduate women • 7 advanced undergraduate women (SEM majors) • 2 graduate students • Approximately 8 graduate students who direct research groups	• Special USB 101 (fall semester) • Introduction to research (spring) • Individual academic advising • Peer study groups/junior mentoring • Evening social activities
2	• 35 undergraduate women • Approximately 8 graduate students who direct research • 2 graduate students	• Social dimensions of science course • Evening social activities
3	• 35 undergraduate women • 2 graduate students	• Individual research • Junior mentoring • Evening social events
4	• 35 undergraduate women • 7 advanced undergraduate women (SEM majors) • 2 graduate students	• Individual research • Junior mentoring • Evening social events • Advising and assisting students in applying to graduate school

tion and have their first opportunity to meet one another and other students and faculty associated with Project WISE, and to learn more about the project, particularly its emphases on collegiality and social support. They are also introduced to their "peer group," made up of four other first-year Project WISE students, and to their "junior mentors," advanced female SEM majors who will lead the peer groups and serve as important resources to the students as they endeavor to adjust to college life. The junior mentors are selected by a subcommittee of the Project WISE working group, based on their strong academic records, particularly in mathematics and science; their ability to teach; their involvement in campus activities; their maturity; and their leadership qualities. We also endeavor to choose a diverse group, comprising women with different majors (e.g., mathematics, engineering, chemistry, etc.) and of different racial and ethnic backgrounds. The latter is particularly important because Stony Brook has the most diverse undergraduate population within SUNY, and our Project WISE students reflect this diversity. Among the 38 students in the 1994–95 group,[4] 8 are "minority" (2 African Americans, 5

Latinas, and 1 Native American), 4 are of Chinese descent, 5 are first-generation students from India, one is Arabic, 6 are first-generation students from
countries in what was formerly the Soviet Union, and 14 are white and born
in the United States.

The junior mentors are key to Project WISE and, according to past and
present Project WISE participants, "the best thing about the program." During
the academic year, each junior mentor meets with her peer group approximately 3 hours per week; at these meetings, she assists them with their
calculus and science course work and engages them in student activities on
campus. As emerging young scientists themselves, the junior mentors serve
as vital links between the social and research environment and good role
models for the new students. As active students on campus, they involve their
younger colleagues in student clubs and organizations and, by example,
demonstrate how extracurricular involvements enrich the college experience.
At the same time, the junior mentors benefit enormously through their
participation in Project WISE because it compels them to think about educational and professional options and gender issues that they might not normally
consider at this stage.

In the first year, Project WISE has three academic requirements. The first
is USB 101 (one credit), a fall-semester course that is a variant of Stony
Brook's regular USB 101 offering, Introduction to Stony Brook, designed to
orient incoming students to the university. The Project WISE version emphasizes aspects of a *research* university, with weekly laboratory tours, faculty
talks, informal discussions, and readings. Wherever appropriate, these involve
women from diverse scientific disciplines and include considerations of social
and professional issues related to gender. The Project WISE sections are
offered by woman scientists and restricted to Project WISE students.

The second requirement is a two-semester college-level calculus course,
"which is the greatest single ticket to admission to and success in science and
engineering careers" or a more advanced mathematics class, and a science
course. To the extent possible, we enroll the women in the same sections of
their calculus and science courses so that they may form study groups and
work on problems cooperatively, aided by their junior mentors.

In the spring semester, the students also take Introduction to Research, a
three-credit course conceived by the working group especially for Project
WISE students. The course gives students direct research experience in a
physical, social, and life science, and in mathematics and engineering, and it
educates them about the definition and parameters of these various sciences.
Working in groups of five led by women faculty or advanced graduate

students, the Project WISE students rotate among different projects in much the same way the high school students do (though at a higher level). The approach adopted in all the projects emphasizes hands-on inquiry using appropriate tools and instrumentation, cooperative activity and experimental, negotiable discovery (Matyas & Malcom, 1991).

Once a month, the students get together with women faculty, graduate students, and researchers from Stony Brook, Brookhaven, and Cold Spring Harbor for an informal evening during which academic and industrial women scientists and engineers, including the students, give talks. As indicated, occasional sessions are attended by the high school girls. The evening sessions are ongoing; as the students advance through their 4 years at Stony Brook, they will be encouraged to take an increasingly active role in them, first by helping to plan some events, and second, as their own research progresses, by giving short presentations themselves.

Sophomore Year

In the second year, the students continue to take SEM courses in accordance with their academic interests. In addition, in the spring semester, they take a unique Project WISE course on the Social Dimensions of Science (three credits) in which they study policy and social issues arising in ongoing research being carried out by Stony Brook and Brookhaven researchers. The idea is to give the students insight into the political and social aspects of science and to make them aware that research is not an isolated event, limited to the laboratory, but rather it occurs within a larger social and political context that influences its operation. In conjunction with the course, the women will do readings, carry out literature searches, and gain experience using a research library, preparing abstracts, citing articles, and referencing papers. They will also give presentations or engage in active debate in which they advocate a position developed during the course.

To advance their research skills, the students will be urged to associate themselves with faculty and to begin to conduct research in a laboratory. The members of the Project WISE working group will play an active role in arranging for research placements. This has already begun to occur as students who participated in the pilot version of Project WISE and are now completing their sophomore year, are making research plans for their junior year, and we are busy identifying appropriate research opportunities for them.

In a new innovation, suggested by the students in the pilot project, in 1995–96, we will pair each second-year student with a first-year student in a "big sister–little sister" arrangement; the big sisters will advise their younger colleagues about courses, teachers, their research, negotiating Stony Brook's bureaucracy, and other aspects of Stony Brook life. In their role as big sisters, the second-year women will provide information and assist the new students in ways that faculty and even the junior mentors cannot. Equally important, by taking a leadership role, the second-year students will enhance their own self-confidence and develop a broader understanding of the social and educational milieu at Stony Brook than would be otherwise possible.

Summer

Stony Brook, Brookhaven, and Cold Spring Harbor all have summer undergraduate research programs. The Project WISE students will be informed of them and urged to apply to those that coincide with their interests. We have also been assisting the students in identifying and obtaining research apprenticeships at universities and research laboratories elsewhere. The Project WISE staff have developed an inventory of these programs, and members of the working group are matching the students to appropriate opportunities. In addition, we have had workshops on preparing a résumé and writing a proposal for these programs. Among the 45 first- and second-year Project WISE students in 1994–95, approximately half have obtained research placements for the summer, mostly at summer programs at universities and national laboratories not routinely associated with Project WISE. Most of the students will receive stipends and, in some cases, free room and board. A small number of students plan to work without pay with Stony Brook researchers.

Junior and Senior Years

Unless they are junior mentors, the students' continuing involvement in Project WISE is more informal than formal. In students' third year, their academic advisement will shift from the project to their major department, where a faculty member will assume responsibility for their guidance. A member of the Project WISE working group will assist them in identifying and choosing an academic advisor who will be helpful and whose interests overlap with the student's. Nevertheless, the students will be encouraged to maintain their relationships with their Project WISE advisor. In the same way, project faculty will urge the students to become actively involved in research and will assist them in locating a good research setting and supervisor. We presume that the network they will have established during the previous 2 years through their attendance at the Project WISE evening sessions will be particularly helpful in facilitating this process and directing them to appropriate researchers. Further, we hope that the acquaintances they have formed, combined with their interest in many of the talks, will spur the students to continue to come to the evening sessions and, eventually, to become presenters themselves. Their continuation will be the best test of Project WISE's efforts to create an ongoing community.

Advising/Mentoring

There are several aspects of the college component that must be emphasized. One is its intense advising–mentoring system. Every fall, Project WISE will offer three sections of its USB 101 course for the new students. The instructors serve as the initial academic advisor to the students in their class. After their first year, the students are given advisors, drawn from faculty associated with or sympathetic to Project WISE. In Year 3, they will be placed with an advisor in their major subject.

The students also benefit from a four-tiered mentoring system that includes the second-year "big sisters," who provide immediate advice and information; the junior mentors, who help them become integrated into the social and academic life of the university, especially in reference to their science and mathematics education; advanced women graduate students who direct the research projects developed for the Introduction to Research course and socialize with them at the evening sessions; and women scientists from Stony Brook, Brookhaven, and Cold Spring Harbor with whom they have frequent contact. The involvement of women scientists from Brookhaven is particularly valuable because it gives the students access to female mentors in disciplines such as physics, material sciences, and other engineering areas in which Stony Brook has only a small handful of women faculty. (There is only 1 woman among 58 faculty in the Physics Department, and only 3 women faculty in the entire College of Engineering.)

We have chosen to "layer" Project WISE with mentors at every level because mentoring has been found to have positive impact on women in their development as scientists (Matyas & Malcom, 1991). Prior to the start of the project each year, the junior mentors take part in an orientation and training session designed and carried out by faculty in women's studies. In addition, the associate director of women's studies and an advanced graduate student in SEM meet with the junior mentors biweekly to discuss mentoring issues that may arise. Within the Introduction to Research course, the women graduate students' formal responsibility is to direct the research groups; as active scientists themselves, they set the tone and provide instruction necessary for carrying out the project. Thus, by example, they enlarge the Project WISE students' perspectives on their own educational choices, and they serve as the next vital link between the research and broader social environments. Older and more advanced in their study than the junior mentors, the graduate students represent a succeeding step in the development of women scientists. At the same time, through their experience with the Project WISE students, the graduate students gain valuable insights into the factors influencing the young women's educational choices and into elements that dissuade women from continuing in SEM. This experience should encourage them to create an environment in their own classrooms and research settings that will address these elements. Finally, in addition to the USB instructor, the Project WISE participants come to know other women faculty and active scientists through their informal interactions at the numerous evening sessions and other Project WISE functions. We hope the students will develop special relationships with some of these scientists and that they will feel sufficiently comfortable to contact any of the women as they advance in their studies and as social and academic situations arise.

Evaluation

A second important aspect of Project WISE is its evaluation component. Because Project WISE is new and because we want to ensure its success, we have instituted an ongoing and comprehensive evaluation to assess what the project considers the three important performance measures for participating high school and college women: engagement, continuation, and skill development in SEM fields. We also are measuring the effectiveness of individual program segments and activities. As problems are identified, the project is being modified to address them. Project WISE has been benefiting from suggestions and input by all of its constituents, including the students, who, for the most part, appear as interested and committed to the project as the working-group members. Perhaps because the project is still in an infant stage, there is a tremendous feeling of good will and ownership among all those involved, and students and faculty are frequently putting forward thoughtful and positive suggestions for making improvements. Many of the students' ideas, such as the big sister–little sister plan and the workshops on resume and proposal writing have been implemented. The fact that they have seen their recommendations acted on seems to be encouraging the students to play an increasingly active role in shaping Project WISE as it matures. This kind of informal evaluation is valuable and will, we believe, enhance Project WISE.

The idea of creating an initiative such as Project WISE originated with a telephone call I received in fall 1992 from a high school teacher who directs a research program at a local school through which academically talented students conduct independent research. Their projects are routinely entered in regional and national competitions, such as the Westinghouse Talent Search Competition and the International Science and Engineering Fair. Approximately 60 students were involved in the program at the time, and most were conducting research with Stony Brook faculty. The teacher was calling to inquire whether I could assist her to obtain funds to support the students' work and to cover such expenses as transportation to the various competitions the students were required to enter. As she proceeded to describe her program, I was struck by two statistics she offered. First, among the 27 seniors who had recently submitted projects to the Westinghouse competition, only 6 were women, and 3 of the women were engaged in social science projects that required minimal quantitative skills. Second, in the 10th grade, when the students begin the research program, the gender balance is much more even, with only a slightly higher number of male students, suggesting a significant drop-out rate among the women.

Curious about these numbers, I began to do research on the gender gap and learned that women drop out of the SEM pipeline at an accelerated rate beginning around 7th grade and continuing through high school, college, and graduate study (Alper, 1993). Although approximately the same percentage of college-bound high school girls and boys take mathematics and science courses in the first few years of high school and the girls perform as well as boys (Alper, 1993), their level of engagement nevertheless seems to be lower. This is evident in their low representation in science clubs and in science and math contests. The boy to girl ratio for participation in the Westinghouse Science Competition in 1992 was 2 to 1. Thus, the situation at the local high school appeared typical. What was especially noteworthy to me were the factors frequently cited as leading to the women's withdrawal: insecurity and self-doubt about their ability to perform well, the highly competitive nature of their SEM classes, lack of encouragement, and the perception of scientists as unattractive people (Keith & Keith, 1989; Wellesley College Center for Research on Women, 1992). It is ironic to note that these factors were likely to be exacerbated in a program like the one at the local school that had preparation for, and success in, competitions at its core and that graded the students based on their participation at these competitions.

I think I was particularly concerned about the gender gap problem because of my own history. As a child and teenager, I had enjoyed mathematics and had entered college with the intent of becoming a math major. My math career ended, however, in my sophomore year when I was only one of four women enrolled in an integral calculus course. I had an instructor, a "macho" male faculty member, who refusing to learn my name, insisted on calling me "dimples," and who invariably brushed off my questions with a witticism. The incident that led me to leave math occurred one day when he responded to a question I had asked by remarking. "Oh, dimples, you don't need to know that. You are just going to get married one day." Although I was not an aggressive young woman, and feminism was not even a concept in the late 1950s, I nevertheless walked out of the classroom and decided to change my major to English. Although I proceeded to earn a PhD in English, I was never passionate about it, and eventually abandoned it for administration. There has always been a lingering interest in mathematics and a feeling that I should have stuck with it.

Thus, when the local high school teacher called, she inadvertently tapped into some deep frustrations and set off a chain of activities that led ultimately to the establishment of Project WISE. It was fortunate that her call also came at a time when, as associate dean for Arts and Sciences with special responsibility for creating or facilitating the creation of an interdisciplinary research and training program, I was in a position to do something.

My first step was to contact several female colleagues in SEM departments to see if they were interested in attending a meeting that would focus on the issue of engaging women in SEM. *Every* woman I called responded enthusiastically and suggested other colleagues who might want to join us. I also invited the high school teacher who had set the wheels in motion with her telephone call to me. Approximately 20 women attended our first meeting; most remained with the project as we continued to meet every week for about 2 hours, discussing broad issues and considering specific strategies. The meetings—which took place for most of the academic year—were congenial, enlightening, and often exciting, and they were defined by a sense of shared purpose as most of the women relayed stories of alienation and humiliation in the predominantly male world of the sciences and engineering. It is interesting to note that although most of the women were in SEM disciplines, and felt alone within their departments, few knew one another, pointing to the isolation that exists even among the female faculty. Nor was this feeling limited to Stony Brook women faculty. When colleagues at Brookhaven heard what we were doing, they expressed interest in joining us and on occasion came to our meetings (even though the drive from Brookhaven to Stony Brook takes about 45 minutes), because they too felt the need for this kind of effort and wanted to be part of it.

Our initial goal was very limited: to create some kind of informal supportive network for female undergraduates. However, the opportunity to do something on a larger, more programmatic scale occurred in the late fall when the National Science Foundation (NSF) issued a solicitation for proposals for "model" programs to encourage girls and women to continue their SEM education. The first-year program within the college component was developed in response to the NSF solicitation. Although there was general recognition among the faculty in our group that intervention was required at *all* levels of education—and the earlier, the better—we decided to focus on the transition from high school to college for several reasons: (a) We were aware that this is the period of "highest risk" in the SEM pipeline, when a high proportion of high-ability, college-bound women become disengaged or discontinue their study of these subjects (Green, 1989; Hewitt & Seymour, 1991; Madison & Hart, 1990; National Science Foundation, 1990); (b) although there are several programs on Long Island, including ones run by the AAUW and by Stony Brook's College of Engineering, directed at elementary and middle school girls, there were none in the region addressing this "bridge" period; (c) this emphasis builds on our strength as active researchers and teachers with whom the young women could interact regularly and become involved in the work we do; and (d) intervention programs at this critical point have been shown to work. Perhaps the most compelling factor, however, was the recognition among all the members of the group that it is in the first year of college that women (and all students) make educational choices that inevitably foreclose many future options for them, and that at least among Stony Brook women their choices did not seem to be including SEM. Although Stony Brook is known primarily for its strength in the physical sciences and mathematics, 1992 figures, for example, showed the following male to female ratio for majors:

- Math and applied math: 51 males, 26 females
- Chemistry: 32 males, 22 females
- Physics: 42 males, 7 females
- Earth and space science: 29 males, 13 females

Within the social sciences, where the gender distribution is more balanced, men dominated the more quantitative disciplines (economics: 146 males, 7 females; political science: 161 males, 94 females), whereas women were clustered in the nonquantitative courses. Further, although women were performing as well or better than men in basic college calculus and statistics courses and in introductory chemistry, they nevertheless tended to take only the minimum number of quantitative courses to satisfy either university distribution requirements or the requirements of their major. Clearly, reflecting national trends, Stony Brook was doing something wrong or, perhaps, more accurately, not doing something positive to motivate women.

When, 6 months later, the NSF issued a second call for proposals—this time for more systemic experimental initiatives—the working group decided to expand Project WISE to include the high school component. Because of our own inexperience with high school students, we sought to engage high school teachers and administrators as early as possible, and we also sought assistance from researchers and staff at Brookhaven and Cold Spring Harbor laboratories, both of which offer extensive educational programs for elementary and high school students. This involved numerous meetings and the slow process of building a coalition among these several participating units so that, more than providing a specific piece, each began have a real stake in the project. Having a stake was deemed necessary if each unit was going to commit itself to the effort and contribute necessary resources and staff time.

Although the initial tendencies were for the Stony Brook group to assert ownership (because it was the lead group) and the high school teachers to feel subordinate ("second class" was the way one teacher put it), as the project progressed, particularly the high school component phase, all the participants came to recognize that the diverse groups (Stony Brook faculty, laboratory researchers and staff, high school teachers and administrators) all had different expertise and interests and that the strength of the project depended on their varied contributions. This recognition came about gradually, as the project began to take shape and suggestions and ideas came in from all participants. As the 10th-grade research projects were being designed, for example, the teachers were constantly reminding the scientists of the level and extent of the students' knowledge and skills; when the projects were implemented, the teachers asked key questions to ensure that the students understood a concept or technique. The researchers increasingly have relied on the teachers to prepare the students for their experiments. A sense of collegiality also developed at occasional social events that have allowed all those involved to become acquainted with one another.

The involvement of Brookhaven National Laboratory has been particularly significant. In terms of coalition building, Brookhaven's Education Department staff has played a key role because its members had prior histories with both Stony Brook and several of the high schools. One education staff member is also a physics teacher at a participating high school, and his class served as a laboratory for assessment of many Project WISE ideas. At present, Brookhaven researchers are designing and conducting group research activities with the high school students; in return, Stony Brook faculty are doing the required evaluation of the projects. Brookhaven researchers also conceived of the Summer Science Adventure for the high school students, and they are currently participating in the development of the proposed college course on the Social Dimensions of Science. The Brookhaven Women in Science group is cooperating with Project WISE in our effort to identify and recruit promising college participants. Last year, for the first time, Brookhaven invited regional high schools to each nominate two outstanding young women scientists, 20 of whom were selected for Certificates of Recognition. Those selected were also awarded $1000 scholarships to Stony Brook to participate in Project WISE. This is going to become an annual event. The Brookhaven Women in Science group is also hosting a special event for all the high school students who were not chosen for Project WISE but who nevertheless have agreed to serve as "controls" in the evaluation.

At the university, Project WISE remains the "child" of all the members of the original working group as they are involved in every phase, particularly of the college component. Faculty members recruit students, provide academic advisement, supervise individual and group research, and develop and teach special courses. The original Project WISE group has expanded, and we now have a working group that includes a female faculty member from virtually every department in the sciences, mathematics, and engineering, as well as one male faculty from physics. Our advisory board has researchers from Brookhaven and Cold Spring Harbor Laboratories and a teacher from each participating high school. A researcher from Cold Spring Harbor Laboratory has just secured an NSF Visiting Fellowship to spend 1995–96 at Stony Brook, doing research and working closely with Project WISE students.

Throughout the academic year, the project hosts numerous social events, planned and attended by women faculty and researchers, graduate students, high school teachers, and Project WISE students. Aided by the NSF funds, we have established a Project WISE office, located in the Physics Building, which is fast becoming a focal point for a myriad of activities of which women undergraduate and graduate students with an interest in science can take advantage. Finally, although the original working group no longer meets weekly, we, and the larger group into which it has been subsumed, still meet at least twice a semester, and members serve on subcommittees and take responsibility for different tasks. Late one afternoon a few weeks ago, I sent out an electronic mail, requesting three volunteers to teach the Project WISE USB 101 sections in the fall semester; the following morning, when I accessed my electronic mail at about 9:30, I had already received six offers. This typifies the entire Project WISE operation.

Project WISE brings together priorities of all the coalition members by providing an attractive opportunity for talented young women and offering them simultaneously a high-quality academic experience and a supportive social environment. The courses and pedagogical approach it fosters can serve as models for other high school and undergraduate courses, as well as special programs at the two participating research laboratories. Project WISE is succeeding, I believe, because everyone involved—students, parents, high school administration and teachers, university faculty and administration, research laboratory scientists and administration and staff, and the local AAUW—believes, or rather *knows,* that they have helped to create it and they have something to gain from it: And they do! This is the first major point I would like to convey to others attempting a similar effort. Second, although there have been glitches and we have modified certain aspects of the project, the problems have been identified and readily addressed largely because of the open and collegial process to which the coalition members are committed and the common goal they all share. Every member knows that her input is valued and that suggestions are routinely considered and, where appropriate, adopted. This practice even relates to the students. When the 10th-grade girls, for example, recommended that the number of research projects future 10th graders carry out be reduced from four (each 2 days), as they were in the project's initial year, to three (each 3 days) so that they have more time think about and discuss the research, their suggestion was discussed, and it has been incorporated for next year. This has given the students, and others who also have introduced ideas, the sense of participation and ownership that we have been stressing throughout. Many recommendations emerge through the proj-

ect evaluation, which is ongoing. Because there is follow up, the students, teachers, faculty, and others take it seriously. Finally, by emphasizing the varied strengths and potential contributions of all the Project WISE constituents, we have minimized issues of "turf" and been able to maintain our programmatic focus.

Several members of the working group have suggested that we have achieved this state precisely because we are all women, concerned with the practical needs of creating and implementing the program; our extraordinary busy schedules and action orientation force us to focus on the immediate tasks and getting things done efficiently, instead of engaging in unnecessary meetings and extraneous discussion. I do not know if this assessment is correct, but I, and the others involved in Project WISE, generally consider the project as the most efficient and collegial undertaking in which we have been engaged at Stony Brook—and we believe this feeling of good will and enthusiasm is being passed on to the students. In a final analysis, the creation of this community of women scientists—which occurred as we developed the program—may be the most exciting, and beneficial, aspect of Project WISE, and it portends well for the project's future.

9

A Reason for Optimism

We want girls to question, observe, record, take things apart, look for patterns, make mistakes, try again, take risks, get messy, and—most important—to be skeptics and not take anything for granted. . . . We thought about the qualities of a scientist, such as the ability to generate questions, to wrestle with uncertainty and to tolerate creative chaos, to have the courage to experiment and learn from failure. We posited that girls' socialization in this culture inhibits the development of these very qualities. Our answer to this problem was scientific inquiry, an approach that encourages questioning, exploration, discovery, and risk-taking. (quoted in Travis, 1993, pp. 412–413)

–Ellen Wahl, director of programs at Girls, Inc.,
describing Operation SMART (Science, Math,
and Relevant Technology), a program designed
attract and nurture girls' interest in science with
the aim of helping girls to acquire an attitude
of scientific inquiry in everything they do

Wendy Katkin's description of Project WISE in the preceding chapter provides a reason for optimism regarding the outlook for women in science. Perhaps one day in the not-so-distant future, women will fondly recall their participation in programs such as Project WISE, crediting them with sparking a lifelong interest in science and instilling a set of values that fostered later success, much in the same way that men analogously ascribe those qualities to participation in Little League Baseball and Pop Warner Football.

It is important to note that Project WISE is not founded on the principle of attaining a "critical mass" of women scientists. Rather its focus is on nurturing the interest of young women in science through meaningful experience and developing an infrastructure of support networks, mentors, and role models. Attainment of a critical mass of women scientists is thus seen as a tangential outcome of the main goals of Project WISE, and neither the program's success, nor that of the individual participants, are predicated on it being achieved.

In addition to Project WISE and Operation SMART, there are several other highly successful programs to support the interest of girls and women in science. Among these is a project launched at Fort Lewis College in Colorado designed to shed the "nerdy" image associated with chemistry. James Mills, chair of the Chemistry Department, commented on the success of the program.

> We've tried to remove the barriers to success. We realized in the 1970s that too many entering first-year students saw our courses as the ones designed to weed them out of science, instead of giving them the foundation they needed to go on in science. . . . We still teach chemistry in a rigorous manner, we just make it more interesting for the students and the faculty. (Travis, 1993, p. 413)

The Fort Lewis College Chemistry Department offers courses in consumer chemistry, global change, science and society, writing, problems and puzzles, and natural products from plants. The practical relevance of these classes to the everyday lives of students appears to be exceptionally effective at attracting women students. Another advantage is that a substantial number of nonscience majors register for chemistry classes as electives, occasionally recruiting new students to the program and establishing chemistry as a dynamic component of the campus culture. Mills noted that the program's success can be largely attributed to their recruiting efforts, which have borrowed from a strategy used by college sports teams. All Fort Lewis applicants scoring high on the SAT or ACT mathematics section receive a personal letter from a faculty member, encouraging them to visit the school and the Chemistry Department, regardless of whether an interest in chemistry has been indicated or not. The track record of the program is spectacular. Fort Lewis College has double the percentage of chemistry majors compared with either

Colorado State University or the University of Colorado; 40% of its chemistry majors are women (Travis, 1993).

A resourceful project spearheaded by Douglas College at Rutgers University seeks to check the trend of isolation often experienced by women in science through rendering 24-hour peer support to a selected group of 100 undergraduate women. Participants in the project live together in the Bunting-Cobb Residence Hall, where they have access to an on-site computer lab, a science and engineering reference library, and a seminar program. Ten female science and engineering graduate students are funded by a special fellowship to reside in the dormitory and act as mentors and tutors. Entrance into the program is competitive and between 20 and 40 students are on a waiting list each year. Ellen F. Mappen, director of the project, commented on its goals.

> We started this whole program because a number of studies showed women were discouraged by the stereotype that science and engineering are not perceived as "Women's careers" and that being around male students seems to reinforce that idea. . . . I don't think we coddle our women students. What we do is provide them with a chance to excel in science, to gain confidence, to be motivated. We don't do their work, and they still have to interact with men. But we do let these students see themselves as professionals, as scientists, mathematicians, and engineers, and this is a message that women have a hard time getting in other environments. (Travis, 1993, p. 415)

The Women in Engineering Program at Purdue University, currently under the direction of Dr. Jane Daniels, has been in existence for more than 25 years—longer than any other formal program of its kind in the United States.

> The mission of the Women in Engineering Program is to increase the participation of women of all ethnic backgrounds in engineering through a comprehensive set of activities which provide encouragement to study engineering, support to successfully complete those studies, and open communication with alumnae and employers to sustain the program. (Daniels, 1994, p. 1)

The Women in Engineering Program is administered in conjunction with the Society of Women Engineers (SWE). At its core is a comprehensive three-pronged strategy of recruitment, retention, and relations with corporate and alumnae sponsors.

> The goals of our recruitment programs are first to help young women view engineering as a viable career choice and then to encourage them to consider Purdue University as an excellent educational preparation for that career. The programs are multi-faceted beginning as early as grade school and continuing through graduation from high school. The programs are diverse in nature so as to appeal to a wide variety of young women at different points in their decision-making process. Contacts with grade school and junior high girls focus on encouraging them to take math and science courses; involving them with female engineering students or practicing engineers who can serve as role models; and giving them some general career information about engineering. Programs aimed at high school students continue to emphasize these three areas but, in addition, give more specific information about fields and functions of engineering. Activities also begin to include information about Purdue University and the Schools of Engineering. The importance of parents, teachers, and counselors is recognized and wherever possible activities address these groups as well. (Daniels, 1994, p. 2)

Retention programs include a buddy system in which incoming students are paired with upperclass women, participate in weekly peer group meetings, and shadow an engineer in an actual job setting, take a women in engineering seminar (a one-credit course designed to give incoming women students an overview of the many vital roles women have taken in engineering and to help them feel supported in their choice of engineering as a career), participate in classroom climate and market-yourself workshops, make plant trips, win merit awards, participate in a leadership program, and participate in separate undergraduate and graduate mentoring programs. In addition, two floors of Amelia Earhart Hall are dedicated to women engineering students (approximately 90% are first-year students), offering a speaker series, tutoring service, plant trips, and other special programs responding to student input and interest (Daniels, 1994).

At the inception of the Women in Engineering Program in 1969, fewer than 1% of the engineering students enrolled at Purdue were women (47 out of 5016). The rate of degree completion for women in those days was less than half that of their male counterparts. Today, the picture has radically changed. Women represent more than half of the 1400 undergraduate engineering students at Purdue, and their rates of degree completion equal that of men.

The success of the Women in Engineering Program at Purdue is dramatically revealed by the fact that the undergraduate enrollment and degrees in engineering conferred at Purdue University have significantly outpaced the national trends (Daniels, 1994).

The Women in Science Program at the University of Michigan extends far beyond the campus boundaries. Director of the program, Cinda S. Davis commented, "We recognized early on that our undergraduate support program couldn't operate in a vacuum, but had to build on and even counteract the precollege experience" (Travis, 1993, p. 414). One of their precollege outreach programs is Summer-Science for Girls, which brings eighth-grade girls from all areas of the state to the Ann Arbor campus for 2 weeks of hands-on experience. The girls are engaged in engineering, natural resources, chemistry, physics, and space science projects, and they participate in seminars on ethics in science, computers, and careers. Science for Life is another precollege outreach program that situates high school girls as interns in the laboratories of women scientists for a 6-week period. Each intern conducts research on her own individual project and communicates her results in a research symposium at the end of the program.

The University of Michigan Women in Science Program is highly active on the campus as well. There is a particular focus on providing opportunities for undergraduate and graduate women to network and support each other. Graduate women attend special workshops on the sources of funding for scientific research and are coached on the techniques for writing a successful grant proposal. Undergraduate women participate in a seminar series exposing them to nontraditional careers in science and women who are successfully balancing scientific careers and motherhood. In addition, the Women in Science Program works closely with individual departments to create a more hospitable classroom environment for women science majors (Travis, 1993).

The highly successful and innovative Women in Science Program at Dartmouth College is a model project designed to create a level playing field for women aspiring for scientific careers. Carol Muller and Mary Pavone outline its history, mission, and specific components in the essay that follows.

The Women in
Science Project at Dartmouth:

One Campus Model for
Support and Systemic Change

_____ *Carol B. Muller and Mary L. Pavone* _____

Sitting in the Women in Science Project office, which is located in the Thayer School of Engineering, I overhear a student tour guide leading a group of parents and prospective students around the engineering school.

"And this is the Women in Science Project Office," she says, rounding the corner. "It may not mean a lot to you (the male high school students laugh) but it means a lot to me. . . ."

Origins

Early in 1990, a number of circumstances and events happened to converge, leading to the creation of the Women in Science Project. Nationally there had been a great deal of discussion about the need for science literacy among all Americans, and concern about the projected shortfalls of qualified entrants to the scientific and technical labor force. Dartmouth's president of 3 years, James O. Freedman, had made plain his goals to develop and encourage opportunities for students to engage in significant intellectual discovery, to achieve gender parity among students at the college, and to support and expand affirmative action. A 1989 study of longitudinal data from Dartmouth indicated that in graduating classes over the previous 5 years, among those students who had indicated an interest in studying science on their arrival at college, women were twice as likely as men to choose a major outside of the sciences. Even when all predicting factors for attrition—high school courses taken, SAT and achievement test scores, grades in introductory science courses—were held constant, there was still a statistically significant gender difference in retention rates. The percentage of Dartmouth seniors majoring in science had dropped to a new low of less than 20% of the class, and a dismal 12% of women students in the class had elected science majors. The National Science Foundation had just issued its newly revised RFP (Request for Proposal) for its Career Access Program, which sought to increase the number of women in science and engineering. Chemistry professor Karen Wetterhahn had just been appointed to serve a term as associate dean of the faculty responsible for the Science Division—and she was the first woman ever to serve in that position. She promptly announced that she had three major goals for her term, one of them being to work on increasing women's representation in the sciences. Then assistant dean at Dartmouth's Thayer School of Engineering, Carol Muller suggested they meet to develop a proposal for the National Science Foundation to fund a program for women in science and engineering. Muller's long-standing interest in gender issues in education and employment, including occupational segregation, had naturally turned to an interest in understanding and improving women's severe underrepresentation in science and engineering.

From that meeting, Muller and Wetterhahn's plans were laid out and tested with other members of the Dartmouth community. Slowly but surely the "architectural" plans for a major, comprehensive program began to take form. Goals and objectives were established: to encourage more women to pursue their interests in science and engineering, by (a) increasing the number of women majoring in science by at least 5% by the time the new incoming first-year class graduated, (b) increasing the number of women taking science courses, and (c) increasing the numbers of women going into scientific and technical careers. That summer, the 450 incoming women students in the class of 1994 were informed by letter that they would have an unusual opportunity to participate in the Women in Science Project at Dartmouth.

Dartmouth College is a private liberal arts university located in rural Hanover, New Hampshire. Founded in 1769 to educate Native American youths and others, it has grown during the course of its 226-year history to accommodate, during the 1994–95 academic year, 4283 undergraduates and 1170 graduate students in the professional schools of business administration, engineering, and medicine, and doctoral students in basic science departments. Once an all-male institution, it began admitting women in 1972. Dartmouth's students come from all 50 states in the United States and 75 other nations. Admission is highly selective; in the class of first-year undergraduates entering in 1995, 50% of students were women, 37% of the students were either valedictorians or salutatorians of their high school classes, and median SAT scores were 650 Verbal, 710 Math.

In designing the program, we drew on existing research and an assessment of student needs particular to the Dartmouth campus to shape the program. Findings about why women do not persist in science shaped our strategies for change. The old explanations of "lack of interest" or "lack of ability" just were not borne out by the facts.

A number of factors contribute to the low number of women studying and pursuing careers in the sciences. Early socialization in families, in schools, and in other media and institutions often leads to an internalized assumption that science is somehow less appropriate for girls and women than for boys and men.

Conversations with college women suggest that schoolgirls are still sometimes counseled to avoid science or scientific careers. A junior chemistry major who is heading for graduate school related an incident clearly recalled from her eighth-grade year:

> When I was in eighth grade, I had all A's in my math and science classes, so I wanted to take biology my freshman year of high school so that I could eventually take an advanced placement science my senior year. My guidance counselor (who was a woman) told me that she didn't think I was emotionally stable enough to take biology and so I should take freshman science instead. I highly doubt she told any of the boys in my class who had straight A's in math and science that they were not emotionally stable enough for an advanced class since emotional stability has absolutely nothing to do with ability. For her, even a girl who was one of the best students in the grade needed an added "emotional stability" in order to be able to hack a harder science class. The fact is she never discouraged me from taking any of the harder English, social studies or history classes, but only sciences.

Another Dartmouth woman was informed by her seventh-grade teacher, despite earning the highest grade in his seventh-grade general science class, that "Women aren't cut out for science; those strange estrogens make it impossible."

The pursuit of science may be perceived or portrayed as isolated, lonely, and incompatible with marriage and raising children. Because there are still comparatively few role models for women in science, some girls and women conclude that scientific pursuits are less appropriate for women. Though role models and mentors need not always be of the same gender, the lack of models who combine the roles of successful scientist and mother can be discouraging to aspiring women scientists.

It has also been suggested that because some girls' early socialization and education give them fewer opportunities to "tinker" and explore machines, equipment, and nature, they have less ease and confidence in experimental and laboratory work. Also, through adolescence, some girls are more likely to suffer from low self-esteem and more likely to internalize failure (Bower, 1991; Gilligan, Lyons, & Hammers, 1989), and are thus less apt to persist in an area in which they have not been particularly encouraged.

Coupled with the effects of socialization are active barriers to women in science in higher education and in careers. Overt, subtle, or inadvertent gender discrimination and lower expectations of teachers, peers, and supervisors may all contribute to a discouraging environment for women interested in science. An engineering sciences major wrote about her peers:

> I've been the butt of jokes that might have been serious, it's hard to tell. Jokes like, "You must be going to college to meet a successful guy" or "The only reason you're an engineer is because women are getting special treatment these days." It makes it hard sometimes to believe that I really am worthy of becoming an engineer.

Actual classroom experiences may also turn girls and women from the pursuit of science. One first-year woman noted, "In my experience men are more hostile when challenged by women than when challenged by other men, which is of great importance in male-dominated classrooms and labs." Bernice Sandler has written about how the "chilly climate" for women in some classrooms and workplaces discourages them from continuing in science (Sandler, 1991). Various research has shown that in group situations, including classrooms, women are more likely to be interrupted than men; people are more attentive when men speak; men are more likely to get more attention, praise, criticism, and feedback than women (Wellesley College Center for Research on Women, 1992). A math major, who is cognizant of males still dominating classroom dynamics, said,

> I know that the old men profs are intimidating, but I don't know whether they discourage equal participation on purpose or not. Sometimes it is just hard to go in to talk to a person you have so little in common with. Some of these old male profs are leftover from before coeducation. A lot [of them] remind us that they have been teaching here for decades, which whether they mean it or not, gives me the signal that they are pre-coeducation and they taught the good old boys. For me, knowing that makes a difference in how I approach a professor.

A senior in genetics and developmental biology observed covert discrimination operating in the classroom:

> It's more a matter of men being seen in a more favorable light in class discussion, because men are traditionally aggressive. If a woman becomes aggressive to make her point be heard (as she usually must do, since the tendency is often to ignore women) she is seen in a negative light because aggression is supposedly undesirable in women.

This woman goes on to say she has learned to modify her classroom participation style even though she does not always feel confident:

> I get nervous about discussion groups, because I've discovered that women who phrase their ideas in the form of a question posed to the professor, or state their ideas and raise their voice in a questioning inflection at the end of the sentence, are far more likely to meet with criticism from a professor than men, who tend to state their ideas firmly, as though they know they are right. I always felt awkward doing this, because I know I don't always have the right answer, and I often want to just offer a tentative answer (with a question mark at the end). I don't do it anymore, because my thoughts get shredded in front of the whole class. I have taken to being very firm in my answers, and I have noticed that I get a better response from profs.

Also, the extreme underrepresentation of women in some scientific fields and specialties makes them more likely to be viewed as tokens, seen in relationship to stereotypes about women, subject to greater scrutiny, and socially and professionally isolated (Kanter, 1977), all conditions that hinder their progress and discourage them from continuing to work in these fields.

Sheila Tobias (1992) has suggested that many of the dynamics of introductory science and math courses in college serve to discourage both women and men students from further study in the sciences. For some able and talented students, the competitive rather than cooperative nature of these classes; the lack of connections to history, philosophy, and applications; and the nature of homework, tests, and other assignments that lead to one right answer, often "found at the back of the book," make these courses dull, unappealing, unrealistic, uncreative, and uninspiring compared with other areas of study.

Though some of these factors may affect more girls and women than boys and men, none can be considered gender specific. Some students appear not to be affected by these phenomena and others may be unaware that their interests have been shaped by external factors. In designing Dartmouth's Women in Science Project, we intentionally incorporated a wide variety of retention strategies under the broad umbrella of the initiative. Solving the problem of women's underrepresentation in the sciences will not be easy, nor does it lend itself to one "quick-fix" solution. Women are not all alike; they leave the study of science for various reasons that differ from one individual to another. No one strategy will work for all. Because women leave the study of science for many of the same reasons as men do, we can anticipate the future extending effective strategies for retention to programs for all students.

Because decisions made during the first college year are crucial in determining whether a student will major in science, and because the proportion of interest in the sciences is highest during the first year of college, first-year women were the initial focus of the Women in Science Project. As an indication of the overall growth of initial interest in science, we found that 25% of the entering women in the class of 1994 were interested in science. Of the entering women in the class of 1998, 63% indicated some level of interest in science, math, or engineering. The entering class continues to be a major area of focus, though by its second year, the project expanded to include all interested students, undergraduate and graduate, in most of its activities and programs.

In addition to considering the reasons for women's underrepresentation in the sciences and engineering, we considered the needs of the women students on our particular campus. Academically, they already represent a rarefied group; remediation is rarely an issue, and certainly no more so for women than for men. But they did have needs that, if addressed, were likely to lead to improved retention in the sciences. These included information, role models, mentoring, encouragement and support, and a sense of community.

It is not surprising that 18-year-olds often lack information about opportunities available to those with scientific and technical backgrounds. Unless a parent or close relative is a scientist or engineer, the only professionals trained in science they are likely to meet growing up are their pediatricians, dentists, and science teachers. "L.A. Engineer" does not yet exist as a television show. We are often asked questions such as, "What can you do with a degree in math besides teach?" and, "What exactly do engineers do?" Helping students appreciate the vast array of interesting and rewarding professions that draw on science and engineering education often helps them see a goal worth working toward.

Role models are important, and not just one, but numerous role models are necessary. These are people who represent the wide variation of individuals who are active in scientific professions. With numerous role models, students are more apt to find someone whose characteristics and interests match their own, and less likely to generalize from a sample of one. For example, a student who talks with just one woman who tells her that scientific research careers are incompatible with marriage and family may make decisions for her future based on that subjective judgment. Another student who may have met the same scientist, but who also has met a number of married women scientists and scientists who are also mothers, may realize just how subjective such a statement may be.

Mentoring has been strongly identified as an effective way to retain women in nontraditional fields. Through an on-going relationship, mentors provide encouragement and support that is particularly important in counteracting the effects of small numbers and lack of a critical mass of individuals. Support and encouragement, which may also be provided by other mechanisms, give a woman student the sense that someone, or some organization, is invested in and cares about her success in her chosen field of endeavor.

A sense of community and belonging is also important to women in science, who may otherwise feel like outsiders because of their underrepresentation. A junior engineering major provided this anecdote:

> I had a conversation with a fellow student (male) in my engineering class over the summer. He and I were talking and I made a reference to a female friend of mine who was also an engineering major. I must have said something to the effect that he "must know her because there were so few women 'engines' majors in our class." He was shocked that I said something like that and asked if I really felt like there were hardly any women in our class. It made me think about how conscious I was about the lack of other women in my classes. He asked if it bothered me, and I realized it did. One of the things I find most intimidating is speaking up in a large lecture class. A lot of times I feel like I am somehow representing the female population of the class. In other words, if I ask a dumb question or get something wrong, it somehow reflects badly on my sex. Sort of proving that women don't belong in the field of engineering. A couple of other women who were listening in on the conversation said that they felt the same thing. The guy I was talking to didn't understand why it would be intimidating. I guess because he has never had to be conscious of being in the minority. . . . With smaller classes I don't mind it as much, possibly because it is not quite as intimidating in a smaller group.

Of course, it is not only women who benefit from information, role models, mentors, support and encouragement, and a sense of community. But given their relatively low numbers in the sciences and engineering, and a greater proclivity to internalize failure and attribute success to luck instead of hard work and talent, women in particular benefit from attention to these needs.

Program Expansion

What the project's cofounders agreed might work for Dartmouth's institutional setting was an overarching organizational approach—a comprehensive program—that would unite the separate resources of Arts and Sciences departments with the Thayer School of Engineering and the Dartmouth Medical School in this educational initiative. What could a campus-wide organizational structure offer? It was more likely to (a) gain the attention and support of top administrators because it served all undergraduate women; (b) make a cohesive presentation to those who would be asked to help fund and support this venture; (c) invest all of the science, engineering, and medical school faculty in helping with the retention effort; and (d) provide a good start to encouraging systemic reform by institutionalizing the program. Because students do not declare majors until the end of their second year, a campuswide program would also serve to (e) build community and identity during their initial years and not fragment small groups of women who were interested in various disciplines.

The needs identified in 1990 were translated into an umbrella of programs collectively known as the Women in Science Project (WISP). The internship and science seminar programs were launched in the fall of 1990 with funding assistance from several small industrial donations, some discretionary College funds, and the in-kind support of faculty using their own research grant money. Over the next 5 years, the original framework of envisioned programs was able to mature and expand with significant grant support from the National Science Foundation, other federal money, corporate and private donations, and multiyear grant support from the Alfred P. Sloan Foundation. During the second year of the project, Mary Pavone was hired as the first project director. Her background in science teaching, graduate research, engineering consulting, and project management was an appropriate mix for the challenge of creating a strong identifiable program.

What's Under the Umbrella?

Perhaps the primary innovation of the project, compared to other women in science, or women in engineering, programs that were developing across the country at the same time, was its cornerstone program: research internships for first-year women. A part-time, paid laboratory research internship fuels the high motivation that first-year women bring to college. It gives women credible, hands-on laboratory work and firsthand experience with scientific inquiry, and complements their introductory science and math classes. The close supervision and one-on-one work with faculty and others in the laboratory helps to demystify science and some of its stereotypes and sets up role models and potential mentor relationships for the interns. Stipends ensure the full participation of economically disadvantaged students. This is an innovative approach to undergraduate instruction in scientific research, which is usually reserved for upper-division science majors, most often seniors, and tends to be focused on preparation for graduate study.

The internships are conducted under the direction of faculty members and other scientists, including the arts and sciences departments of biological sciences, chemistry, earth science, engineering sciences, environmental studies, geography, mathematics and computer science, psychology,[1] and physics and astronomy, the medical school's departments of anesthesiology, biochemistry, medicine, microbiology, radiation oncology, pathology, pediatrics, pharmacology and toxicology, physiology, and psychiatry, the Veterans Administration Research Center, the U.S. Army Cold Regions Research and Engineering Laboratory (CRREL), and the local Montshire Museum of Science. In 5 year's time, 140 faculty and researchers connected with Dartmouth have sponsored 360 first-year interns. Many of these faculty stay in contact with students as long-term mentors and invite students to return to work in their laboratories in later years. Some students use the familiarity and confidence gained from one laboratory experience to explore other scientific disciplines their next year.

A fascinating gender phenomenon was observed in 1995 within the Presidential Scholars Program and Senior Honors Thesis Program, both of which are selective research opportunities open to juniors and seniors. For the first time, equal numbers of upperclass men and women had undertaken scientific research in both of these academically intense programs. In no small part, we think that early hands-on research experience contributed to an increase in women's self-confidence and desire to continue in research and has provided them with access to faculty they would not otherwise meet.

Research interns are expected to work 10 hours per week for the winter and spring academic terms (quarters), and the internships offer the opportunity for substantive, thematic employment in lieu of work study or other part-time jobs in the dining hall, library, or elsewhere on campus. Approximately 40% of the student body receives some amount of financial aid.

As a culminating experience, interns participate in a science poster symposium at the conclusion of their internship, developing a poster representing their work, and informally addressing questions from interested students, faculty, and others attending the symposium.

Because not all students have the time or inclination to invest 10 hours a week in an internship nor are all the problems that contribute to the underrepresentation of women addressed by internships, the Women in Science Project has other components. A comprehensive or umbrella approach to creating the project allows students to get involved in programs based on their own needs and recognizes that their needs will likely change over time. Male students are invited to participate in all programs other than the first-year internships. These other programs include a peer mentoring program, a women-tutored science study room, special science seminars, panel discussions, lunch conversations with women scientists and engineers, and visits to industrial sites.

The peer mentoring program actually began as a student-generated idea to satisfy the need for more connections between upperclass women science majors and first-year women who were interested in science. Because of Dartmouth's unique year-round operation, the undergraduate classes do not have the opportunity to interact very much nor know each other in ways that establish mutually beneficial relationships between older and younger students. This 3-year-old program has experienced growing success in making positive connections; during 1995, nearly half of the women in the class of 1998 requested an upperclass peer mentor in an area of science of interest to them. The volunteer peer mentors offer the insight of someone who has experienced the courses, concerns, and particular challenges typically faced in the introductory year. There are mutual benefits to be gained by both mentors and mentees. One woman noted her "culture shock" after arriving at Dartmouth from an all-female, private high school and finding out that there would be few women teaching her. She later commented that the WISP peer mentor program was her greatest aid in meeting upperclass, science-oriented women who could be her role models. Her assigned peer mentor was a math major, and though her own interests were in biology, she still looks to her mentor for answers and encouragement. Meanwhile, this particular student, like many others who found themselves enriched as mentees, offer their services in the following years as mentors to new students.

The women-tutored study room is another young program with multiple benefits. Four nights a week, upperclass women provide free tutoring and collaborative study focusing primarily on introductory science and math classes. This program supplements the organized study groups and private tutors that are also available through the College's Academic Skills Center. WISP specifically employs women in science as tutors. The tutors' understanding and confidence in the material are enhanced by their tutoring, and plus they provide role models for students who are seeking help and encouragement of their own. As a supplement to other campus tutor assistance where, at times, there may be only male tutors available, some women find working with another woman on problem sets or class material much more comfortable and not as intimidating as working with male tutors who are perceived by some to be "amazing in science." WISP tutors enjoy their roles in helping students develop confidence as well as mastery of the material. In giving feedback on the program, one of the tutors related, "Helping [women] get over this anxiety about not being good enough, or smart enough, was really important to me." Both men and women frequent the science study room for this assistance.

Each term inspiring women scientists and engineers are invited to Dartmouth to speak to Dartmouth students. Sometimes the best conversations are those that occur during informal sessions, perhaps over lunch or a pizza dinner, where these successful women share stories of their own career paths, the challenges they have met and how they were surmounted, and candid accounts about how they have combined their scientific careers with marriage and families. This comment came from a student who was writing her impressions in the newsletter to share with others after attending a visiting women scientist luncheon: "As a '96 attending my first WISP event, it was very encouraging to hear Dr. Jemison say that she did not have every detail of her education and career planned ahead of time." Notable speakers for the Women in Science Project have included biochemist Lucile Smith, AIDS researcher Phyllis Kanki, astronaut and physician Mae Jemison, MacArthur award–winning chemist Jacqueline Barton, engineering dean Eleanor Baum, Kenyan environmentalist Wangari Maathai, and many others. Indicative of the collaborative spirit of the Dartmouth community and the broad acceptance WISP enjoys on campus, it is common for other departments bringing visiting lecturers to campus to share their visitors with WISP students.

Occasionally, WISP sponsors site visits to local and regional science and engineering firms. These special opportunities expand women's understanding of how science is conducted outside of academia. Site visits allow students to see technology applied in the workplace, recognize the important role of communications within technology, and see how scientists are integrated into businesses and industry. Students are strongly encouraged to seek preprofessional experiences during their off-residence terms from campus to further explore research, government, or industrial opportunities before making decisions that would eliminate these possibilities.

Not all skills for future scientists are taught in the science classroom. WISP offers various workshops, panels, and seminars that inform students about career opportunities, the process of seeking preprofessional experiences, and the development of personal skills. Some programs are cosponsored with other campus offices, such as Career Services, the Academic Skills Center, or the Women's Resource Center, to accomplish mutual objectives.

A WISP newsletter is distributed every 2 weeks via electronic mail to all participants and numerous faculty and administrators around the campus. Dartmouth's BlitzMail system connects everyone on campus electronically. The newsletter serves as the figurative "glue" for the project, reminding all of the project's existence and goals and featuring notices of colloquia, campus activities and programs related to science, opportunities for internships, scholarships, and profiles of women faculty and students in the sciences. The newsletter is written and disseminated by a paid student administrative intern for the project with guidance provided by the director. Quite intentionally, many student "voices" are published in the newsletter, giving their reactions to and support of WISP programs they have attended and passing along their wisdom and experiences to their peers. By 1995, nearly 1000 undergraduate women were receiving the newsletter. For many, this electronic connection serves as their reminder that there is a growing community of women pursuing science at Dartmouth. The persona of WISP as supportive, inclusive, and welcoming is conveyed to all through this publication and its contents.

Faculty Development and
Cultural Change

Many efforts designed to encourage greater participation of women and minorities in science and engineering are primarily "band-aid" efforts that address the symptoms but not the roots of the problem. There is a growing contingent who feel that we need to look beyond providing women students the tools to "survive" in an environment that fails to adequately support and encourage them. Until we begin to restructure the organizations most involved—schools, universities, corporations, and other institutions—to change organizational culture, beliefs and behaviors, incentive and reward systems, we will not be creating long-lasting change.[2]

In contemplating change in an institution of higher education, we realized that it was essential to involve the faculty, as well as others. The faculty has both the opportunity to create change, both in policy and in the actual delivery of education, and also the ability to thwart and actively resist change. By enlisting faculty members directly in providing retention efforts, through their supervision of students involved in research internships and involvement in other activities, they are likely to learn more about and appreciate more fully the experiences of women students. Like most sensible professionals, faculty members "do not replace strongly held views and behavior patterns in response to fiat or the latest vogue; instead, they respond to developing sentiment among respected colleagues, to incentives that reward serious efforts to explore new possibilities, and to the positive feedback that may come from trying out new ideas from time to time." (Reforming Education, 1989, p. 154).[3] We have already found that some science faculty members who were initially skeptical that first-year students could be involved in any meaningful way in research projects have, through talking with their own colleagues and observing their behavior, found ways to involve first-year students in research. A few others have confessed to us their surprise in finding the Women in Science Project's success in encouraging women students in science corroborated in direct conversation with students.

In the project's fourth year, 1993–94, a major grant from the Alfred P. Sloan Foundation enabled us to expand faculty development activities associated with the project. Regular faculty seminars, held twice each academic quarter, focus on science teaching, including current innovations in teaching on our own campus, results of studies of attrition and retention in the sciences, gender issues in the classroom, student perspectives on teaching, and issues related to minority underrepresentation in the sciences. In most cases, these seminars have provided an unusual opportunity for faculty in the sciences to discuss teaching and to do so across departments. Last summer, we launched the first of a series of summer institutes for faculty focusing on science teaching, retreats that allow the faculty to explore and discuss issues related to science teaching with greater depth and thoroughness, leading to action plans for the future. Small grants are available to faculty for curricular innovation. Through these programs, the institution begins to amplify its interest in effective teaching, adding, albeit modestly, to the incentive and reward structure for faculty to encourage innovation and improvement in teaching science.

Some Results to Date

How well is this comprehensive 5-year-old program working? The Women in Science Project has grown in each year of its existence, in participation of faculty and students, in program activities, and in supporting resources. In the first year, 115 first-year women (25% of the women in the class of 1994) signed up to participate in the project's activities; 45 of these worked as research interns. Of this first intern cohort, 60% became science majors. Nearly half of the science faculty offered to supervise interns, many using their own research funds to pay the students. Four years later, the original goal of increasing the number of women science majors by 5% had been exceeded. The class of 1994 graduated nearly 100 women science majors, or 21% of the female senior class. Over the course of 5 years, student participation has grown to 1000 students receiving the newsletter every 2 weeks, 60% of the incoming women in each class interested in participating in programs, approximately 100 research internships offered to first-year students each year, and about 250 first-year students paired with older peer mentors. At least 160 faculty are active in some aspect of the project including faculty seminars and the faculty teaching institute.

The percentage of women selecting science majors has grown, even as the total number of students majoring in science has increased (men and women) and the number of women in each entering class has grown in the past 5 years. This year, 42% of the students graduating with science majors are women. In engineering, which is counted as one of the undergraduate science majors, 24% of senior majors are women and that percentage is projected to climb to 26% of the engineering majors who will graduate in 1996, both in advance of the national average of 18%, and a considerable increase from the 15% of women engineering majors in 1990.

It appears that our strategy of linking a series of programs under a major, visible umbrella has been successful. Even students who do not actively participate in many programs report that they feel a strong sense of institutional support just because of the project's presence on campus. Some participants have noted that project activities were clearly instrumental in affecting their choice of a major:

> I would say it made a huge difference in my deciding to study and even major in science here. Before I came, I was definitely not attracted to math and science because of unappealing high school math and science courses. I had no plans to do anything other than fulfill the minimum requirements in science here. I became interested in taking an earth science course in the fall, however, and received an

internship for the winter and spring terms. Because of my experiences in my internship and my classes, I am now planning to be a science major and also to pursue it for a career.

Although the project was designed to address retention of women in science, recent program evaluation suggests that some women are selecting Dartmouth as the college of their choice because of the presence of the Women in Science Project (Cunningham, 1994).

External evaluations of the Women in Science Project have shown that within the research internships, mentoring was often the most valuable aspect of an intern's experience (Horizon Research, 1993). As one intern commented,

> The days I loved the most were not necessarily the times that a lot was accomplished—because each day something happened from which I learned—but the days I was working with Professor Gibson. It was working with another person in a field that interested me that really satisfied all my needs.

Interns particularly appreciate their role as a part of the team within a laboratory and feeling their work is important. Although most students find their internship experience stressful at first, as they become familiar with their work, their confidence increases. One of the class of 1998 interns said,

> I am personally very grateful for my WISP internship this term. Honestly, I think I would have given up on the sciences and research after this term because of my horrendous experiences in chem. But being able to go into a real lab to do real research (and be able to do it alongside real scientists and understand what I am doing) has made me see the light at the end of the tunnel. Science is about learning through both failure and success. No one gets it right the first time around.

Between 50 to 60% of all first-year interns have declared science majors at the end of their sophomore years. Another "hidden" layer of students—hidden in the sense that we are not easily able to track them within the Dartmouth system—continue to pursue science classes in a premed curriculum that accommodates nonscience majors.

Other findings have reinforced the likely benefit and value of a model project such as the Women in Science Project. A 1991 study that examined efforts made by U.S. institutions to increase the participation of women in science suggested there are too few of these efforts and that the absence of a "nurturing" environment leads many students to feel that no one cares about whether or not they pursue studies in these areas (Matyas & Malcom, 1991).

Another report issued in the same year by the National Academy Press (1991) suggested that institutions must shift attention from recruitment to retention. The National Research Council convened a conference to assess effective programs in retaining women in science and engineering in 1991, and conferees specifically recommended that institutions provide early, hands-on research experience, create a network of faculty and student mentors, arrange visits with technical professionals outside academia, and offer financial aid packages that enable students to spend their time on laboratory work rather than on part-time jobs outside the institution (Continuing Shortage of Women, 1991). All of these strategies are reflected in our project's design.

Future Issues

What issues face the Women in Science Project, now and in the future? An ongoing issue is that of adequately educating both male and female students, and faculty, to the concept of the "unlevel playing field" that still remains for women pursuing the sciences. We find that the undergraduate population, particularly in their early years, has disparate views and generally a minimal understanding about the issues of gender equity in the sciences, the rationale for the inequities, and the role that covert discrimination and subtle discouragements can play in affecting women's lives, and hence, the need for the specific benefits provided through WISP programs. Although male students are invited to participate in all programs except for the internships, and a few do participate, it is the structured first-year research opportunity for women that has caused the most resentment among male students. The male backlash is unfortunately directed at their female peers, some of whom "feel bad for the men who do not have this opportunity," or hypocritical that they are the beneficiaries but not their male friends.[4] There are faculty who readily admit that the system has traditionally existed as a "men in science" organization all along, with professors informally inviting the best performing and most articulate students (usually male) into their laboratories to join them in research endeavors or to hold after-class academic conversations that encourage those students to further pursue their interests. Role models and mentoring relationships can grow out of these opportunities. The opportunities have existed, and still do exist, for enterprising males seeking early exposure to research and mentoring connections. For upperclass men and women at Dartmouth there are a number of structured research programs as well as unstructured opportunities that students can seek and develop on their own. It is the immediacy of the comparisons being made between first-year men and women that appears to create this alleged bias against men—conjuring up the image of schoolchildren who have been told to always share their toys and cookies equally. One woman's rationale, perhaps a bit naive, was,

> I don't see why they [the internships] should not be available [to men]. It seems like everyone should start on an equal basis, and I think it doesn't seem fair to limit, to keep men out of these opportunities, just because of the assumption that later in life they're going to have so many more opportunities than women. I think that the goal should be to make things even every where, and even if it is not [equal] later on, I think that it should be even now. (Horizon Research, 1993)

In program evaluations of both faculty and interns there are divided opinions on this issue, with no clear majority sentiment at this time. Perhaps most telling of women's attitude is that Horizon Research found there to be stronger agreement among interns with the statement, "My male friends think that WISP internships should be available to males as well as to females" than the statement "Even though the number of internships is limited, I think they should be available to males as well as females" (Horizon Research, 1993).

Certainly we are interested in maintaining the momentum established at Dartmouth, staying responsive to student needs and maintaining the vital participation and partnership from faculty and the college administration. We recognize the importance of tracking project outcomes and evaluating our programs and their effects on participants. Long-range planning and project funding are also issues with which we stay involved. Project dissemination and learning from others is an ongoing effort through reports, conferences, presentations, electronic media, advisory committees, and individual conversations. Sharing advice, encouragement, and advocacy is an indispensable part of being an agent of change.

What does the Women in Science Project offer for those bright and academically talented women who come to Dartmouth interested in science? They can choose from a comprehensive array of programs designed to give them mentors, role models, skills, information, hands-on experience, connections, support, and community. A graduating senior in engineering sciences offered her "famous last words" to others in the May WISP newsletter: "I have definitely felt a lot of support here at Dartmouth for women in science, and I would not have stuck with it had I not been so encouraged." The pathways beyond Dartmouth need to be welcoming and supportive as well to retain this woman, and all women, in science.

It is my sincere hope that the two programs detailed in this volume—the Women in Science Project at Dartmouth College and Project WISE at SUNY-Stony Brook—will serve as models for other institutions serious about addressing the needs and challenges faced by women in science. Both are dynamic, highly innovative programs that regularly take the pulse of student participants and adapt accordingly.

Although Muller and Pavone accent the preceding essay with student insight, it is specific to certain points that they are making. To complement these perspectives, it would be informative to gain a picture of the overall college experience among selected participants in the Women in Science Project at Dartmouth. Such an opportunity was serendipitously afforded me when two women taking part in the program autonomously answered the general call for papers that I circulated through several electronic mail lists, and subsequently contributed essays. Thus, neither woman was recruited through the Dartmouth Women in Science Project to participate in this project. On the contrary, it was in response to receiving essays from these two women that I contacted Pavone and Muller and invited them to provide a detailed description of the Women in Science Project.

It is important to note that the two essays that follow are not contributed by women speaking *for* the Women in Science Project at Dartmouth College. Instead, they are contributions speaking *about* their encounters with the program within the context of their overall college experience. Neither participant paints a utopian picture. However, this is not the objective of the project at Dartmouth. Rather it is to create a level playing field for women in science. Although each woman appears to be fully aware of the additional challenges and boundaries to success that women often face in establishing a scientific career, both are confident, optimistic, have a clear sense of their capabilities and talents, and carry a set of strategies for transcending any obstacles they may confront along the way. Again, this does not mean that the Dartmouth environment is ideal for women pursuing science and engineering degrees because of the Women in Science Project. There is still much work to be done. A case in point is that, despite existence of the program, Michelle Montejo outlines a situation in which a Dartmouth faculty member advised her that pursuing a doctorate in biochemistry would not be conducive to marriage and a family—council that she cites as strongly influencing her decision to aspire to a career in medicine. Nevertheless, perhaps the best indication of the success of the project at Dartmouth College in supporting women students on the road to success in scientific careers is to compare the optimistic tone of the two essays that follow to several others appearing in this volume.

From Eden to the Seashore

_____ *Michele Montejo* _____

The day I realized that every person's life is scientifically oriented in some way or another was also the day that my interest in science became something more than simply wondering why the sky was blue. My epiphany came on a characteristic Miami summer day, where even at the crack of dawn it is already hot and humid. Perhaps I was anxious that morning, perhaps a little nervous. It was my first day of summer school, where I had voluntarily enrolled to take an honors course in high school biology.

I found a seat among the other confused faces at a black granite desk. After some introductory remarks, the instructor took up a piece of chalk, and asked a very simple question.

"How many of you are scientists?"

That was it! No explanation; no indication of what a good answer might entail. He just left the class hanging. I suppose that everyone was contemplating something during those few seemingly eternal moments because not one student was gutsy enough to raise her or his hand. Slowly, though, a few bold hands poked out above the sea of heads in the room, uncertain of what to expect from such an audacious response. Jealously afraid that I might be the only student who did not qualify as a scientist, I began to think about the question and about the work of a scientist. I soon realized that perhaps I, too, was curious in my nature, continually seeking solutions to the riddles of life—so yes, I too was a scientist. As I impishly raised my hand, and was greeted by an explanation from the teacher about the purpose of the question, my interest in science increased tenfold. Only then did I realize that science is the foundation for everything, and I decided right then and there that I would someday become a professional scientist.

Okay, okay. So maybe my fond memory of the experience has embellished the facts to some degree. Life is rarely that poetic. But now, with a handful of meaningful scientific experiences behind me, I am a sophomore at Dartmouth College in New Hampshire studying chemistry and planning to attend medical school. And, although the significance of my little anecdote has become exaggerated somewhat over the years, it is true that along the way I always have referred back to that question our biology teacher had challenged the class with at such a vulnerable time. It is true, also, that this question lit the candle of scientific thought in my heretofore chaotic and unenlightened consciousness.

My first hands-on laboratory experience came in the 11th grade, when I applied to participate in a program called Community Laboratory Research. Students were matched with local researchers based on their responses to a general questionnaire. I was assigned to conduct my research project at the Miami Museum of Science and Wildlife Center. Confounded by all of the possibilities, I wanted to begin every project with which my director tempted me. However, in the end, I chose to initiate a project with the goal of establishing baseline parameters for the blood serum chemistry of bald eagles and other birds of prey, both captive and wild. These data could then be used in the diagnoses of injured birds of prey and to determine whether or not a bird is fit enough to be released into the wild. I continued this research for 2 years, and, although it was not the most technical of laboratories, I learned a great deal about laboratory procedures and data analysis.

Bolstered by my new experiences and continually seeking more, I left for Dartmouth College, a private, liberal arts college with an undergraduate enrollment of approximately 3,800, located in Hanover, New Hampshire. Maybe Dartmouth, being a liberal arts college, is not renowned as a "science" school, but I have, nevertheless, found taking science courses there to be a very fulfilling experience. At first, I was hesitant about attending a school where I would be forced to concentrate so much effort into classes that would have nothing to do with my major. But now this is perhaps what I like most about Dartmouth, for in only a year I have had the opportunity to translate Cicero's speeches against Catiline, read *Paradise Lost* from cover to cover, study the presence of American landscapes in Thomas Cole's paintings, and learn about anorexia nervosa as a culture-bound syndrome. All of this while I continued to hone my chemistry skills.

Overall, I find the atmosphere at Dartmouth to be pleasant. For one thing, I do not think that there is the level of competitiveness that exists at other schools. This is not to say that the students lack a spirit of competition, however, but that we, in general, approach schoolwork with a more relaxed attitude that puts cooperation first. What I think makes the school most comfortable, though, is the amiable relationship between the students and the faculty. Questions and debates are encouraged in the classroom, and the professors almost always honor students' ideas with an open mind.

One other aspect that makes Dartmouth a comfortable school is the fact that I have never been made to feel like I was a woman on a male campus. This was slightly surprising for me because I had always heard that Dartmouth was the utmost of chauvinism, dominated by the "frat boy," football jock mentality, such as depicted in the movie *Animal House,* which flourishes on degrading women. I was quick to learn that this was simply a stereotype and that men generally treated women as their equals.

I assumed that this equality should trickle down to the individual departments at Dartmouth. A little research into the Chemistry Department, however, soon proved me partially wrong. With a male to female student ratio of roughly 67 to 42[5] and a male to female faculty ratio of 17 to 2,[6] the Chemistry Department seems to be further away from equality, at least in number, than I expected.

In other "hard" sciences such as biology and physics, the numbers are similarly disappointing. In the Biology Department, for example, the male to female faculty ratio is about 28 to 3, and in the Physics Department the ratio is 11 to 1.[7] Aside from this, however, it is not as though women tend to hold inferior positions to men, for I do not see a concentration of women in entry-level positions, nor are there any faculty levels where female representation is absent. Rather, women are simply underrepresented at all levels of faculty.

At this point, it would be quite simple, and probably expected, for me to jump up on my soapbox and deliver a short feminist dissertation, criticizing the establishment and the men who run it. But I guess that I hold some rather unorthodox[8] views on the subject. Some may say that it is just a lack of experience that causes me to think this way; others may say that I am naive, but I suppose that until something drastic happens to change my mind, I will never feel subordinate to my male counterparts.

It is not as though I have never been part of a female minority, for there have been plenty of occasions. Whereas the two chemistry classes that I have taken at Dartmouth have had reasonably even distribution of females and males, my physics class was definitely tipped in favor of the men. Even in high school, I witnessed the gross underrepresentation of women in the "hard" sciences. In my advanced placement physics class, for example, I was one of only 2 women in a class of about 20 students.

Nevertheless, this inequality in numbers has never made me feel uneasy. I do not feel that I have been treated any differently than my male classmates, nor have I been in a position where I felt degraded because I am a woman. Perhaps I am being too conservative, perhaps I am simply an anomaly in a world of ever-changing roles. I am sure that plenty of Dartmouth women would disagree, vehemently, with my previous statement about not feeling like a woman on a male campus. I have heard all of the horror stories. I know about the daily injustices toward women. I have seen all of the statistics on sexual abuse and harassment. I have often read about the salary disparities between men and women. And I sympathize from the bottom of my heart, I really do. But as ruthless and apathetic as I may seem, I do not think that I will ever truly feel the agitation, the anger, the raising of my consciousness, unless I become a victim myself.

Please do not misinterpret this statement. I certainly *do not* wish to become a victim and am perfectly content to remain on friendly and peaceable terms with my male colleagues as long as I possibly can. In the next couple of years, as I aspire for a career in the sciences, I plan to rely heavily on the self-confidence that leads a quiet and unobtrusive life deep within my soul. And, as long as I remain strong, I know that I will be less vulnerable to injustice, more viable to compete with men, better able to change the things I dislike, and more at ease with myself. I can only hope that my self-confidence will somehow keep me sufficiently strong—enough, that is, to prevent me from becoming an embittered victim of society's imbalances.

I often wonder if I am traversing through life with tunnel vision, because I seem to be blind to instances where other women have been openly mis-treated at Dartmouth. I am sure that there have been several cases in which men and women have been treated unequally or judged under separate sets of criteria by the faculty or by their peers, but I do not recall witnessing any, nor have I been on the receiving end of such subjugation.

It is ironic that there is one particular instance in which I see men being treated unfairly. There is an organization at Dartmouth called the Women in Science Project, affectionately referred to as WISP. Among other things, this program is responsible for arranging mentors for the incoming first-year women interested in science, bringing speakers to the school, setting up study rooms, and planning for the annual egg drop contest. The most memorable and meaningful part of WISP, however, is that each year it matches first-year women with researchers from a variety of scientific fields. After an application and interviewing process, the student, if selected, is ready to begin her paid internship. It is a special experience, and the program is one that is definitely unique to the school.

Nevertheless, I have heard several first-year male students complain about the lack of a MISP program. Why should women be fed research opportunities on a silver platter and men be left wandering from door to door in search of scraps? I can never find an argument to counter their complaints, except for, "Well, if you don't think it is right, why don't you start your own program?!" I know full well, too, that this is not the kind of answer they want, for it does not even satisfy me. It dodges the question and never explains why women, in their pursuit of equality, rely on an organization that, by its definition, implies that a woman is unable to do anything for herself. Yet I do not hesitate to take advantage of the resources offered to me by WISP.

It is through this program, in fact, that I came to work in Sudikoff Laboratories for Computer Science. I do not know what compelled me to seek an internship there: At the time, I knew next to nothing about computers. My work at Sudikoff, however, has been a learning experience—one that has been both gratifying and frustrating. I was one of six first-year women to obtain an internship working in the computer laboratory. Our mission: to create a multimedia "kit" that would attract women and minorities to the fields of computer science and computer engineering. Still in the rough stages, our project is part of a new wave of technology that permits personal research to be done more efficiently simply by using a computer and software to access information. At first I must admit I was pretty frustrated, mostly because I started a little later than the rest of the team and also because I felt my computer skills were lacking. Looking back, though, I am happy that I got a job outside of the field of my major, and even more happy that I stuck with it, for I learned a great deal about computers, about working within a group, and about how to put my creative talents to work.

It is perplexing to me why more women do not follow through in the "hard" sciences. The lack of women faculty in such areas as chemistry, physics, and biology is clearly evidence of this. I tend to consider a career in medicine to be a departure from the "hard" sciences. A medical doctor is usually not, after all, involved in research or teaching undergraduates. I specifically remember one occasion when I was discouraged from entering the "pure" sciences. However, this may have been some of the most valuable advice I have ever been given. It came at a time when I was trying desperately to decide whether I wanted to go to medical school or whether I wanted to obtain a PhD in biochemistry and spend my life in research. On learning of my dilemma, one woman professor at Dartmouth was quick to tell me her story and about all of the drawbacks and obstacles that I would face if I decided to pursue a career in biochemistry. What I heard was certainly disconcerting, on the one hand, but on the other, it made me become more enthusiastic about studying medicine. I think that her story goes a long way in explaining the underrepresentation of women in "hard" science careers.

She informed me that scientific research is not conducive to having children and that medicine, rather, was a much more flexible career when it came to establishing a family. She added that it is very difficult and requires many years for a researcher to secure a position as head of a laboratory, and that medical doctors have a much higher rate of succeeding. Finally, she pointed out that the earning potential of a medical doctor is much higher than that of a researcher. I thought her arguments were pretty convincing, so much so that I decided at that precise moment to set my sights on medical school and aspire to become a doctor of medicine.

It is interesting how much our culture lives by stereotypes. Once adopted, a stereotype dictates how we see the members of our society and what we expect of them. In the world of science, it is an unwritten expectation that men are more likely to become surgeons, engineers, mathematicians, and computer scientists. Women, on the other hand, supposedly make better pediatricians, biologists, and psychiatrists. Although this is quite a stride from the old days of women nurses and men doctors, it is still a shame that members of both gender often feel the need to adhere to such preconceived notions.

I hope to overcome one of these stereotypes by becoming a surgeon. I dream that I will someday perform the spectacular miracles that change or even save lives, and look forward to becoming a master of precision, flawless in my efforts to perfect the human body. I expect, though, that the road getting there will be long and hard. Not only will I spend many sleep-deprived years traveling it, but along the way I expect to encounter many detours, enclosing fences, and guarded borders. The obstacles will be abundant; conquering them will be an exciting part of the challenge. I have many doubts and fears about wanting to become a surgeon, for I often worry that I lack the tenacity, the stamina, the swift and graceful hands, the concentration, and the self-confidence. Will I be able to cultivate within myself those assets that are so valuable in the operating room? Will I ever have the bedside manner that touches patients' hearts and puts them at ease?

Perhaps I will find in my years of medical school that I am simply not cut out for surgery. As disappointing as this may seem to me now, I know that I would quickly be able to find a new passion. I am excited about medicine in general and will remain open-minded to other specialties, always trying new things in the process. In the end, I am sure that I will look back and be pleased that I chose a career in the sciences. It is, I believe, in my nature, in everyone's nature, to be a scientist. I find science to be a fascinating and endless source of challenges and puzzling questions.

I am presently working at the University of Miami School of Medicine conducting research on glycogen synthesis. And, as I sit here collecting fractions and reading absorbances, I cannot help but think about all of those individuals who helped me reach the point where I am today. For without having read the writings of Lewis Thomas or studied the work of science greats such as Albert Einstein and Linus Pauling, without parents who always encouraged me to explore, without my first high school science teacher, without my guardian angel who is always somewhere watching out for me, I do not think that I would have been as motivated to achieve or as enthusiastic about becoming a scientist. Thus far, I think that I have done a pretty good job.

"Oh, the Places You'll Go . . . "

_____ *Natalie M. Bachir* _____

I am from a city of 4,000 people in the northern part of Wisconsin. Because only 25% of my graduating class would go on to attend college, and only two would endeavor to leave the state, and only one (me) was able to gain admittance into an Ivy League school, I suppose that I was always considered the smart one. The brain. The hard-working, well-mannered, goal-driven girl. I was never really in competition with any men, or any women, for that matter. I was just me. My being female did not make a difference to my aspirations or my thoughts, my grades or my relations with teachers and classmates. If anything, I was much more uncomfortable with the fact that I was the only first-year student in my chemistry class. I did not even notice the fact that I was the only woman until the day my teacher made a big deal about whether or not he should address us as "you guys." I told him that I really did not mind either way.

Sexual harassment was something that women on television were shouting about. But I was not sure what it was, exactly, that they were fighting against. It was most certainly not anything I had ever encountered in my little protected part of the world.

When I received my college acceptances in the mail, I was both excited and overwhelmed. How would I choose? I narrowed down my choices to three or four. What was it about Dartmouth College that finally made it the right choice for me? My parents liked it because it was a small Ivy League college located in the wilderness of New Hampshire. That assured them of their daughter's safety. I liked it because it was a small Ivy League college located in the wilderness of New Hampshire. That assured me that I would be able to obtain a great education and still have fun in the outdoors, without an incredibly competitive atmosphere. In addition, there was a bonus: Dartmouth's Women In Science Project (WISP). I had remembered my father showing me an article about the internships offered through WISP, and mentioning that one day, maybe I would be fortunate enough to be offered such an internship. That cinched it. In the fall I headed off to Hanover, a town not much larger than my own hometown, to follow my dreams. After all, as the quote from Dr. Seuss, a Dartmouth alum, pointed out in the Dartmouth brochure, "I had brains in my head, and feet in my shoes. I could direct myself in any direction I chose."

I had wanted to be a doctor since the fifth grade. I was so sure of my aspirations that when asked, in college applications, to outline my goals, I always provided the following idealistic answer.

My goal in life is to improve society. Possibly by educating the people of our country, promoting freedom and justice, fighting against discrimination, or striving for international peace. To reach this goal would mean a great deal to me, which is why, after much thought and consideration, I decided to become a physician. As a physician, I feel that I would be closer to humanity than in any other profession. For a physician is more than just a "body repairman," he or she is an advisor, and a confidant. With my constant desire for knowledge, I hope to learn as much as I possibly can in the field of medicine. With this knowledge, I want to further medical progress and accomplish the goal that every physician, I believe, should have: to reduce suffering and prolong life. I not only want to succeed in my career, but also succeed in keeping up that great American tradition of raising a family on the principles of love, trust, and integrity. If I accomplish these goals, I will surely enjoy my life and be happy. The biggest barometer of success to me is that I will be satisfied that I have lived my life for an honorable and worthwhile purpose.

At that point in my life, I had never taken a college-level science course. I had never conducted research in a laboratory with a professor. I knew the compassionate side of myself that was needed in order to be a good doctor, but I was not sure whether I had enough interest in the sciences. The study of

English, foreign languages, and art had always come easily to me. Would I be able to compete with students who had come from science magnet or private schools? Would I be able to take on the heavy course work and the laboratories, while still enjoying my favorite extracurricular activities? Or would I be one of the first-year students who, after taking the introductory courses in biology and chemistry, were "weeded out" of the system?

To be honest, I had a rough start. Adjusting to college life in itself was difficult. There were all kinds of people to deal with, decisions to make, and serious study habits to attain. In addition, I was intent on finally becoming an "independent woman." I refused to seek advice from deans, professors, and, most important, my parents. The term did not end with straight A's, as every other term in my life had. In retrospect, it is a good thing it did not. My grades forced me to take the time to think about my reasons for studying at Dartmouth, my reasons for wanting to become a doctor, and how I planned to attain my goals in life.

At first, I was a bit confused. Did I really want to go into medicine? Or had my father's influence, as a general surgeon, been so strong that I had never even bothered to explore any other areas of study? What were the reasons for my not performing up to my usual par in the fall term? Was the tough course load too much for me, or did I just have a difficult time adjusting to college life? Had *I* been "weeded out"? Was it time for me to change course, and think about pursuing another career?

Every year, the Women in Science Project at Dartmouth offers first-year women the opportunity to engage in paid hands-on research internships with science faculty members or researchers in nearby industrial or government laboratories. In order to obtain such a position, one has to go through both an application and interview process. I applied, and was later notified that I had both been accepted into the program and awarded my first choice of research projects. I would be working with Dr. Daubenspeck, a professor in the Physiology Department of the Borwell Research Building of the Dartmouth-Hitchcock Medical Center. I was excited!

Working in a laboratory was an amazing experience. I worked side by side with professors, PhD candidates, and postdoctoral research associates. I learned about muscle control in the respiratory system, the scientific method, and analyzing data. Everyone was willing to help me, teach me, and listen to my ideas. I worked hard, and tried to learn as much as I possibly could from my research. Needless to say, I was enthralled when Dr. Daubenspeck asked me if I would like to continue to do full-time research in the laboratory over the summer.

In the meantime, the Ethics Institute at Dartmouth was planning to offer a multidisciplinary course on the technology of assisted reproduction. An intern for the summer was needed to conduct library research for this course. I applied for the job, went through an interview process, and was selected.

Working in the physiology laboratory during the summer proved to be even more fascinating, as I was able to work longer hours and take part in more aspects of the research. I gave more of my input on the design and execution of the experiments. In addition, I attended engineering and physiology seminars with Dr. Daubenspeck, and enjoyed working in the company of a variety of scholarly and enthusiastic professionals and graduate students.

Conducting research for the Ethics Institute was equally invigorating. When I first began, I could see a potential problem associated with such technologies as in vitro fertilization and surrogate motherhood: women being misinformed, women being manipulated, women being used . . . so I decided to focus on how reproductive technologies affect the health of women. I was somewhat upset by my findings. I had never really cared to be sensitive to women's needs or pay any attention to the way in which women were treated. However, through this research experience, I came to realize women are more likely to be overlooked or mistreated. In the area of assisted reproduction, most researchers and doctors are men, but, of course, the primary patient is the woman who wants to bear a child. As a woman in science, this frustrates me, and drives me to persist in my scientific endeavors.

WISP had a great impact on my first-year experience. Through all of my disappointments, surprises, and realizations, it was quite beneficial to be constantly exposed to "the big picture," and be able to experience and take part in the dynamics of scientific research. The project helped to keep me focused on my ultimate goal at Dartmouth. There was a reason for trudging through all of those hypercompetitive science courses, after all! Throughout my first year, my WISP internship sustained my interest in the sciences, and lifted my spirits.

Over the course of the summer, I thought a lot about the Women in Science Project's impact on my life, and, most important, its potential impact on the lives of many aspiring women scientists at Dartmouth. However, there was one area of weakness that concerned me. Although the Women in Science Project did a fantastic job of supporting women students in science career tracks, it did not really address the issue of our being women at Dartmouth, as well. Balancing both at the same time is no easy task! I had an idea. The gap could be filled by arranging a discussion group, through WISP, to identify problems and challenges women faced at Dartmouth, and share advice on how to cope with those problems. The atmosphere of the discussion group would be friendly and open to all points of view. It would be expansive in that through discussing obstacles women had to face at Dartmouth, we might be able to come to some conclusions on the problems women in science confront in our society as a whole. I immediately arranged to meet with Mary Pavone, director of the Women in Science Project, and outlined what I saw as a need along with my strategy for addressing it. She said she thought my idea was fantastic, and immediately offered me a position as an intern for WISP. My job included leading discussions once a week, researching prominent issues that arose during discussion, and writing articles in the WISP newsletter. I worked toward identifying the obstacles women in science face at Dartmouth, researched their causes, and attempted to arrive at solutions.

Before coming to Dartmouth, I had read and heard that my college of choice had a problem. It was only in 1972 that Dartmouth began admitting women, and it is still labeled as a "male-bonding" school. More than 50% of the male population are affiliated with fraternities, and correspondingly fraternities more than double the number of sororities. I was informed that at Dartmouth, women and men cannot relate. The dating scene is almost nonexistent. The men are overpowering. Dartmouth is male territory. Drinking at fraternity parties is a prevalent part of the Dartmouth social life. The number of women with eating disorders at Dartmouth is appalling. Women are just too worried about how they look and what men think of them. Women cannot relate to one another or form strong friendships. Dartmouth is a conservative "boys' club." In terms of tolerance and political correctness, I was to discover that the college I planned to attend was behind the times. This is what I was told before coming to Dartmouth. It is also what I hear now as I study at Dartmouth. Is it all true?

I can give personal accounts. I can tell you of things I have seen and situations I have encountered. I can say, as I recently admitted to my sophomore dean, that yes, in a way, I was disappointed after I came to Dartmouth. When I had read that at Dartmouth the students played hard, but worked hard, too, I had no idea what all of the playing was about.

I have experienced the fraternity scene. I have watched women playing the fraternity game. What are they doing? This is not the way my mother taught me to behave.

"It's funny," remarked an acquaintance of mine last year, "But you can tell which women will be going to the fraternities tonight."

It was the winter term and we were eating dinner in the dining hall. She was referring to the tight, low-cut shirts that most of the women were wearing. Hers was black. In the fraternities, I saw first-year women more easily able to obtain beer than the first-year men. I saw the men ask the women to get them beer, after beer, after beer, after beer. I have been approached by men who have made idle chit-chat for a few minutes before ever-so-gallantly proposing, "Hey, want to get out of here, and go upstairs?" To this I can do nothing but laugh, and reply, "No, thanks." My rejection never appears to be a blow to their egos. They simply mumble a few more words, and then move on. Such occurrences can make one cynical. After all, these are Dartmouth students, the leaders of tomorrow.

I have watched women smile coyly as they drink themselves into inebriation at fraternity parties. I have seen women treated without any respect at all, in the fraternity basement, on the dance floor, on the way upstairs . . . and yet they go back. Is there no other way to relieve tension and have fun on this campus? What do women feel they are missing in themselves that they participate in activities that compromise rather than build self-esteem?

It may seem that I have diverted from my topic. However, it is my belief that it is impossible to separate what it is like to be a woman majoring in the sciences at Dartmouth from what it is like for a woman to exist in the culture at Dartmouth. From my description, it should come as no surprise to learn that I have encountered sexual harassment. There were four instances last summer alone. One of the most embarrassing moments was when my family was visiting the campus and my younger sister and I were sitting outside peacefully reading. Two men tossed a tennis ball over to us, expecting that we would welcome the opportunity to toss it back in a flirty fashion. When we made no attempt to play along, they began to whistle at us and point at the ball. It was at that point that I gathered my belongings and, with my sister in tow, walked away. Unless we are with a man, it is generally viewed by the male population at Dartmouth that *all* women are approachable in *all* circumstances.

There was also the time that the technician working in the physiology lab where I was conducting research thought himself quite witty. He sarcastically commented to the other men in the room that I was involved in "ChISP," an acronym for the "*Chicks* in Science Project." Despite this being a laboratory providing internships for WISP, headed by a man that is highly supportive of the project's goals, I still was not exempt from taunting and demeaning remarks. Stereotypes about women are deeply ingrained in the social fiber. His statement, which for him probably amounted to no more than incidental, mindless play, upset me. I told him what he had said was not appropriate, and let it go at that, not wanting to pay him any more attention. The culture at Dartmouth has made me cynical.

My research with the Ethics Institute brought me to the office of a fascinating professor. I had met her through a workshop sponsored by the Ethics Institute in the summer.

"I was lucky," Professor Sokol remarked, a smile spreading across her face, "That the high school I attended had a good academic curriculum, as my initial reason for choosing that particular high school was that it had a good dressmaking and design program!"

At this, she could not help but laugh, and I could not help but join her. Dressmaking and design? Professor Sokol? I was speaking to an endocrinologist; a professor of physiology; an ardent feminist: a powerful, independent, assertive woman. Born to immigrants who were quite unfamiliar with the educational system in the United States, Professor Sokol had, as an undergraduate, to make her own decision about majoring in biology and going on to graduate school at Harvard.

"We felt we were somewhat different," she replied.

In 1961, when Professor Sokol came to Dartmouth, there were 2 full-time women professors and 1 part-time woman professor, out of a total of 12 professors, in the Physiology Department. I smiled when she related this to me. I looked at Professor Sokol with admiration. She was a pioneer; a woman of perseverance and courage. Of course, in 1961, Dartmouth was still an all-male school. It was only in 1972 that women were first admitted. "So, what do the numbers look like now?" I asked, a knowing tone in my voice. We would surely laugh together at the fact that "back then," there were so few women involved in science. How fortunate I am to live in an era in which women are encouraged to achieve up to their full potential, even in a typically male-dominated field! Professor Sokol smiled at me; the reason would soon become apparent.

"Hmm, I'll have to count," she said, whirling around at her desk to look at the list of professors in the Physiology Department. She turned and addressed me with the results: "There are 5 women out of a total of 24 professors."

I was shocked. I expected that there would at least have been a slight increase from 1961 to 1994. However, the ratio has remained exactly the same.[8]

I have decided on a double major in chemistry and philosophy. Researching the Chemistry Department at Dartmouth, I found that there are active research programs in subfields of organic, bio-organic, inorganic, physical polymer, and laser chemistry. Although the graduating class of 1995 consisted of an estimated 112 women compared to 152 male science majors, the numbers for the Chemistry Department were very different. In the class of 1995, there were 6 female and 13 male chemistry majors. But that does not upset me. Thus far, my classroom and laboratory experiences in general chemistry have revealed that professors tend to treat students equally and hold the same expectations for females and males. I have found that they are always willing to listen to ideas and encourage women to pursue their interests in chemistry.

In contrast, I have found attitudes in the student population to be much less favorable. For example, last year my laboratory teaching assistant behaved in a condescending manner toward me. When I asked questions, he would automatically assume that they were the typical questions of an uninterested science student who had not taken the time to read the book beforehand. He unnecessarily focused on tangential areas and I had to repeatedly remind him of my initial question. When he found out that I wanted to major in chemistry, he laughed out loud. According to him, I did not "look like a science person." Now what on earth must I possess to look like a stereotypical "science person"? I do not even want to attempt a guess.

Curious about the situation, I went to talk to Dr. Karen Wetterhahn, a professor of chemistry and cofounder of the Women in Science Project at Dartmouth. I hoped that there would be more than a few female role models to whom I could go for advice in my field. I found that the numbers were quite different for female professors in the Chemistry compared to the Physiology Department. Since Professor Wetterhahn had come in 1976, the number of female chemistry professors has doubled. On the surface, this might seem encouraging until one learns that in 1976, Professor Wetterhahn was the *only* woman in the department! Now there are 2, out of a total of 16 professors. This is not acceptable.

My research and classroom experiences at Dartmouth have solidified my goal to become a physician. I would like to practice medicine, to teach, and to conduct research. In one respect, my goals are the same as when I was typing all of those college applications. However, unlike before, my aspirations now come from serious thought and experience. Thus, they are more real to me. No longer an abstract dream, they are ambitions, desires, and attainable goals.

I have discovered that science encompasses everything. It is embedded in our ideas, the knowledge we attempt to acquire, and the interactions we have every day of our lives. To be able to learn and be successful in science, one must be able to communicate effectively. A science major must be able to develop ideas, ask questions, and share thoughts. To be knowledgeable and proficient in an area of the "hard" sciences is a power. With this power, one can enlighten some, anger others, and in the end, it is hoped, benefit society. With this power, one can change the world. Although I am less ignorant about the obstacles I have to face as a woman interested in pursuing a career in the sciences, and although I am more aware of the disappointments and hardships I likely will encounter along the way, I still remain as idealistic as I was before I matriculated to the college. I firmly believe that my college experience will be largely what I make of it. I plan to make mine the best and most productive experience possible, as a woman in science, and as a student ready to face the challenges of changing our society for the better. After all, "I have brains in my head, and feet in my shoes. . . ."

Science has much to offer to women, and women have much to offer to science. It would seem to be a perfect combination. However, women's representation in scientific fields has been historically low and we have a significantly higher percentage of derailment at all points along the career continuum compared to men. It is my sincere belief that one of the best ways to effect a reversal of this trend is to create a pool of women that enter the field informed about the challenges and boundaries to success that they will potentially encounter. The probability for success will be further enhanced if, in addition to being aware of the potential obstacles, women carry with them an assortment of strategies for circumventing these obstacles. This has been the work of this volume. Although there is no such thing as a magic formula, a catalog of steps, which if properly taken will universally guarantee success for all women, the volume does expose the extra stuff and provides a number of suggestions for negotiating through it. For example, a major lesson of this volume is that isolation should be avoided at all costs. It impedes progress and ultimately leads to career derailment. Thus, it would be wise for a budding female scientist or engineer to take the steps necessary to make sure that she does not become isolated. If no organized support system for women exists at your institution, or if the one available is not meeting your needs, it is then incumbent on you to develop your own. Complaining about the lack of adequate support may place you in the company of a group of individuals where you can be collectively miserable, but without action it will get you absolutely nowhere. Find people who will help and support you even if they are in unrelated fields. Take charge of, and responsibility for, your career.

A major theme running throughout this volume is that competence, although necessary to get your foot in the door, is not enough. You must be *seen* as capable and dependable by others. Do not allow your talent to be neglected or discounted. The scientific arena is competitive. Those who sit around waiting to be noticed usually watch others secure the best opportunities while they become further marginalized. Therefore, manage your own public relations campaign to ensure recognition and rewards for your accomplishments. Take the initiative to forge networking connections and collaborations that will place you in the mainstream. You can do this even if your area of research is considered risky or controversial. Above all, avoid dead ends. If you are in a situation in which your ability is not appreciated or you are not viewed as a meaningful part of the group, get out. In the long run, it will be better for your career and your emotional well-being.

The contributors to this volume make it clear that we have no choice about facing the extra stuff. Women entering the scientific or engineering career track will inevitably encounter it to some degree. This is because we have little control over the attitudes and actions of others. Nevertheless, we *do* have a choice about how we will react to the extra stuff. We can either resign ourselves to an oppressed status, focusing on the notion that we have no power and therefore no hope, or we can refuse to act like oppressed people. It is my opinion that if women are to truly succeed in science and engineering disciplines, we must shed our underprivileged, oppressed image. Being conscious of our difference, that we are women in a field dominated by men, adversely affects the creative thought process, our willingness to participate in group forums, our eagerness to take risks, our career decisions, and ultimately impedes our growth as individuals. Just as attainment of a critical mass does not ensure that all women in a department will be supported and respected, sheer numbers alone should not mean that men must dominate science. Women must step up to the table expecting to be served, and if we are refused, demand to know the reason why. For too long we have accepted the status quo, and attempted to shape our careers around it.

Without a doubt, this is an exciting time for women in science. New organized efforts to facilitate women's success are being launched on what seems like a daily basis. The future prospects for primary-age schoolgirls demonstrating an interest and aptitude for science seem brighter than ever before. However, we must not become intoxicated by positive progress reports. The surface has barely been scratched. Rather than being a time to sit back and relax, it is a time to build. It is a time to solidify gains so that their affects are long lasting. Women must claim ownership of science rather than seeing ourselves as trespassers on the private property of men. To this end, we must strive to cite the research of women colleagues in our lectures, providing a much needed balance for aspiring students that has been previously absent. We must integrate ourselves into the structure of the academy by stepping up to serve on study sections, review panels, and editorial boards; to assume leadership roles in societies and organizations, and to participate in academic committees and in campus–corporate women in science programs. We must not only be visible, but also vocal. We must recognize that our gains will be marginal if our influence is limited to women. Thus, it is important that we assume responsibility for mentoring young men as well as young women.

It is my sincere hope that this volume will prove to be a valuable resource for women aspiring for professional careers as well as for those whose careers are already established, for administrators and leaders hoping to create a more hospitable environment for women at their institution, and for those attempting to construct programs designed to support women through the career process. However, perhaps its greatest contribution will be to serve as a reference for struggling women to realize that they are not alone; that others have gone before them; that others have faced the challenges and boundaries they are encountering and successfully transcended them; that there is hope.

Notes

Chapter 2

1. Those familiar with the music of James Brown—the Godfather of Soul—will recognize this as a paraphrase of his classic song "Say it Loud! (I'm Black and I'm Proud!)."

2. Although it is true that both girls and boys *can* play Little League Baseball, girls' participation and achievement is still not uniformly encouraged by parents and coaches.

3. Based on a batting average of 300.

4. The facility had a "clean room." Everyone who entered was required to wear special clothing to reduce the possibility of outside contamination.

5. Ethnic minorities and other disenfranchised groups are also seen by some in the majority as "stealing" jobs.

Chapter 3

1. In these instances the woman's femininity is almost always subject to question as well.

2. See essays by Molly Gleiser, Sue Nokes, and Patricia Eng, this volume, for additional examples of this behavior.

Chapter 4

1. Bernadine Healy was director of NIH from 1991 until 1993, when she was forced to resign. She has been an outspoken advocate for women's health research.

2. See Sue Nokes, this volume, for another example of using affirming language with students.

3. Dr. Mancl was appointed to the faculty at Ohio State in 1986.

4. See Patricia Eng, this volume, for an additional example of this phenomenon.

5. See Carol Muller and Mary Pavone, this volume, for a discussion of animosity toward programs focusing solely on women students.

6. See Molly Gleiser, this volume, for additional discussion regarding lack of parental support for women in scientific career tracks.

Chapter 5

1. Sex mosaics refer to fruit flies in which a specific genetic event (e.g., the spontaneous loss of an unstable ring X-chromosome) leads to an adult fly with clonal patches of cells that are genotypically male (X0) surrounded by cells that are female (XX).

2. See Susan Franks, this volume, for a discussion of this concern as a major factor behind her decision to leave research science. As Dr. Tompkins points out, research and education are not at diametrically opposite poles. Although some compromises are inevitable when accepting a faculty position, there are "nontraditional" departments at colleges and universities in which a person interested in conducting research can still spend a significant amount of time at the bench. One of the best sources of this information is to speak to people at meetings about their departments.

Chapter 6

1. This estimate is based on 4 years of undergraduate study, 4 to 6 years of graduate study, and 2 to 4 years of postdoctoral training. In many scientific subdisciplines, it is par for a PhD graduate scientist to complete two separate postdoctoral fellowships before being considered eligible for an entry-level faculty position.

2. The events that Naomi Weisstein describes all occurred coincident or directly subsequent to passage of the 1964 Civil Rights Act.

3. That is, encompassing the period from 1974–1984.

4. See Molly Gleiser, this volume, for an additional example of this behavior.

5. See Sue Nokes, this volume, for a parallel example of this type of ostracism.

Chapter 7

1. It is beyond the scope of this volume to provide a complete review of feminist analyses and critiques of science. Interested readers will find a good starting point with Sandra Harding. (1986). *The Science Question in Feminism*. Ithaca, NY: Cornell University Press; Sandra Harding, *Whose Science? Who's Knowledge?* Ithaca, NY: Cornell University Press; Sandra Harding and Jean F. Barr (Eds.), *Sex and Scientific Inquiry*. Chicago: University of Chicago Press; Helen Longino. (1990). *Science as Social Knowledge: Values and Objectivity in Scientific Inquiry*. Princeton, NJ: Princeton University Press; Evelyn Fox Keller. (1985). *Reflections on Gender and Science*, New Haven, CT: Yale University Press; Mary M. Gergen. (Ed.). (1989). *Feminist Thought and the Structure of Knowledge*, New York: New York University Press; and the references cited by these authors.

2. See Noretta Koertge, this volume, for a more thorough examination of the stance of some radical feminists toward science.

3. My recounting of Noether's career path is based on this biography, which includes the full text of three intellectual obituaries.

4. For an account of her reaction to Feynman's 1974 address to the first integrated graduating class, see Mary E. Eichbauer's letter to the editor in *The Chronicle of Higher Education,* October 19, 1994, and my letter in reply on November 9, 1994.

5. See Molly Gleiser's essay, this volume, for an elaboration on the treatment of women scientists at MIT.

6. For a humorous description of an NWSA Conference, see Sommers, 1994. My novel describes the atmosphere at music festivals (Koertge, 1984).

7. An early, influential version of this interpretation is Merchant (1980). An early rebuttal appears in Koertge (1980). A comprehensive rebuttal is found in Soble (1995).

8. A description and a critique of this approach appears in Koertge, N. (1993). Ideology, Heuristics and Rationality in the Context of Discovery. In S. French & H. Kamminga (Eds.), *Correspondence, Invariance and Heuristics* (pp. 125–136). Dordrecht, the Netherlands: Kluwer.

9. This is not a quote but an aphoristic summary of Longino, H. (1990). *Science as Social Knowledge* (pp. 191–193). Princeton, NJ: Princeton University Press.

10. For an actual history of the approach now labeled as *feminist,* see Persky, J. (1995). The Ethology of Homo Economicus. *Journal of Economic Perspectives, 9,* 221–231.

Chapter 8

1. It is rare that a single cause can be unequivocally attributed to a suicide and far more common that it is a multiplicity of factors interacting simultaneously that create a mind-set in which suicide is viewed as the only option. However, I find it significant

that work-related isolation was a common thread experienced by nearly all of the women studied.

2. This project is supported in part by two grants from the National Science Foundation: Grant No. HRD9353771 and Grant No. HRD9450023.

3. Prior to September 1994, with the exception of the AAUW, the upper levels of administration at all the participating institutions consisted of men only. In September 1994, Stony Brook had its first woman president appointed, and she has been highly supportive of Project WISE as well.

4. Among the 35 students who started in Project WISE in the fall 1994, three were unable to continue in the spring semester; they were replaced by three alternates.

Chapter 9

1. Although psychology is considered a social science at Dartmouth, the department's research is experimental and behaviorally focused rather than clinically oriented.

2. Change also will be required in arenas other than institutions, such as social and family belief systems, communications media, and so forth, but these are beyond the focus and scope of this project. In addition, it is clear that even with institutional change in higher education, systemic change is also required in precollege education to ensure full participation of women in science. Our project is thus limited to a still-ambitious program of institutional change within one university, and an effort to influence other institutions of higher education toward similar change.

3. This wording, which seems most appropriate, is taken directly from chapter 14, "Reforming Education," In *Science for All Americans.* Washington: AAAS (1989, p. 154).

4. See Michele Montejo, this volume, for an example of this position.

5. Data obtained from the Dartmouth College chemistry department. The numbers include majors and minors in the classes of 1994, 1995, and 1996.

6. Data obtained from the Dartmouth College Bulletin: Organizations, Regulations, and Courses, 1993–1994.

7. Considering the part-time faculty position as one half of a full faculty position, the ratios are 2.5 women to 12 men in 1961, and 5 women to 24 men in 1994.

8. Or perhaps traditional views, depending on the audience.

References

Alper, J. (1993). The pipeline is leaking women all the way along. *Science, 260,* 409–411.

American Association for the Advancement of Science (1989). *Science for all Americans.* Washington, DC: Author.

American Association of University Women. (1992). *How schools shortchange girls: A study of major findings on girls and education.* Wellseley, MA: American Association of University Women.

Associated Press Report. (1989, December 8). Montreal shooting spree.

Association of American Colleges. (1986). *A guide to non-sexist language.* Washington, DC: Author.

Barnett, G. C., & Baruch, G. K. (1985). Women's involvement in multiple roles, role strain, and psychological distress. *Journal of Personality and Social Disorder, 49,* 135–145.

Baruch, G. K., & Barnett, G. C. (1986). Role quality, multiple role involvement, and psychological well-being in midlife women. *Journal of Personality and Social Disorder, 51,* 578–585.

Bayer, A. E., & Astin, H. S. (1975). Sex differentials in the academic reward system. *Science, 188,* 796–802.

de Beauvoir, S. (1952). *The second sex.* New York: Vintage Books.

Belenky, M. F., Clinchy, B. McV., Goldberger, N. R., & Tarule, J. M. (1986). *Women's ways of knowing: The development of self, voice, and mind.* New York: Basic Books.

Benditt, J. (Ed.). (1993). Women in science '93: Gender and the culture of science. *Science, 260,* 383–432.

Benditt, J. (Ed.). (1994). Women in science '94: Comparisons across cultures. *Science, 263,* 1467–1496.

Bernard, J. (1976a). *Women, wives, and mothers.* Chicago: Aldine.

Bernard, J. (1976b). Where are we now? Some thoughts on the current scene. *Psychology of Women Quarterly, 1*, 21–37.

Best, R. (1983). *We've all got scars: What boys and girls learn in elementary school.* Bloomington: Indiana University Press.

Bloom, D. E. (1986). Women and work. *American Demographics, 8*, 25–30.

Bower, B. (1991, March 23). Teenage turning point: Does adolescence herald the twilight of girls' self-esteem? *Science News*, 184.

Bowers, J. (1987). Special problems of women medical students. *Journal of Medical Education, 43*, 532.

Brooks, D., Smith, D., & Anderson, R. (1991). Medical apartheid: An American perspective. *Journal of the American Medical Association, 266*, 2746–2749.

Caplan, N., & Nelson, D. S. (1973). On being useful. The nature and consequences of psychological research on social problems. *American Psychologist, 28*, 199–211.

Caputi, J. (1993). *Gossips, gorgons, and crones: The fates of the earth.* Sante Fe, NM: Bear.

Carr, P. L., Friedman R. H., Moskowitz, M. A., & Kazis, L. E. (1993). Comparing the status of women and men in academic medicine. *Annals of Internal Medicine, 119*, 908–913.

Chancellor's Workshop on Women in Science and Engineering report to the chancellor. (1994, April 16). Urbana-Champaign: University of Illinois.

Choate, P. (1986). *The high-flex society.* New York: Knopf.

Coe, D. B., & Dienst, E. R. (1990). Women in podiatric medicine: Experience during training. *Journal of the American Podiatric Medical Association, 80*, 334–339.

Cole, J. R. (1981). Women in Science. *American Scientist, 69*, 385–391.

Cole, J. R., & Zuckerman, H. (1991). Marriage, motherhood, and research performance in science. In H. Zuckerman, J. R. Cole, & J. T. Bruer (Eds.), *The Outer Circle: Women in the Scientific Community.* New York: W. W. Norton.

"Continuing shortage of women in science decried; Many drop out." (1991, December 11). *Chronicle of Higher Education*, A31–A32.

Cosell, H. (1985). *Woman on a seesaw: The ups and downs of making it.* New York: Putnam.

Culotta, E. (Ed.). (1993). Minorities in science '93: Trying to change the face of science. *Science, 262*, 1089–1136.

Cummings, M., & Wise, D. (1974). *Democracy under pressure* (2nd ed.). New York: Harcourt Brace Jovanovich.

Cunningham, C. M. (1994). *Women in Science Project interim evaluation report.* Ithaca, NY: Women in Science Project.

Cutler, J., & Canellakis, Z. (1989). Pacing a career and setting priorities. *FASEB Journal, 3*, 1781–1784.

Daly, M. (1978). *Gyn/Ecology: The metaethics of radical feminism.* Boston: Beacon Press.

Daly, M. (1987). *Webster's first new intergalactic wickedary of the English language.* Boston: Beacon Press.

Damarin, S. (1995). Gender and mathematics from a feminist standpoint. In W. G. Secada, E. Fennema, & L. Byrd (Eds.), *New directions for equity in mathematics education* (pp. 242-257). London: Cambridge University Press.

Daniels, J. (1994). *Annual report: Women in engineering programs.* West Lafayette, IN: Purdue University.

Davenport, D. (1971). Intrepid analysis of female scientists. *Science, 171,* 521–522.

Davidson, M. J., & Cooper, C. L. (1987). Female managers in Britain: A comparative perspective. *Human Resource Management, 26,* 217–242.

Deaux, K. (1979). Self-evaluations of male and female managers. *Sex Roles, 5,* 571–580.

Deaux, K., & Emswiller, T. (1974). Explanations of successful performance on sex-linked tasks: What is skill for the male is luck for the female. *Journal of Personality and Social Psychology, 29,* 80–85.

Dick, A. (1981). *Emmy Noether: 1882–1935.* Basel, Switzerland: Birkhauser.

Dickstein, L. J. (1990). Female physicians in the 1980s: Personal and family attitudes and values. *Journal of the American Medical Women's Association, 45,* 122–126.

Eichbauer, M. E. (1994, October 19, 1994). [Letter to the editor]. *The Chronicle of Higher Education,* pp. 83, 85.

Entwisle, D. C., & Baker, D. P. (1983). Gender and young children's expectations for performance in arithematic. *Developmental Psychology, 19,* 200–209.

Etaugh, C., & Kasley, H. C. (1981). Evaluating competence: Effects of sex, marital status, and parental status. *Psychology of Women Quarterly, 6,* 196–203.

Etzkowitz, H., Kemelgor, C., Neuschatz, M., Uzzi, B., & Alonzo, J. (1994). The paradox of critical mass for women in science. *Science, 266,* 51–54.

Fausto-Sterling, A. (1992). *Myths of gender: Biological theories about women and men* (2nd ed.). New York: Basic Books.

Feminist Majority Foundation. (1991). *Empowering women in business.* Washington, DC: Author.

Fennema, E., & Peterson, P. (1985). Autonomous learning behavior: A possible explanation of gender-related differences in mathematics. In L. Wilkinson & C. Marrett (Eds.), *Gender influences in classroom interaction* (pp. 17-35). Orlando, FL: Academic Press.

Final Report of the Committee on the Status of Women Graduate Students and Faculty in the College of Engineering. (1993, June 18). Urbana-Champaign: University of Illinois.

Frieze, I. H., Whitley, B. E., & McHugh, M. C. (1982). Assessing the theoretical models for sex differences in causal attributions for success and failure. *Sex Roles, 8,* 333–343.

Geppert, L. (1995, May). The uphill struggle: No rose garden for women in engineering. *IEEE Spectrum,* 42.

Gergen, M. M. (Ed.). (1989). *Feminist thought and the structure of knowledge.* New York: New York University.

Gibbons, A. (1992a). Key issue: Mentoring. *Science, 255,* 1368.

Gibbons, A. (1992b). Creative solutions: Electronic mentoring. *Science, 255,* 1369.

Gibbons, A. (1993). Traveling without maps. *Science, 260,* 399.

Gilbert, L. A. (1983). Female development and achievement. *Issues of Mental Health Nursing, 5,* 5–17.

Gilbert, L. A., Gallessich, J., & Evans, S. (1983). Sex of faculty role model and students' self-perceptions of competency. *Sex Roles, 9,* 597–608.

Gilligan, C., Lyons, N. P., & Hammers, T. J. (Eds.). (1989). *Making connections: The relational worlds of adolescent girls at Emma Willard School.* Troy, NY: Emma Willard School.

Glazer, M. (1983). Ten whistleblowers and how they fared. *Hastings Center Report, 12,* 33–40.

Goldstein, E. (1979). Effect of same-sex and cross-sex role models on the subsequent academic productivity of scholars. *American Psychologist, 34,* 407–410.

Grant, L., & Ward, K. (1996). Gender and academic publishing. In J. Smart (Ed.), *Higher education: Handbook of theory and research* (pp. 175-215). New York: Agathon.

Green, K. C. (1989, September/October). A profile of undergraduates in the sciences. *Scientific American,* 475–480.

Gross, P. R., & Levitt, N. (1994). *Higher superstition: The academic left and its quarrels with science.* Baltimore: Johns Hopkins University Press.

Gutek, B. A. (1985). *Sex and the workplace.* San Francisco: Jossey-Bass.

Hamilton, J. A. (1989). Emotional consequences of victimization and discrimination in "special populations" of women. *Psychiatric Clinics of North America, 12,* 35–51.

Haraway, D. (1991). *Simians, cyborgs, and women.* New York: Routledge.

Harding, S. (1986). *The science question in feminism.* Ithaca, NY: Cornell University Press.

Harding, S. (1991). *Whose science? Whose knowledge? Thinking from women's lives.* Ithaca, NY: Cornell University Press.

Healy, B. (1992). Women in science: From panes to ceilings. *Science, 255,* 1333.

Hewitt, N. A., & E. Seymour. (1991). *Factors contributing to high attrition rates among science, mathematics, and engineering undergraduate majors: A report to the Sloan Foundation.* Denver: University of Colorado, Bureau of Sociological Research.

Hirshberger, N., & Itkins, S. (1978). Graduate student success in psychology. *American Psychologist, 33,* 1083–1093.

Holland, D. C., & Eisenhart, M. A. (1990). *Educated in romance: Women, achievement and college culture.* Chicago: University of Chicago Press.

Horizon Research, Inc. (1993). *Women in Science Project internship evaluation report.* Chapel Hill, NC: Author.

Jensen, M. B. (1971). Intrepid analysis of female scientists. *Science, 171,* 522.

Jensvold, M. F., Hamilton, J. A., & Mackey, B. (1994). Including women in clinical trials: How about the women scientists? *Journal of the American Medical Women's Association, 49,* 110–112.

Jensvold, M., Muller, K. L., Putnam, F. W., & Rubinow, D. R. (1989). *Abuse and PTSD in PMS patients and controls.* Presentation to the International Society of Psychosomatic Obstetrics and Gynecology, Amsterdam.

Jensvold, M. F., Reed, K., Jarrett, D. B., & Hamilton, J. A. (1992). Menstrual cycle related depressive symptoms treated with variable antidepressant dosage. *Journal of Women's Health, 1,* 109–115.

Kanter, R. M. (1977). *Men and women of the corporation.* New York: Basic Books.

Kaufman, D. R. (1978). Associational ties in academe: Some male and female differences. *Sex Roles, 4,* 9–21.

Keith, S. Z., & Keith, P. (Eds.). (1989). *Proceedings of the national conference on women in mathematics and science.* St. Cloud, MN: St. Cloud University.

Keller, E. F. (1983). *A feeling for the organism: The life and work of Barbara McClintock.* San Francisco: W.H. Freeman.

Keller, E. F. (1985). *Reflections on gender and science.* New Haven, CT: Yale University Press.

Kelly, D. N. (1976). A school for tokens. *Supervisor Nurse, 7,* 7.

Kessler, R. C., & McRae, J. A. (1982). The effect of wives' employment on the mental health of married men and women. *American Sociological Review, 47,* 216–227.

Koertge, N. (1980). Methodology, ideology, and feminist critiques of science. In P. Asquith & R. Gierge (Eds.), *PSA 1980: Proceedings of the 1980 biennial meeting of the Philosophy of Science Association Vol. 2* (pp. 346–359). East Lansing, MI: Philosophy of Science Association.

Koertge, N. (1984). *Valley of the Amazons.* New York: St. Martin's Press.

Kramarae, C. (Ed.). (1980). *The voices and words of women and men.* London: Pergamon Press.

Lenny, E. (1977). Women's self-confidence in achievement settings. *Psychological Bulletin, 84,* 1–13.

Levinson, D. (1978). *The seasons of a man's life.* New York: Knopf.

Li, F. D. (1969). Suicide among chemists. *Archives of Environmental Health, 19,* 518–520.

Long, S. R., & Zakian V. (1994). Women in biomedicine: Encouragement. *Science, 263,* 1357–1358.

Longino, H. (1990). *Science as social knowledge: Values and objectivity in scientific inquiry.* Princeton, NJ: Princeton University Press.

Lorde, A. (1984). "The master's tools will never dismantle the master's house." In *Sister outsider* (pp. 110-113). Freedom, CA: Crossing Press.

Macoby, E., & Jacklin, C. (1974). *The psychology of sex differences.* Stanford, CA: Stanford University Press.

Madison, B. L., & T. A. Hart. (1990). *A challenge of numbers, Committee on the Mathematical Sciences in the Year 2000.* Washington, DC: National Academy Press.

Mann, J. (1994). *The difference: Growing up female in America.* New York: Warner Books.

Martyna, W. (1980). The psychology of the generic masculine. In S. McConnell-Ginet, R. Borker, & N. Furman (Eds.), *Women and language in literature and society* (pp. 69-78). New York: Praeger.

Mason, J. (1991). The invisible-obstacle race. *Nature, 353,* 205–206.

Mason, M. (1987). Do you have any daughters? *Journal of the American Dietetic Association, 87,* 283–284.

Matyas, M. L., & Malcom, S. M. (Eds.). (1991). *Investing in human potential: Science and engineering at the crossroads.* Washington, DC: American Association for the Advancement of Science.

Merchant, C. (1980). *The death of nature: Women, ecology, and the scientific revolution.* San Francisco: Harper & Row.

Merton, R. K. (1973), *The sociology of science: Theoretical and empirical investigations.* Chicago: University of Chicago Press.

Morell, V. (1992). Speaking out. *Science, 255,* 1369.

Morrison, A., White, R. P., & Van Velsor, E. (1986, October). The glass house dilemma: Why women executives dare not fail. *Working Woman,* 146.

Morrison, A. M., White, R. P., & Van Velsor, E. (1992). *Breaking the glass ceiling: Can women reach the top of America's largest corporations?* Reading, MA: Addison-Wesley.

Musil, C. McT. (Ed.). (1992). *Students at the center: Feminist assessment.* Washington, DC: Association of American Colleges.

National Academy Press. (1991). *Women in science and engineering: Increasing their numbers in the 1990's.* Washington, DC: Author.

National Research Council. (1989). *Everybody counts: A report to the nation on the future on mathematics education.* Washington, DC: National Academy Press.

National Science Foundation. (1990). *The state of academic science and engineering. Directorate for Science, Technology and International Affairs, Division of Policy Research and Analysis.* Washington, DC: Author.

Nelson, M. B. (1994). *The stronger women get, the more men love football: Sexism and the American culture of sports.* New York: Harcourt Brace.

Osborn, M. (1992). Prospects for women in science. *Science, 360,* 101.

Osborn, M. (1994). Status and prospects of women in science in Europe. *Science, 263,* 1389–1391.

Pagels, E. (1988). *Adam, Eve, and the serpent.* New York: Vintage Books.

Pagels, E. (1989). *The Gnostic gospels.* New York: Vintage Books.

Pankhurst, E. (1914). *My own story.* New York: Hearst's International Library.

Patai, D., & Koertge, N. (1994). *Professing feminism: Cautionary tales from the strange world of women's studies.* New York: Basic Books.

Pendergrast, M. (1995). *Victims of memory: Incest accusations and shattered lives.* Hinesburg, VT: Upper Access Books.

Report on the Institutional Training Grants, Study Groups EPMC Subcommittee on Equal Opportunity for Access in Extramural Programs. (1984). Unpublished NIH report.

Report on the Task Force on the Status of NIH Intramural Women Scientists. (1993). Bethesda, MD: National Institutes of Health.

Rhode, D. L. (1985). *Reflections on gender and science.* New Haven, CT: Yale University Press.

Rosser, S. (1990). *Female-friendly science: Applying women's studies methods and theories to attract students.* New York: Pergamon Press.

Sadker, M., & Sadker, D. (1979). *Between teacher and student: Overcoming sex bias in the classroom.* Unpublished report by the Non-Sexist Teacher Education Project of the Women's Educational Equity Act Program, U.S. Department of Health, Education, and Welfare, Office of Education.

Sandler, B. R. (1991). Women faculty at work in the classroom, or why it still hurts to be a woman in labor. *Communication Education, 40,* 6-15.

Sandler, B. R. (1992). *Success and survival strategies for women faculty members.* Washington DC: Association of American Colleges.

Sandler, B. R., & Hall, R. M. (1986). *The campus climate revisited: Chilly for women faculty, administrators, and graduate students.* Washington, DC: Association of American Colleges.

Sanford, K. K., Parshad, R., Price, F. M., Jones, G. M., Tarone, R. E., Eierman, L., Hale, P., & Waldmann, T. A. (1990). Enhanced chromatid damage in blood lymphocytes after G2 phase X irradiation, a marker of the ataxia-telangiectasia gene. *Journal of the National Cancer Institute, 82,* 1050–1054.

Schmidt, D. A. (1987). The cradle of success. *Dental Economics, 77,* 37–40.

Schmuker, D., & Vessell, E. (1993). Underrepresentation of women in clinical drug trials. *Clinical Pharmocology and Therapeutics, 54,* 11–15.

Schrier, D. K. (1990). Sexual harassment and discrimination: Impact on physical and mental health. *National Journal of Medicine, 87,* 105–107.

Seachrist, L. (1994). Disparities detailed in NCI division. *Science, 264,* 340.

Seiden, R. H., & Gleiser, M. (1990). Sex differences in suicide among chemists. *OMEGA, 21,* 173–185.

Sherman, J. A. (1976). Social values, femininity, and the development of female competence. *Journal of Social Issues, 32,* 181–195.

Shilts, R. (1987). *And the band played on.* New York: St. Martin's Press.

Soble, A. (1995). In defense of Bacon. *Philosophy of Science, 25,* 192–215.

Sommers, C. H. 1994). *Who stole feminism?* New York: Basic Books.

Stryer, L. (1995). *Biochemistry* (4th ed.). New York: W. H. Freeman.

Swaffield, L. (1988). Is it still jobs for the boys? *Nursing Times, 84,* 17.

Tidball, M. E. (1973). Perspectives on academic women and affirmative action. *Educational Record, 54,* 130–135.

Tobias, S. (1992). Women in science. *Journal of College Science, 21,* 2.

Travis, C., & Offir, C. (1977). *The longest war: Sex differences in perspective.* New York: Harcourt Brace Jovanovich.

Travis, J. (1993). Making room for women in the culture of science. *Science, 260,* 412–415.

U.S. General Accounting Office. (1992). *Women's health: FDA needs to ensure more study of gender differences in prescription drug testing.* GAO/HRD 93–17. Washington, DC: Author.

van der Hoeven, K. J., & Doss, P. K. (1994). High school student perspectives of the geosciences: A gender related study in central Maine. *The Maine Geologist, 20,* 9.

Vare, E. A., & Ptacek, G. (1987). *Mothers of invention*. New York: William Morrow.

Vetter, B. M. (1994). *Professional women and minorities: A total human resource data compendium* (11th ed.) Washington, DC: Commission on Professionals in Science and Technology.

Walrath, J., Li, F. P., Hoar, S. K., Mead, M. W., & Fraumeni, J. F. (1985). Causes of death among chemists. *American Journal of Public Health, 75,* 883–885.

Weaver, J. L., & Garrett, S. D. (1978). Sexism and racism in the American health care industry: A comparative analysis. *International Journal of Health Services, 8,* 677–703.

Weisstein, N. (1976). Adventures of a woman in science. *Federation Proceedings, 35*(11), 2226–2231.

Wellesley College Center for Research on Women. (1992). *How schools shortchange girls*. Washington, DC: American Association of University Women Educational Foundation.

Wermeling, D. P., & Selvitz, A. S. (1993). Current issues surrounding women and minorities in drug trials. *The Annals of Pharmocotherapy, 27,* 904–911.

Widnall, S. E. (1988). AAAS presidential lecture: Voices from the pipeline. *Science, 241,* 1741.

Widom, C. S., & Burke, B. W. (1978). Performance, attitudes, and professional socialization of women in academia. *Sex Roles, 4,* 549–563.

Winter, R. E. (1983). *Coping with executive stress*. New York: McGraw-Hill.

Woolf, V. (1929). *A room of one's own*. London: Hogarth Press.

Wylie, A., Okruhlik, K., Morton, S., & Thielen-Wilson, L. (1989). Philosophical feminism: A bibliographic guide to critiques of science. *Resources for feminist research, Vol. 19,* 2–36.

Zimmerman, D. H., & West, C. (1975). Sex roles, interruptions and silences in conversation. In B. Thorne & N. Henley (Eds.), *Language and sex: Difference and dominance*. Rowley, MA: Newbury House.

Index

Ali, Muhammad, 45, 71
Alper, Joseph, 10

Baum, Eleanor, 87, 257
Benesch, Ruth, 69
Best, Rafaela, 51
Borg, Anita, 88
Brown, Jan, 169
Burton-Nelson, Mariah, 44, 51

Career assessment, gender differences in, 57-80, 60, 80-81, 99-100, 103, 127, 132, 138, 146, 185, 270. *See also* Stereotypes
Career derailment, 109, 129, 132, 146, 198-199, 220, 237, 247-248
Career status, of women, 7, 11. *See also* Gender bias
Carr, Phyllis, 150
Castellana, Maureen, 9
Chase, Martha, 69
Civil Rights Act of 1964, 147
Coe, David, 42
Condescending behavior, 29, 48, 63, 76-77, 91, 138, 182, 185, 207, 236, 276, 278. *See also* Devaluation of women
Cooperative learning/working environment, 9, 20, 55, 223-224. *See also* Support networks
Cosell, Hilary, 34, 103

Critical mass, 10-13, 145, 165, 243, 280 defined, 11
Criticism, science establishment's resistance to, 7, 54, 131-132, 174-175. *See also* Support system
Curie, Marie, 72

Daly, Mary, 184
Daniels, Jane, 244
Davis, Cinda S., 246
Deaux, Kay, 60
de Beauvoir, Simone, 23, 50
DeLucia, Paula, 69
Devaluation of women, 18, 24, 122, 149, 159, 237. *See also* Stereotypes
Dickstein, Leah, 140
Dienst, Evelyn, 42
Differences, male-female, 44-45, 52. *See also* Gender binaries
Discouragement, from science career, 28, 75-76, 91, 123, 148, 163, 249, 264, 269-270. *See also* Career derailment
Discrimination, 7, 74-75, 92, 96, 123, 136, 140, 142-143, 148-149, 160-162, 209-210, 217, 250, 262. *See also* Extra stuff

Eccles, Jacquelynne, 31
Eisenhart, Margaret, 199

About the Editor

Ángela M. Pattatucci, PhD, is the Student Assessment Coordinator for the Puerto Rico Statewide Systemic Initiative (PR-SSI), a joint effort to promote excellence in science and mathematics for all students by the Resource Center for Science and Engineering of the University of Puerto Rico (RCSE), the Commonwealth Department of Education, the General Council of Education, and the National Science Foundation. She began her career at Northeastern Illinois University in Chicago, where she was conferred with a BS in biology in 1986. She conducted research on aging in the fruit fly, *Drosophila melanogaster,* with Dr. Jules Lerner, and served as an educational consultant to the Chicago Public Schools during her undergraduate tenure. She conducted doctoral dissertation research under the mentorship of Dr. Thomas Kaufman at Indiana University in Bloomington, focusing on expression and regulation of homeotic genes in *Drosophila melanogaster,* and received her PhD in 1991. She moved to Bethesda, Maryland, to conduct postdoctoral research in the laboratory of Dr. Dean Hamer at the National Cancer Institute, a branch of the National Institutes of Health, where she gained international recognition and acclaim for her research on human sexual orientation and sexuality. She subsequently served on the faculty of the Ponce School of Medicine in Ponce, Puerto Rico, for 2 years before joining the RCSE. In addition to her academic achievements, she is an accomplished athlete and musician, and is currently producing a work of fiction.

About the Contributors

Susan S. Allen, MD, MPH, is president and CEO of Advances in Health Technology, a nonprofit corporation to assist in the development and introduction of new technologies for improving the health of women and men, especially their reproductive health.

Natalie M. Bachir is a senior at Dartmouth College. She has a double major in philosophy and either chemistry or biology, with plans to go on to medical school. She currently holds a position as a writing tutor at the Composition Center at Dartmouth College and engages in research with the Ethics Institute.

Jennifer M. Cramer is a graduate student in the Department of Electrical and Computer Engineering at Carnegie Mellon University.

Patricia L. Eng, PE, is currently chief of the Transportation & Storage Inspection Section of the Spent Fuel Project Office at the Nuclear Regulatory Commission (NRC), where she has developed inspection procedures for spent fuel storage and coordinated the development of NRC guidance documents. She is also the national secretary for the Society of Women Engineers.

Suzanne E. Franks, PhD, is a medical writer at Covance Clinical and Peri-approval Services in Princeton, New Jersey, where she prepares clinical study reports and other documents to be submitted to the FDA as part of the new drug approval process. She previously conducted cancer research at the

Department of Nuclear Magnetic Resonance and Medical Spectroscopy, Fox Chase Cancer Center, in Philadelphia.

Laura J. Gaines is a natural therapeutics specialist and certified massage therapist working in the area of alternative medicine. She holds a BS in public health from the University of North Carolina at Chapel Hill.

Molly Gleiser, PhD, studied chemistry at the Imperial College of Science in London, where she received a doctorate in 1950. Her research specialties include thermodynamics and suicide prevention among scientists. She currently makes her living as a freelance writer and has published more than 100 articles.

Denise Gürer, PhD, obtained her doctorate degree in computer science in 1993 from Lehigh University. While at Lehigh, she was awarded the Vision Leadership Award (1992), a Graduate Student Leadership Award (1990), and Physics Award (1985). She is currently working at the Applied Artificial Intelligence and Technology Program, SRI International in Menlo Park, California, where she specializes in applications of artificial intelligence to real-world problems.

Wendy Katkin, PhD, is the associate provost for Educational Initiatives at the State University of New York at Stony Brook. She is also director and cofounder of Project WISE.

Noretta Koertge, PhD, is a professor in the Department of History and Philosophy of Science at Indiana University at Bloomington.

Marybeth Lima, PhD, is an assistant professor in the Department of Biological and Agricultural Engineering at Louisiana State University.

Minna Mahlab is the assistant director of the Science and Math Learning Center at Grinnell College in Iowa.

Beth Martin is a graduate of the program in science communications at the University of California, Santa Cruz. She currently works as a technical writer in the Silicon Valley computer industry and as a popular science outlet writer for *Science News.*

Michele Montejo attended Dartmouth College for 2 years and recently spent the summer studying at St. Anne's College in Oxford University. She is presently enrolled at the University of Miami with a triple major in chemistry, biochemistry, and English literature. She plans to attend medical school.

Carol B. Muller, PhD, is executive director of MentorNet, a national program of industrial electronic mentoring. She operates Blue Sky Consulting, Inc., as well.

Sue E. Nokes, PhD, is an assistant professor in the Department of Biosystems and Agricultural Engineering at the University of Kentucky in Lexington. In 1993 she was awarded the Towers Faculty Recognition award for resident instruction from the College of Agriculture at the Ohio State University.

Kimberly Groat Olsen, PhD, is an assistant professor in the Department of Chemistry at Loyola College of Maryland. She is the recipient of a Department of Education National Needs Fellowship, the 1993 Eli Lilly Predoctoral Fellowship, and the 1994 Kraft Corporation Fellowship.

Mary L. Pavone, PhD, is director of the Women in Science Project at Dartmouth College in Hanover, New Hampshire.

Angela Rella earned a BS in electrical engineering and a BA in English literature from the State University of New York at Binghamton in 1994.

Donna Riley is a doctoral student in the Department of Engineering and Public Policy at Carnegie Mellon University. Her primary research involves stochastic optimization and environmental design.

Ann Saterbak, PhD, is an associate research engineer in the Environmental Directorate of Shell Development Company in Houston, Texas. Her work focuses on the application of natural biodegradation processes to remediate soil and groundwater contaminated with petroleum hydrocarbons. She also provides technical and regulatory support on environmental issues to personnel at Shell Oil's Exploration and Production facilities.

Laurie Tompkins, PhD, is professor in the Department of Biology at Temple University in Philadelphia.

Katrien J. van der Hoeven graduated from Colby College in 1995 with a major in geology and a minor in chemistry. She spent 6 weeks in Wyoming, South Dakota, and Montana studying field geology before entering the master's program in geology at Arizona State Unversity.

Janet Vorvick, MS, is a graduate of the computer science program at Portland State University. St. Olaf College awarded her the BA degree in 1982.

Nina Wokhlu is currently pursuing a Doctor of Medicine degree at the University of Medicine and Dentistry of New Jersey, New Jersey Medical School. She is a recipient of the Tau Beta Pi National Laureate Award for Community Service and the Howard R. Swearer Humanitarian Award for New Jersey.